Dyslexia-friendly Str
Reading, Spelling and

Many pupils with dyslexia have poor spelling and handwriting, even when their reading is adequate. This practical yet evidence-based book shows teachers who work with pupils with dyslexia how they can effectively address these areas of weakness. Diane Montgomery introduces her popular Cognitive Process Strategies for Spelling (CPSS) and provides guidance on how this direct action can be successfully used in both primary and secondary contexts.

The book describes dyslexia-friendly approaches in Logographic, Alphabetic and Orthographic phases – 'the three faces' of dyslexia. Best literacy practice for all children is illustrated in a developmental reading and spelling approach, handwriting as a support to literacy teaching is explained and strategies for overcoming handwriting difficulties are detailed from Reception onwards.

Dyslexia-friendly Strategies for Reading, Spelling and Handwriting is full of new research, case examples and practical methods that have been tried and tested in the classroom. This is a must-read guide for all teachers and SENCOs in primary and secondary settings working with pupils with dyslexia.

Diane Montgomery is Professor Emerita in Education at Middlesex University.

Dyslexia-friendly Strategies for Reading, Spelling and Handwriting
A Toolkit for Teachers

Diane Montgomery

Routledge
Taylor & Francis Group

LONDON AND NEW YORK

First published 2017
by Routledge
2 Park Square, Milton Park, Abingdon, Oxon OX14 4RN

and by Routledge
711 Third Avenue, New York, NY 10017

Routledge is an imprint of the Taylor & Francis Group, an informa business

British Library Cataloguing in Publication Data
A catalogue record for this book is available from the British Library

Library of Congress Cataloging in Publication Data
Names: Montgomery, Diane.
Title: Dyslexia-friendly strategies for reading, spelling and handwriting
: a toolkit for teachers / Diane Montgomery.
Description: New York : Routledge, 2017. | Includes bibliographical
references and index.
Identifiers: LCCN 2016048449| ISBN 9781138223141 (hardback) |
ISBN 9781138223158 (pbk.) | ISBN 9781315405582 (ebook)
Subjects: LCSH: Language arts (Elementary) | Learning disabilities. |
Dyslexia.
Classification: LCC LB1576 .M65 2017 | DDC 372.6--dc23
LC record available at https://lccn.loc.gov/2016048449

ISBN: 978-1-138-22314-1 (hbk)
ISBN: 978-1-138-22315-8 (pbk)
ISBN: 978-1-315-40558-2 (ebk)

Typeset in Galliard
by Saxon Graphics Ltd, Derby

Visit the eResources: www.routledge.com/9781138223158

Printed and bound by CPI Group (UK) Ltd, Croydon, CR0 4YY

Contents

Preface

It has been ten years since *Spelling, Handwriting and Dyslexia* (Montgomery, 2007) was published. It discussed dyslexia research and practice and in the last chapter identified ways in which the practical implications of the research would be developed. This book contains those developments, some of which were prefaced in *Teaching Gifted Children with SEN* (Montgomery, 2015).

In the interim, research has confirmed the pervasive effect of handwriting difficulties across the ability range in causing underachievement. It is a difficulty in plain sight and its role in literacy development and cognition had been greatly underestimated and frequently ignored in some schools. This has been especially so since computers have become widely used from pre-school onwards. The need to learn handwriting has been questioned when the time can be given to other subjects. Neglecting handwriting will be shown to be an unwise choice based on new evidence from neurological research.

Recent research on spelling difficulties has shown that there is also a wide range of individuals who have spelling problems without necessarily having any reading difficulties. These spelling problems are similar to those of dyslexics but are overlooked as carelessness and want of effort when the authors desperately need some structured help.

Spelling problems also limit achievement as writers have to find vocabulary they can spell and this limits their ability to think about the message and argument they are trying to make. It places a cognitive overload on the system just as handwriting coordination difficulties can also do.

The situation regarding reading teaching and reading standards appears to have changed very little in many schools since the 1950s (Tymms, 2004), despite the National Literacy Strategy (DFEE, 1998) and many other corrective guidelines since. There is in the guidelines a strong emphasis on reading teaching with phonics now introduced at the outset. Remedial support follows a similar pattern focusing on reading teaching and more phonics but with small groups or one-to-one support. It will be argued that the type of phonics and methods used are not yet fit for purpose.

This text will seek to show how the problems experienced by dyslexics and dysgraphics lead to some different strategies than those currently employed and that have been shown to be effective in helping overcome their problems. The recommendations are based upon analysis of multiple case studies as well as cohort research.

The incidence of dyslexia varies in the different countries with a lower incidence in languages that are 'transparent', meaning they have a simple sound-to-symbol association to learn – one letter one sound as in Turkish and Italian. In English there are 26 letters of the alphabet (graphemes) and 44 sounds or 'phonemes'. It is also an 'opaque' language and has a complex orthography (spelling system) – not only because of this but also because it has roots in many languages such as Celtic from the original settlers, Latin from the Roman invasion, Anglo-Saxon (Old English) from seventh-century settlers, Norse from later invaders, French from the Norman conquest, and borrowings from Greek, Spanish, Hindi and so on.

It is said that 10 per cent of people in the UK have dyslexia, with 4 per cent being severe cases (BDA, 2017). Studies for this book suggest the incidence is higher, at around 20 per cent.

The book begins with a profile of 35-year-old James, a severe dyslexic, his experiences of school and his advice to us. In the opening chapter we learn from Nicholas what reading and remedial teaching methods involved for him two decades later. Unfortunately these still bore little relationship to his needs but show what dyslexic children are still generally offered by schools.

Nicholas was fortunate in that his support teacher was on a specialist MA SpLD programme and decided to evaluate what was reported as a dyslexia-friendly approach as part of her coursework.

However, looking at the new casework from 2012 to 2016 it would seem that many schools and dyslexia research are still caught up in a cycle of failure to address the needs that dyslexics actually have. Why this might be so is explored in Chapter 4.

Katy (aged seven) wrote the message below (Figure 0.1) to me in 2006. Like others in her class she did not enjoy writing and this was the general picture discovered by Alston in 1993 and across the decades during appraisal research in 1,250 classrooms (Montgomery, 2002). Teachers were widely observed to experience the groan that would follow when they said, 'Now write that down'.

Katy's view was borne out in the contents of the 20-minute essays for a handwritng research project in 2008 (N=531) when many pupils chose to write about writing. When we might expect children to want to write and to enjoy it they regard it as a chore and many find it difficult and even painful.

The original book (Montgomery, 2007) contained the background theory and research with implications for practice. But for all the books and all the research on dyslexia we seem to have failed them. We have not paid the necessary close attention to their needs or what they know of what we do to them. We seem not to have learnt from them but keep applying our own theories of what is dyslexia-friendly.

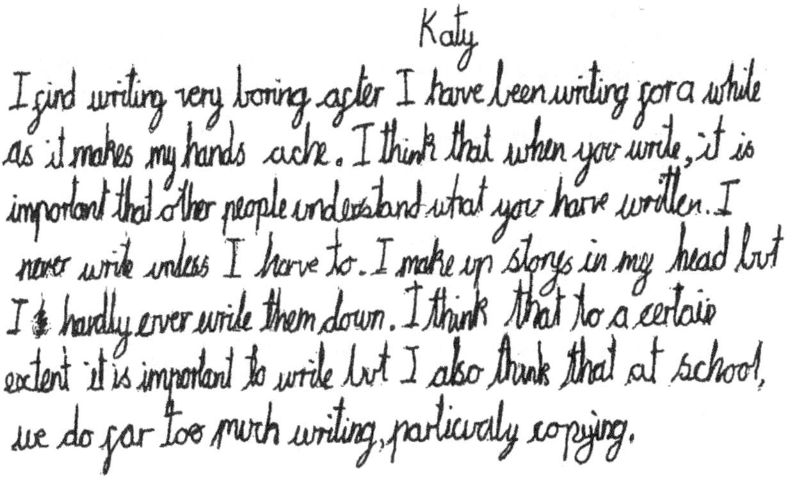

Katy

I find writing very boring after I have been writing for a while as it makes my hands ache. I think that when you write, it is important that other people understand what you have written. I never write unless I have to. I make up storys in my head but I & hardly ever write them down. I think that to a certain extent it is important to write but I also think that at school, we do far too much writing, particularly copying.

Figure 0.1 Katy, aged seven

This book emphasises case analysis as a way of revealing pupils' needs, linking this information to relevant practice and research. It aims to be a hands-on book for teachers and mentors or adults interested in self-help and family help. It also draws on recent research with families in Potential Plus UK who have been concerned about their gifted children's hitherto unexplained underachievement and their writing problems.

Below is James's experience and advice.

James R., aged 35 in 2016

HI PROF,
WRITING FOR THIS LONG IS GOING TO BE THE LONGES I H
WRITER FO SINS I DID MY GCSES!
WHEN AT PRIMARY SCHOOL I FOUND MOST THINGS NOT
TO CHALENGIN.
X EXSEPT THE 3R
IT WAS HARD TO GET ACROS THAT IT WAS NOT JUST
LAZYNES.
IN SECONDRY SHOOL I RECEVD A STATMENT AND STARTED
GETTING 1 2 1 SUPORT. THIS WAS IN THE FOR OF AN
AMANUENSES AND 1 2 1 TO BILD ON LITERY SKIS.
X
X I AChVED 9 GCSES C – A AND 3 A LEVES. I THEN WENT TO
ROHAMPTON UNIVERSATY A TO DO A BSC BIOLO LOCI CAL
SCIENES. AS AT THIS TIME AND STIL TODAY I HAD NOT RED
A BOOK SO ALL OF MY ESAS AND NOTES WHER ACHVED BT
WItH HELP.
I FIND THE //

James wanted to share his experiences of dyslexia with us and joined in the writing research project. Here he is writing at a speed of 13.4 words per minute in a ten-minute test and 46.7 letters per minute. The average speed for a university-educated adult is between 35 and 45 words per minute.

His speed is at the average speed of pupils in Year 7 and this is not surprising given his dyslexic history and failure for this to have been identified and given support until the secondary stage. He has therefore done very well to achieve so much.

He has written the whole piece in capital letters, which is also typical of unremediated dyslexics or to which they revert under stress. The script shows that considerable effort and pressure has been exerted in the act of writing and demonstrates a lack of fluency that would lead to fatigue.

James's spelling is in what is termed the alphabetic phase (Frith, 1985) where he uses a phonetic skeletal basis for spelling, adding to it some of the more complex word structures that he has acquired over time. It is more typical of a beginning speller.

Because he came so late to obtaining support his development was arrested before full phonic and more correct orthography had been achieved. He has therefore done exceptionally well to obtain his impressive list of GCSEs, A-level qualifications, his degree and now a career in teaching.

At the age of nine he started playing the saxophone and had no problem reading musical notation. He gained Grade 5.

Figure 0.2 James's handwritten notes for his solo train journey to London. Age 18

James's story in his own words in year 9 recorded by his scribe

What itches you?

This is a very personal 'what's itching me'. It would not apply to most other people. Because I have specific learning difficulties the work that is set for me I find very difficult if I don't have anybody there to help me. I have the ideas but they are not the easiest things to transfer from one person to another. Often teachers forget this when they set work. I find it extrememly tedious and hard to do it on my own.

Specific learning difficulties occur when someone is otherwise quite normal and intelligent except for reading, writing and remembering aspects of schooling. Quite intelligent people can have specific learning difficulties. For example, the actresses Susan Hampshire and Ruth Maddox, and even Albert Einstein.

Literature is full of unhappy school days. For example, the early chapters of *Jane Eyre* by Charlotte Bronte. In the *Portrait of the Artist as a Young Man* by James Joyce, Stephen, the hero, hands in his essay and is publicly embarrassed by the teacher who accuses him of heresy. Stephen did not realise he was heretic. Charles Dickens, in his book *Nicolas Nickleby*, created the monster teacher Wackford Squeers.

Here are some of the things teachers have said to me and my mum which have been hurtful but not intentionally. Remember – I find it incredibly hard to read and write unaided:

'You are just being lazy.'

'If you really try you can read that James.'

'Will you make your writing neater.'

'Surely you can spell better than that.'

'Oh no, you haven't lost your jumper/tie/book/etc. again James.'

'Now where is James R.? You stand up please. You're the one with problems aren't you? (Done in front of the whole tutor group in Year 7.)

'James please read this to the class.'

'Why haven't you filled your homework diary in?'

'You will have detention and you will copy this work from the blackboard and you stay there till you get it right.'

Comments to my mum:

'Mrs R. I have taught children with problems before and your son is just having me on.'

'Give it time, it will all click together soon.'

'Oh, he's not so bad as some, I've had plenty worse.'

What it is like to be dyslexic?

When I see letters I can read the separate letters but I am unable to put them into a whole word. I am not sure how the sounds go together.

Try reading this:
  'This is what it is like to read from my point of view'
  'Τηισ ισ ωηατ ιτ ισ λικε το ρεαδ φρομ μυ πσιυτ σφ υιεω'
  The top sentence is the same as the second one.
  Try to write with your wrong hand with your thumb tied up. Using a mirror to read your work. Then you will just about get the same effect!

I also have difficulty remembering. I can remember the first two weeks back at school in the second year I lost about £110 worth of stuff because I'd forgotten where I'd left it. Even with a mental check list I can forget to put things on the list in the first place.

What could teachers do?

The British Dyslexia Association makes a number of suggestions. These are the ones I find the most helpful:

1 A scribe to write for the dyslexic.
2 Do not ask them to read extended pieces of text. They will volunteer if they feel confident enough.
3 Provide fact sheets where possible.
4 Give instructions in short stages.
5 Allow them plenty of time to write down homework – or write it down for them. Allow them plenty of time to do the homework.
6 Make sure they know what homework is due and when.

Pointless homeworks

When I do homework it probably takes me half an hour to do what would be ten minutes for anyone else. I have had some stupid homeworks. The most often stupid homeworks are when we are given a worksheet to take home and copy work from. Other homeworks are just pointless for anyone but are even harder for me because there is so much reading. My mum has spent ages down at the library for me.

Home stress

There is also lots of stress at home to do homework. As I was saying, most of my homeworks are writing so I have to depend completely on my mum or my dad to write things out for me which leaves me only being able to do a few homeworks on my own which does not give you too much satisfaction in what you are doing.

My present situation

I now have quite a lot of help in many of my lessons and Mrs H. gives me one to one specialist teaching. With the people to write for me it allows me to be in the sets I really should be in for example I'm in set 2 out of 6 for English, set 2 out of 6 for science, 2 out of 6 for humanities and in set 3 for French (but I don't actually go!).

For the future

For my exams I do have some hope. My mum told me that in the newspaper a girl with dyslexia got an A in English without writing a word!

Do remember there are more like me in the school.

James was given a commendation for this English topic. It included four cartoons that vividly described his feelings.

In 2016 James left the school in which he had been teaching and moved to a new school nearer his home where he is teaching music, science and A-level music technology.

Acknowledgements

This research began with 17 junior school pupils officially diagnosed as dyslexic by the local authority educational psychologists and attending an off-site Reading Centre. They all gave up two of their remedial lessons to help me understand their particular needs.

I explained that the research would not be finished in time to help them but might help young people like them in the future and they gave up their time to share their thoughts, knowledge and experiences and to try to do my 'games'. My special thanks to all of them, who will by now probably have their own families and some dyslexic children and grandchildren of their own.

My thanks too, to all those dyslexics since then, especially James, Robert and Nicholas and their teachers and parents, who have contributed to this book.

Introduction to dyslexia, dysgraphia and underachievement

The first chapter on dyslexia-friendly reading strategies begins with a case study on Nicholas. It illustrates his dyslexic needs and how they were not met by the usual classroom practices and then shows what happens when they are directly addressed with dyslexia-friendly methods.

Chapter 2 shows how his needs could have been addressed in the Reception year, in the logographic phase. New research with cohorts of Reception children identified the problems they have and the techniques that have proved successful in addressing them. It is here that the handwriting difficulties from immaturity through to dysgraphia also emerge and the next two chapters show how these are identified and assessed. The types of interventions that can prove effective are then illustrated through more case work.

Chapters 5 and 6 return to the needs of dyslexics in the alphabetic and orthographic phases. The successful specialist remedial programmes that deal with the alphabetic phase are discussed and evidence is presented to show why they work and their effects on particular cases.

The needs of dyslexics at the end of the alphabetic phase or those who have spelling problems without reading problems are dealt with in Chapter 6 through a new morphemic and strategic programme. Research has shown that it can also give an uplift of at least two years in each year and a series of case study interventions show how the techniques work. The programme consists of Cognitive Process Strategies for Spelling (CPSS) that also transfer to reading, and 'The 15 Spells'. Both can become part of a school policy on spelling that all teachers can easily incorporate into their specialist lessons not just the English and Special Needs Departments.

The final chapter illustrates dictionary work and gives examples of a 'Spelling Detective's Dictionary' in which pupils and teachers can look up CPSS strategies.

Dyslexia

Dyslexia is an unexpected difficulty in learning to read and write by the methods normally used in classrooms. It appears to be a universal problem even in writing systems that use ideographs such as in Chinese. However, it is particularly problematic in alphabetic writing systems even when the relation between sound (phoneme) and symbol (grapheme) is regular or one-to-one such as in Turkish and Italian. It even occurred when Pitman's (1961) Initial Teaching Alphabet (i.t.a.) was introduced for a brief period into some English schools. The i.t.a. alphabet had 44 symbols for the 44 phonemes used in English and used the standard 26 letters and 18 new graphemes to regularise the relationship between symbols and sounds. A small number still found it impossible to learn and others had difficulties in transferring at seven or eight to traditional orthography. The scheme did, however, speed up the acquisition of reading skills by about a year (Downing and Thackray, 1970) in 'normal' pupils.

Dyslexia even occurs when traditional phonics is the only method of teaching (Chall, 1967, 1985) as well as when it is not. The only difference Chall found was that the incidence of dyslexia with phonics first systems was lower, about 1 per cent, and that with Look and Say and meaning emphasis systems it was in the order of 4 per cent.

In Scotland, where they were using phonics methods from the outset, Clark (1970) and the Scottish Education Department (SED, 1978) found the incidence was 1.5 per cent, whereas Rutter et al. (1970) found in the Isle of Wight survey, in the Look and Say teaching context, that it was 4 per cent.

In the current era with the national guidelines from DfE (2014) and 'phonics first' and 'synthetic phonics' initiatives (Rose, 2006) the British Dyslexia Association (BDA, 2017) confirmed that there is an incidence of 10 per cent dyslexia in British schools and that 4 per cent of these had severe problems.

Thus, despite 125 years of investigation into the origins of dyslexia and attempts to remediate it and billions of pounds of time and effort, it still exists to plague children and their parents and stays with them into adulthood. Its residual effects are usually slow reading and spelling problems.

It will be suggested in this book that we have been looking in the wrong place for much of this time, leading to an emphasis on the wrong methods and following research paradigms and conventional wisdom that are inappropriate.

Dyslexia was identified as a developmental disorder by Frith (1980), in which development may be arrested in one of three phases – logographic, alphabetic or orthographic. This approach has been adopted in this book and the different needs in each phase are analysed and interventions illustrated. However, the concept of 'disorder' will be questioned and replaced by the notion of 'developmental delay'.

Currently the needs of dyslexics are still only formally identified after they have failed to learn to read and write by the normal methods and are entering the junior phase or even the secondary school. Unfortunately they are then offered more of the same methods that have failed them but in individual tuition.

In subsequent chapters it will be shown how to identify dyslexia in the different phases – logographic, alphabetic and orthographic – and the form of remediation most suitable to meet their needs at those periods.

The current specialist remedial programmes are mainly directed at addressing the needs of dyslexics in the alphabetic phase and their effects will be illustrated. As a criterion for success it is essential that a remedial programme gives two years uplift in literacy skills in each year of use in order to bring the pupil up to at least grade level otherwise their difficulties are not being remediated. A table of outcomes from the different types of remedial programme can be found in Chapter 5 (Table 5.1) and illustrates this point.

Before dyslexics reach the alphabetic phase they are usually identifiable in Reception and Year One and are in the logographic phase. New research will be presented to show how potential dyslexia can be identified there by the class teacher as part of the usual work and methods for addressing it that are proving successful.

Once pupils reach the orthographic phase or Level 3 dyslexia their needs become different again and a new type of programme is required. This is provided by a strategic and morphemic approach to intervention termed Cognitive Process Strategies for Spelling (CPSS). These also give two years' uplift in literacy skills.

The advantages of CPSS methods is that they can be applied with all pupils as mini lessons for class groups or individually in short one-to-one remedial sessions. Adult dyslexics have also found them useful. These cognitive methods have proved more effective than the widely used rote learning techniques. The improvements in spelling have been found to have a marked transfer to reading to raise its performance whereas concentrating solely on uplifting reading skills does not seem to transfer to spelling in the same way.

Dysorthographia

Dysorthographia is the term I have given to the learning problems of pupils who had a severe spelling difficulty but were good or very good at reading (Montgomery, 2000). They were often gifted children who had learned to read self-taught before school began. Others learned to read easily on entry to school and had never had a reading problem but did have the spelling difficulties seen in dyslexics. For these pupils the CPSS programme is essential. Case work with these pupils is illustrated in Chapter 6.

The term dysorthographia distinguishes these pupils from those with handwriting difficulties or dysgraphia.

Dysgraphia

Children with dysgraphia have difficulties in handwriting with or without difficulties in spelling. Their difficulty is in learning and developing the fine motor skills and precision needed for handwriting. It may result from poor muscle tone and control or a general weakness in hand coordination. The coordination difficulties may be confined to fine motor skills such as handwriting or may be part of a more general difficulty in movement skills such as in walking, running and ball skills. Such children are often referred to as 'clumsy'. The earlier term for this was 'dyspraxia' but now it is referred to as DCD or Developmental Coordination Difficulties or 'Disorders' in US literature.

The result of poor handwriting skills is that the pupils get little practice in writing and so it can delay spelling development too. There are, however, many strategies that can help overcome some of these difficulties so that their effects on literacy development are minimised. A range of these techniques will be demonstrated, as well as the identification and assessment strategies that are needed to accompany them.

Because handwriting is essential to the specialist dyslexia multisensory programmes to underpin the other work on the alphabet and phonics it will be investigated first in conjunction with early learning and then as remedial support to lay the foundation for the rest. Recent neurological research has shown why handwriting is essential to the literacy process as a whole, not just for dyslexics but also for other learners and this will be discussed in Chapter 2 in relation to Reception class developmental teaching and learning and then as part of remedial work in the later chapters.

Dyslexia with dysgraphia

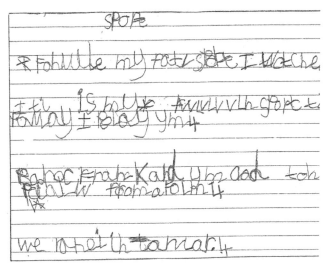

Year 5 pupil: 29 words in 15 minutes

Writing speed approx. 2 words per minute

If you study Ian's writing closely you can see that he has spelled many words correctly, has done some mirror writing, written very slowly for his age and has great difficulty constructing his letters and words.

Figure 0.3 Ian's writing age 9 years 4 months in Year 5 – he has dyslexia and dysgraphia

Some 30 to 50 per cent of dyslexics also have dysgraphic problems and when they co-occur it makes the dyslexia more difficult to remediate. The dyslexia problems are made more severe because there are two learning problems to overcome and one is dependent on the other. Many of these children are the ones who are found in specialist dyslexia centres or schools. This means that the numbers there with both problems are higher than in the general population and can lead to some people including coordination difficulties in the dyslexia diagnosis rather than as co-occurring.

James (see case study on pages ix–xiii) was a dyslexic entering school in 1986 soon after the Warnock Report (1978) had been implemented in schools in 1983. Dyslexia had been identified as a specific need and Statementing procedures had been implemented but had not reached down into his primary school.

In the case of Robert (see below), we see him entering school ten years later than James but very little seems to have changed in the schools. This is despite the fact that by then there had been a significant change in the remedial field. In the 1990s it had been widely disseminated from the research studies that a phonological deficit underlay the dyslexic's difficulties and phonological awareness training was the new 'cure'. This research was to underpin the need for phonics teaching and phonological awareness and the need for multisensory training. It moved remediation from an emphasis on visual training and sequencing methods to phonological awareness training – a necessary but not sufficient move, it will be argued.

In the case example below we find Robert in this period of 'enlightenment' with his experiences of remediation.

Robert: seven years and two months, dyslexic and dysgraphic, 1998

Classroom behaviour:
Robert is quiet and tries hard but is making little progress in reading. The school is providing some in-school extra tuition but has not yet referred him for formal assessment and diagnosis with a view to Statementing.

His mother has asked for a private assessment and would send him to a local private school but this school will not accept him if he is dyslexic. She has already paid for two private remedial lessons per week for the last term but is now very worried because Robert has made no progress at all and is coming home from school each day and 'Going crackers, presumably from frustration'. She is very understanding and concerned.

She reports that Robert has a clumsiness problem. He manages to spread food over himself at meals. When he was younger he continually fell off his bicycle but he persisted and finally succeeded. She had been worried about these difficulties and took advice about them when he was in pre-school. She was told that at this stage she should not worry about them and the dressing turmoils – he put his clothes on the wrong way round and shoes on the wrong feet, etc. She was told that these difficulties 'might not lead to any problems later such as in learning to read and write'.

Although he was not markedly late in walking or talking, now he tends to avoid talking in new company and 'goes off on his bike or digs the garden'. He is now a skilled swimmer, water skier, sail boarder and dinghy sailor. As can be inferred, the family is rich. However it has a lower social ethos. There has been recent family discord and separation so that Robert and his older sister now live in a separate house with their mother.

The 'Remedial' teacher introduced the 'Fuzz Buzz' books and gave individual coaching on reading using the Look and Say approach and copy writing, e.g. 'There are three red boxes'. Robert copied this and coloured in the red boxes.

After about ten lessons the remedial teacher began to introduce some phonics and taught all five vowel sounds in the same session with their key words. When checked a week later Robert names one of them 'E' but can recall none of their sounds. The keyword pictures that he had drawn were too tiny and obscure to identify what sound they might represent.

Robert talked sensibly about his problems and the attempts to help him. He considers the Fuzz Buzz scheme 'too stupid' – meaning 'childish'. Even so, he says it is too hard for him as he only knows two words and only reads it because the teacher helps him on every word.

In this assessment session he read a page or two of his reading book with help on most words, missed the picture clues and relied on memory to tell him who was being discussed. He used no word attack skills and predicted from syntactic and semantic clues.

He was unable to attempt to spell any of the words on the Daniels and Diack (1979) spelling test, scored zero; scored a span of four on digit span; scored zero on the Neale Analysis of Reading Ability (Neale and Christophers et al., 1994) reading test number one story comprehension questions. He was able to write the numbers 1 to 10 unaided but most of them were reversed. He was able to engage in some mental arithmetic.

His knowledge of the names of randomised alphabet letters was a score of 6 correct out of 26 letters (O, X, Z, S, I, J). None of these would be very useful in word attack. He gave the correct sounds of two of the letters of the alphabet (m and z). On an articulation awareness test (Chapter 5) he scored 4 out of 10, which was found to be typical of the low score of unremediated dyslexics. Independent reading on the Schonell (1979) test showed that he knew two words – and, the. He then also volunteered 'mummy'.

His Draw-a-Person (Harris, 1963) test score suggested a mental age consistent with his chronological age but interestingly the head was in profile, which is advanced for his age group. His coordination problems would be likely to lead to a lower or depressed score on this test so the assumption would be that he is above average in ability.

Observation of his behaviour:
When he arrived to be tested Robert came in and sat down and fell off the chair. He accidentally flicked a pen onto the floor. As he regained his seat he scattered the pens and pencils across the table. He settled and then concentrated.

His concentration span was short, his eyes drifted or flicked away. On digit span he forgot the digits but then got the third list correct (span of 4). After this he lost concentration and could not regain it and became confused.

His movements were twitchy, random and slightly choreiform. There were some contra-lateral movements and tonguing.

All the time he was pleasant and responsive, trying so hard at everything.

As can be seen from the case examples of James and Robert in the era of Look and Say methods of teaching reading and copy writing for spelling, dyslexics' needs were not met. The introduction of phonics first, which might have helped in mild dyslexia, was unlikely to have helped them because of their severe cases. What is of concern is that dyslexia programmes that had already been in existence in the UK for more than two decades were not known about by their remedial teachers. Robert's school was sent a copy of the *Teaching Reading Through Spelling* (Cowdery et al., 1983–7) series. Later reports indicated that someone in the school was using it successfully.

As will be seen this picture is still to a large extent the situation today. It shows an emphasis on addressing reading skills, with spelling and handwriting the poor relations in what should be a family partnership. It points to a lack of training in initial teaching at least to advise teachers that specialist programmes do exist and what they are. Even so, there has been a blight upon such programmes that reduces their effectiveness. This is part of the history of intervention and conflict in dyslexia that is explained in Chapter 5 as the 'back story'.

Since the beginning of the new millennium we have seen changes to the schools' reading and writing curricula so that phonics was introduced early in the National Literacy Strategy (DfEE, 1998) and later, phonics first and synthetic phonics (DfES, 2006, 2014). Despite these changes the schools and teachers have not all responded to these initiatives and custom and practice still pervades what they do.

In 2017 the British Dyslexia Association still identified 10 per cent of pupils as having dyslexia and 4 per cent of them with severe difficulties. In more disadvantaged areas the numbers rise even higher. It means that despite all the research and remedial attempts dyslexics' needs have not yet been met. This leads people to conclude that dyslexia cannot be remediated or prevented and so they focus on compensatory strategies.

Even where the recent changes in the national curricula have been incorporated into the teaching practices in classrooms, dyslexics still emerge from the system and this shows that phonics alone was not the answer to dyslexic difficulties. But we knew this anyway from four decades of remedial teaching where phonics was the first resort of the remedial teacher and still did not work for dyslexics. Severe dyslexics, however bright, failed to learn to read and write while those with a milder form acquired some knowledge but were still slow at reading and remained poor spellers. Phonics in all its forms proved necessary but not sufficient to meet their needs.

However, it was also important to provide phonics teaching in a 'structured, cumulative and thorough' manner. This was the advice from the BDA expert group in 1981 but its interpretation has been varied. Having a phonics scheme has not meant that it is cumulative or structured to meet the dyslexic's needs. How it was to be achieved was illustrated in the specialist programmes but they were not necessarily followed by practitioners and scheme writers who came from a different ethos in early years literacy teaching.

It is the purpose of this book to investigate the needs of dyslexics, identify what meets them and then show how it can be implemented.

In Chapter 1 we are introduced to Nicholas in 2006. Will we find that the national initiatives and the research have improved his lot? In Chapter 4 we meet Oswald in 2016, three decades after James's case and find perhaps that little has changed.

Dual and Multiple Exceptionality (DME)

Twice exceptional children have been identified as those who are potentially more able or gifted intellectually but who have a specific learning difficulty (disability in the US). Frequently they have a co-occurring disability such as Asperger Syndrome or Attention Deficit Hyperactivity Disorder and so have a multiple exceptionality. To this pair we must add DCD as another 'disorder'. This means that a bright dyslexic might have DME.

In the case of dyslexia with dysgraphia it is important to recognise it as a dual exceptionality and if the child is more able it is a multiple exceptionality.

At this point it is important to record that slower learners (those with lower measured IQs) may also be dyslexic. They can be identified by having literacy skills that are much lower than predicted from their 'mental age', e.g. a dyslexic ten year old with a mental age of eight years will have the literacy skills of a six or seven year old or even lower. Their remedial needs are for a 'whole way of life' literacy curriculum rather than the expectation of them making progress in remedial 'catch up' sessions.

Underachievement (UAch)

UAch is identified as a lack of achievement consistent with ability or perceived potential. It may be seen in uneven performance over a range of subjects requiring the same type of skills or an apparent lack of effort put into tasks. Characteristically a pupil may be excellent at explaining ideas and what has been learned but is unable to write it down with the same ease and clarity.

Underachievement in schools is widespread but much of it goes undetected. Studies show that it affects pupils across the ability range and is more common and more damaging to some groups than others. In general terms underachievers show an inability to sit still, pay attention, and stay on task. Deeper investigation shows that they have a very poor self-image. What they typically say of themselves is, 'I'm useless at this or that... I hate school... school hates me... it's boring.'

Baum, Cooper and Neu (2001) found from underachievers that everyone in the school knew what they couldn't do but absolutely no one knew what they could do.

It shows we need to celebrate what pupils achieve and help them do better. Concentrating on the negatives causes them to become depressed, demotivated and even feel like failures.

It would be a mistake, however, to locate underachievement as a problem only intrinsic to the pupil. There is a range of external factors that can also cause underachievement that the pupil can do little about. Such factors are underachieving schools whose aspirations for pupils are too low; underachieving departments and teachers whose teaching and learning strategies need to be improved; and underachieving environments whose children cannot be given quality nurturance that enable them to take advantage of schooling. Finally, the ethos and the models of schools, families, popular culture and modern ways of life may not encourage pupils to value schooling or education in the wider sense.

The profile of more able underachievers in school has been well-researched but less is known about underachievement in the middle and lower ranges. What we do know is that they share common characteristics but that there are additional features to consider in this wider group.

A checklist to aid identification of UAch across the ability range:

- Large gap between oral and written work.
- Poor literacy skills.
- Failure to complete school work and homework.

✳ • Poor execution of work.
   • Dissatisfaction with own achievements or complacency in low
   • achievement.
   • Avoidance of trying new activities.
   • Perfectionism and extreme self-criticism.
   • Sets unrealistic goals and aspiration.
   • Does not function well in groups or subverts group work.
   • Lacks concentration.
   • Poor attitudes to school.
   • Claims school work is boring.
   • Fear of failure or fear of success.
   • Negativism, refuses to do tasks or obey rules.
   • Absents self from school or classes.
   • May have difficulties with peers.
   • Low self image.
   • Attention seeking or clowning and calling out.
   • Antisocial behaviour, name calling, bullying.
   • Problem behaviour and disruption.
   • Overassertiveness or oversubmissiveness.
   • Fear of teachers and school.
   • Evades school work.
   • Performs satisfactorily in all areas at a level with peers.
   • Finds plenty of dead time to socialise in lessons.
   • Constantly wandering or out of seat.
   • Consistently mumbles and grumbles while teacher is talking.
   • Has a special educational need perhaps not yet identified.
   • Has very high ability.

Underachievers do not show all these characteristics; there are patterns or clusters of indicators. It is probably difficult to find a pupil who does not show at least one or two of these characteristics at some time – most of them mask our ability to see the real potential underneath. The underachievement may be temporary and related to a difficult period in the pupil's family life or in school. The most important thing to do is to identify the difficulties and help the pupil overcome them so that the UAch does not become permanent.

In secondary schools, where a lot of written work is required, the general profile is of an inability or a refusal to produce written work of a suitable quality or to sit still and pay attention in class.

There may be an uneven pattern of performance across subjects with higher performance in arts and sports or good behaviour and performance in just one subject with a favoured teacher. Out of school achievements may be significant in a number of spheres at home and in the neighbourhood yet school achievements are low. Some only attend for favourite subjects.

While looking across the board at achievement and commitment there are also those individuals who make no impact and function at an average level consistent with that of peers. The 'rhinos' – 'Really Here In Name Only' who are serving time until they can escape from school and get into the real world. Some disappear from view and some become highly successful entrepreneurs. Some of the most gifted pupils may show only average performance in school.

Most often it is in the middle and lower ranges of ability that mismatch goes undetected, but my observations in 1,250 lessons over a period of years (Montgomery, 2002) suggested that some 80 per cent of pupils underachieved a large part of the time even in the best of lessons. Whitmore (1982) found 70 per cent of pupils identified by IQ were underachieving; however, even IQ tests do not identify many of the most able.

In our own schooldays few of us can claim to have spent all day on task totally focused. It is too tiring. We need time for thinking, consolidation and mental relaxation within a lesson's timeframe. Good lessons arrange for these to happen in legitimate ways without allowing 'dead time'.

Persistent underachievement is a great waste of potential and a careful analysis is needed to identify it and find ways of overcoming it. Addressing the writing difficulties as shown in the following chapters can make a strong contribution.

Figure 0.4 (Montgomery, 2009: 8) summarises the major contributing factors to underachievement in the presence of an individual's particular potential and ability.

The **internal factors** are the motivational ones or the drive to behave in particular ways, the personality factors or the type of people we are and the traits that we have. These interact with the barriers we bring to learning. Such barriers exist in a range of general and specific learning difficulties (learning disabilities) and these can undermine progress in all school and life subjects.

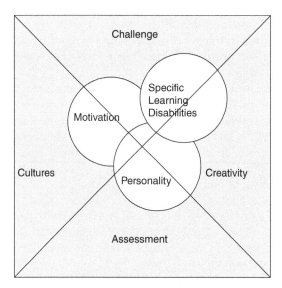

Figure 0.4 The internal and external barriers to learning in UAch

Intrinsic barriers are modifiable but will interact with others, which we have acquired in interaction with the environment. For example, Ryan and Deci (2000) found that extrinsic rewards such as gifts and prizes actually caused a decline in motivation to learn and study whereas a positive, supportive learning environment raised intrinsic motivation.

The **external factors** can conspire to raise or to diminish achievement. For example, a punitive assessment system with multiple targets and objectives and an overloaded curriculum reduced intrinsic motivation (Feller, 1994; Ryan and Deci, 2000). Thus while we aspire to encourage pupils to become lifelong learners our current objectives-based, assessment-driven, audit culture system militates against this (Edgington, 2016).

Some personalities are more vulnerable to this than others and their self-esteem is radically lowered. Some will cease to try, others can become alienated, school averse and exhibit behaviour problems. A coercive system cannot gain the best from pupils unless the teachers unite under strong leadership to make the difference.

It is thus teachers who are the prime source of motivation for pupils in classrooms, providing interest, enthusiasm, positive developmental feedback in assessment for learning and who Catch them Being Good (CBG, Montgomery, 1989), not off task being a nuisance. The second key component is to have appropriate and relevant curriculum tasks and teaching methods, which generate interest and maintain enthusiasm. It is teachers who design the tasks to offer the cognitive challenge and creativity. This consists in developing problem-based approaches to learning and real problem-solving activities, not just asking more challenging questions or making tasks more difficult.

Greater pupil activity, and more open-ended and individualised learning approaches have enabled disaffected pupils to stay on task and become involved in school learning. This needs to be reinforced by positive and supportive use of formative assessment and behaviour management (Montgomery, 2015).

The cultures and subcultures into which we are born and brought up determine many patterns of our behaviour. Some cultures provide models inconsistent with education and learning which become attractive to disaffected youngsters seeking emotional support of the peer group and gang. Difference, however, should be enriching yet is often seen as perverse in a traditional schooling culture modelled upon a nineteenth-century education that pervades much popular and political debate.

For some pupils the intrinsic and extrinsic factors may be in advantageous forms that help them to progress in school and later life. In particular, intrinsic motivation, an inner drive, to go on and pursue studies for their own sake, to be able to plan ahead and follow the plan without anyone encouraging them to do so, is very important. A family background that is supportive and educative and uses extended language is also well known to enhance a child's learning experiences and capabilities.

When we understand these interacting factors and identify those that are operating as barriers we can set about dismantling them. This means we need a range of tools, instruments and strategies to help us. Of great importance, however, is the need for **clarity, consistency, confidentiality, fairness** and **cognitive challenge** in identification and provision. The best way in which these can be achieved is by **identification through provision, high-quality provision**.

1   Dyslexia-friendly teaching of reading

Introduction

Dyslexia has generally been characterised in education as 'dyslexia or reading difficulties' (DfE, 1997: 15). In the research field it was defined as reading out of line with expectation based on age and IQ (Yule and Rutter, 1985) and Snowling (1991). Poor readers were those whose reading was in line with their lower ability and general attainments.

The whole history of dyslexia research and practice from the 1950s to the beginning of this new millennium reflects this concern with reading difficulties as the centre of the problem. However, knowledge about dyslexia first came to public attention over 120 years ago because of a bright boy's inability to spell (Morgan, 1896). Throughout the intervening period it has been known that dyslexics not only have reading difficulties but also an even more severe spelling problem.

Even when dyslexics do learn to read, and most of them do, their spelling difficulties persist into adulthood to trouble them. In the past, people who spelled badly would be regarded as stupid and in academic studies their work would be downgraded despite good content. In SATs and GCSEs governments had ordered that poor spelling must have marks deducted. This seems unfair, because when literacy practices since the 1950s are analysed little or no attention was given to systematic spelling teaching in most English classrooms until after the Rose Report (2006).

Peters' (1967, 1985) analysis of the literacy teaching scene found that spelling was generally 'caught' during reading not taught. This was confirmed in appraisal research in infant classrooms (Montgomery, 2002) and in research for this book. Misspellings were corrected at all levels by two main strategies: 'Look-Cover-Write-Check', a rote learning technique, and by visualisation – 'does it look right?'. Teachers and lecturers of older students would write on the work 'You must use a dictionary' or 'Careless work'. But dyslexics and many other poor readers have difficulties using dictionaries and need to be specifically taught dictionary skills. Carelessness is not the problem.

Reading is of course a very important skill to acquire but it is difficult to understand why; given dyslexics' other difficulties in spelling, the major focus of research and practice has been devoted to reading. Bright pupils with no reading difficulties but with severe dyslexic spelling problems also appear to have been ignored.

Over the 100 years the definitions of dyslexia have changed from it being regarded as a reading disorder (Critchley, 1971) to a reading and spelling disorder (BDA, 2000). Its origin was regarded as a result of 'word blindness' up until the 1970s and then as a 'phonological processing' problem in most instances since (Vellutino, 1979). During these changes the causes of dyslexia have been variously attributed to visual perceptual difficulties, auditory processing problems, working memory deficits, sequencing and organisational problems and so on.

The definition of a problem is an important consideration in both research and practice. This is because how we define something will direct how it is investigated and the results that will be obtained (Snow, 1973). Thus if dyslexia is defined as 'reading problems' or 'reading disorders' that is what will be investigated and other factors will be ignored.

If the cause is thought to originate in working memory deficits then the results will be interpreted within this framework. For example, poor scores on digit span may be interpreted as an indication of a working memory deficit and lead to time spent in remediation on boosting working memory. However, when we find dyslexics with difficulties in recalling and repeating the sets of numbers in the digit span test in comparison with non-dyslexic peers it is more likely to be the result of their verbal processing difficulties. This means that as they try to memorise and then repeat the numbers they are deleted or confused by the cognitive coding, subvocal and vocal processing. Digit span recall has been found to improve as reading and spelling scores improve (Koppitz, 1977; Montgomery, 1997a) and so remediation would be better directed to improving literary skills not working memory.

At times definitions have been over-inclusive as in BDA (1991). The definition included motor skills and orientation difficulties as part of or integral to the syndrome. It reflects the complexities of the cases referred for specialist help and indicates that in addition to the literacy problems the dyslexic may have co-occurring difficulties in the DCD and dysgraphia areas, a dual exceptionality.

In this book it is argued that dyslexia in the majority of cases results in both a reading and an even more severe spelling problem. It is a result of a minor neurological dissociation that inhibits the normal association of sounds and their symbols in the early acquisition phase. When this is remediated then development follows a normal pattern.

If dyslexia can be remediated in Reception instead of waiting for three to five years of confusion to set in then it may be possible to clear up the problems it creates. The subgroup of dyslexics with spelling-only problems will also need to be investigated.

In addition to the problems of definition of the term dyslexia and its origins there is a further issue to be addressed and that is the nature of 'good' or 'effective' provision. This is a major issue of definition for education and remediation providers. It is perhaps even more crucial than theories emerging from research. For example, when Anna Gillingham and Bessie Stillman were putting together their original remedial programme, Samuel Orton was proposing the origin of dyslexia as 'twisted symbols' (Strephosymbolia) resulting from the representations in the non-dominant hemisphere of the brain not being suppressed. The remedial programme addressed the children's actual needs with marginal relationship to the twisting of the symbols except perhaps in helping overcome mirror writing by using cursive handwriting.

A group of remedial teachers in the 1990s strongly held different dyslexia theories about visual, auditory and memory problems, and all taught the same G and S based programme for which they had personal evidence as 'best' practice having seen other methods fail. Now most remedial teachers have converted to the phonological awareness and processing difficulties and spend much time and resources on training to overcome it. The result has been that dyslexia still exists and has not been overcome in most cases, even after remediation lasting for four or more years. What is noticeable over that period is the change in title of the remedial teacher to 'learning support teacher' – possibly an admission that they were not able to remediate the problems and could face legal action if they claimed to do so in a period when tribunals were rapidly increasing.

During that period, Pumfrey and Reason (1991), in an NFER survey, found that there were no effective methods in use across the country and Snowling (1991), in her critical review of 'reading' research in dyslexia, found none able to demonstrate effective remedial teaching methods except perhaps for that of Hornsby and Farrar (1990), because of the lack of adequate controls.

Finding a lack of success of the remedial techniques was not necessarily because effective methods for use with dyslexics did not exist but that the prevailing educational paradigm conflicted with them and did not admit them as any kind of 'good practice' and so their use was not permitted/ encouraged. This issue will be discussed further in Chapter 5.

These NFER findings that there were no effective remedial methods in operation was despite the fact that an unpublished HMI (1991) survey of specialist remedial reading centres had identified a number of 'centres of excellence' operating in the south east. These included the Beve Hornsby Centre in Wandsworth, Joy Pollack's Centre in Fulham, the Dyslexia Institute at Staines run by Jean Augur, and Lucy Cowdery's centre at Kingston on Thames. All these centres operated highly structured cumulative programmes based on or related to aspects of the Gillingham, Stillman and Orton programme (1940, 1956). They all dealt with a structured, cumulative and integrated programme of reading, spelling and handwriting.

Only the Kingston Reading Centre was funded by the local authority and the NFER survey was investigating local authority provision and must have missed it.

Many of these dyslexia centre specialist teachers were recruited on t of having a child of their own with dyslexia and finding that the Gillingh Stillman approach worked with them. The integration of the three s reading, spelling and handwriting placed the specialist programmes in a se position from the rest of early years literacy teaching and the general orth␣␣␣xy of remedial teaching that focused almost entirely on remedial reading strategies.

It is interesting to note that Snowling's paper of that period spent 23 pages on reading research in dyslexia and 12 lines on spelling deficits. It is little wonder that with such a plethora of research devoted to reading that teachers have also focused their interventions for dyslexics on improving reading. The teachers themselves had been taught by Look and Say methods and brought up in an ethos of reading research and debate in a Look and Say and 'real books' context and the colleges appeared to have endorsed this. In this context spelling and handwriting were not regarded as important or relevant to reading. Spelling was mainly to be caught during reading and copy writing and this still appears to be the view – at least implicitly – of many teachers today.

A survey of provision by HMI in 54 schools and one LEA special support service in ten Local Education Authorities was published by Ofsted in 1999. It found that provision was frequently delayed until the year before entry to secondary school. However, better progress was made by pupils who were identified earlier in their primary schools.

General attainment was lower in pupils with Specific Learning Difficulties (SpLD) than expected for their chronological age in two-thirds of primary and half of secondary pupils.

> In some cases, pupils who had received well-targeted specialist help made very significant progress in reading. For example one pupil recorded four and a half years' progress in reading-age terms in 18 months.
>
> (OFSTED, 1999: 6)

The four inspectors found that good progress in reading was usually linked to a highly structured programme often involving a multi-sensory approach, teaching letter clusters and word-building. Pupils made progress in spelling but not to the same extent as in reading. Spelling and writing remained a difficulty for many after transfer to secondary school. The assessment of writing was not well-developed.

In secondary school almost all the pupils needed further help with reading, especially with higher order skills such as skimming and scanning.

Thus we now see that in some schools there is satisfactory and even good provision for dyslexic pupils but this focuses mostly upon reading, as does the survey. The good provision programmes are not named so that they cannot be more widely shared and the rates of progress in terms of reading and spelling ages are not given.

The National Literacy Strategy (DfE, 1998) was introduced after a year of the pilot study with lower attainers. Its format was highly structured and did not meet the needs of good readers and moved too fast for slower learners. New surveys and literacy research culminating in the Rose Report (2006) led to the DfES (2006) guidelines on phonics first and synthetic phonics.

However, the synthetic phonics recommended appeared not to be in the toolbox of many teachers. The guidelines advocated blending or encoding strategies for spelling, such as 'a-n-d' and 's-a-n-d' to make 'and' and 'sand' and decoding strategies that required children to split syllables into their component phonemes, e.g. 'c-a-t' when syllable splitting by ear is not possible for them (Liberman et al., 1967) and running a blend through a word is not the best or easiest for early learners.

It was clear that the guidelines were still not geared to the real needs of learners but derived from a top-down interpretation of what learners should be given. The implications of such erroneous advice will be discussed in later chapters.

Even today teachers still seem wary of teaching spelling and rely on the rote learning of weekly spelling lists with some phonics and a few rules thrown in. The phonics taught in Reception and later is directly related to decoding words for reading. Sometimes it is only basic phonics that is taught and the differences between analytic and synthetic phonics are not understood.

The **developmental approach** to classifying reading and spelling disorders identifies the phase or stage in which the development had been arrested (Frith, 1985) and this is the approach that has been adopted in this book. However, Frith writes that dyslexic children classically have difficulties moving from an early phase of acquisition in which reading is visually based (logographic) to the alphabetic phase when children are able to use letter-sound associations for both reading and spelling. It has to be remembered that she was also working in the context of a Look and Say regime and this may have defined what was written about the logographic phase.

Is it different in a phonics first regime? All we know is that in phonics-based and phonics first regimes fewer dyslexics are created, 1 per cent (Chall, 1967, 1985). Read's (1986) creative spellers began by making single letter sounds represent whole words in phonics first regimes.

At a later stage some dyslexics fail to move from the alphabetic phase to the orthographic phase where reading and spelling are automatic and considered to be independent of sound. Some of them may learn to read very well but their spelling remains poor and at the phonetic level. Why this is so is put down to their 'disordered' system but this notion of disorder will also be challenged in later chapters.

Reading and spelling

Reading is a recognition skill. This means that all the letters making up the words are already present on the page. The reading task is to decode the written symbols to find out what meaning the word or sentence makes. This means the reader already needs to know the names of objects and events and by four and five years most children will have a well-developed grasp and use of the English language, its meanings (semantics) and its structures and tenses (syntax).

Nevertheless language development in speaking and listening activities is of primary significance in the early years and throughout education. The alphabet letters like words have individual patterns and features. We do not store images of the actual letters or words when we learn but apparently we do store features in the brain and rules for recognition (Farnham-Diggory, 1978). Thus the reading task is to identify the features that call up the word's meaning on a consistent basis. How the eye and brain do this features analysis is not fully understood but most children in an environment of print can learn to read by 'paired associate' learning in a purely Look and Say regime. The written word is paired with its sound and calls up the meaning. Some children need more pairing exposure than others. Dyslexics can fail to learn by this system.

In addition to this visual recognition strategy for words children learn to use picture clues to help them decode the story or message. This is supported by syntactic clues indicating the need for good language development. The learning of phonics adds to this mix of cognitive strategies so that children can learn to guess the unknown word from the context in the sentence and the story even more precisely by using its initial sound.

They are 'code-breaking' or decoding in reading. It helps if the stories have a controlled vocabulary at first so that the main task is accomplished and the eye and brain learn which features are important and the patterns that recur. It is usually at this stage that the emphasis changes in reading teaching towards a code emphasis and the role of phonics in helping decoding so that the basic vocabulary is increased.

Spelling is a recall skill. To write a word we have to drag to mind all of a word's letters precisely formed and in the correct order. The page is blank. We may try to visualise the word and copy what we see in the mind's eye. This usually results in the middle letters becoming muddled and we write 'from' instead of 'form', 'was' for 'saw' and 'on' for 'no'.

Alternatively we may try to sound out the word as separate letter sounds and this only works with regular words but not with 'said' and 'come'. Good spellers learn to use a range of strategies to support their spelling and one such strategy is the use of analogy. The word sounds similar to a word they already know so if they can spell 'time' correctly they can by analogy spell 'slime' using their knowledge of the 'sl' blend. This may also mean that for a time they will also spell 'rhyme' as 'rime'.

This is not the only problem in spelling. We not only have to know which letters and in the correct order but we have to write them. This means we must learn to command writing implements and our hand to scribe the small graphemes. To spell automatically, the motor memory for graphemes and words has to be connected to their meaning and flow along with our thoughts.

The amazing thing is that during the Look and Say era of literacy teaching that by only teaching reading most children eventually learned to spell correctly without being explicitly taught, except perhaps being exposed to some later spelling drills. However, inadequacies in pupils' spelling knowledge have been frequently complained of by employers and governments and there is still apparently a long tail of underachievement.

The reason for this lack of skill and slow acquisition rates it will be suggested is because of the lack of an integrated system of teaching reading, spelling and handwriting despite claims to the contrary and that multisensory teaching practices are followed.

Dyslexia-friendly lessons from Nicholas

Nicholas was 4.2 years old when he entered the Reception class. He was very young to start school but was a bright child. For the whole of the Reception year he failed to make any progress in reading, spelling or writing and had only reliably learned numbers from one to five.

During this Reception year he received much one-to-one attention and a variety of reading teaching approaches were used to try to help him. Because he was young his teacher was reluctant to push him and his parents were not willing to reinforce the work at home because 'he was too young'.

When the 'Precision Teaching' method promoted by Ainscow and Muncey (1979) as part of SNAP (Special Needs Action Programme) was tried it did not work because as soon as new words were begun Nicholas forgot the old ones. The class teacher used the 'Letterland' pictogram scheme (Wendon, 2003) as do many other Reception teachers because it is user friendly and the stories and pictograms of the letters are very popular with the children. Letterland also failed to help Nicholas because he could never remember the letters without the character and when the class moved on to the next letters he was lost.

Because he could copy or draw any writing in front of him his mother assumed he could write but he had no recognition of anything that he had written.

At the beginning of Year 1 his learning support teacher decided to investigate with him the use of an APSL (Alphabetic-Phonic-Syllabic-Linguistic) scheme, 'Beat Dyslexia' (Stone, Franks and Nicholson, 1993). This is in a worksheet mode based on the Gillingham and Stillman format and the anglicised versions including articulatory and synthetic phonics aspects of TRTS (Cowdery et al., 1994) and Hickey (Augur and Briggs, 1991) and the Edith Norrie letter case (Norrie, 1973) but without most of the Linguistic elements.

The computerised form of the Cognitive Profiling System (Singleton, 2000) identified Nicholas had weaknesses in visual-sequential memory, phonological awareness, using rhyme and visual-verbal associative memory and sound-symbol correspondence). He had good scores in visual and associative memory and auditory-sequential memory. A note of caution is needed here. We often find that such test scores are a result of a lack of literacy learning rather than some underlying cause of it because all the items involve some form of verbal coding and processing. In essence Nicholas had failed to learn to read and spell by the normal methods used in schools, he was dyslexic.

After 12 weeks of two half-hour sessions per week with one-to-one tuition using 'Beat Dyslexia' Nicholas had made progress. He was able to recognise all the sounds in his reading pack, and able to write all the letters in his sound/spelling pack that the lessons had covered. He was also able to read any words that these letters could make by the time he had completed the first book in the programme (see example below) with the letters: i, t, p, n, s, sp, d, a, c, o, r, dr, cr, tr, pr, spr, scr, and str.

He could also spell by himself any three or four letter words using these letters. His teacher reported that he was also beginning to transfer this knowledge to other school work and especially use it in his free writing.

The teacher (Vallence, 2006) reported that,

> Within the first few sessions it became clear that the key for Nathan in being able to remember the sound was the 'clue word'. He would look at the letter and needed to be shown the clue word, say the word and then the sound. He learned the sounds of the first two letters 'i' and 't' in this way, getting to the stage of knowing the sound with the clue word. Adding the third letter, again he learned it in the same way and when he read his first word using these three sounds, his face lit up and he began to see success for the first time.
>
> However it was slow progress since Nicholas needed to see all the clue word pictures as well as the letters. His mind had a great deal to do. However, he was very pleased with himself.

The question was, could he move on and not need the clue words to support him. Clare Vallence decided that he would not move on in the programme until he could sound out the letters without having the clue word. This was a critical decision and at various points in the school day they used the reading pack. Within a week he knew all three letter sounds and at about the same time he was also able to write them in fully cursive style. He was easily able then to put the letters together to make words. 'His face was beaming and his joy at his success was wonderful to see.'

By the time he had learned the first five letters in the programme he no longer needed to be reminded of the clue words. What is of importance is the significant amount of time that had to be dedicated to this very early stage of learning. This is consistent with the suggestions made earlier that areas around the neurological dissociation have to be trained to take over the function. Once this has occurred the process speeds up. It is however the point at which the remedial teachers and researchers baulk. It is too slow and boring for them so they move on too fast!

> Another big result was Nicholas's first sentence written by himself using the first 7 letters. Whilst he was restricted with words, he wrote, 'it is in a tin' without any help and in full cursive. Again his delight at his success was marvellous to see. He understood that he had been able to make

sense of letters like the others in his class and his self esteem rose significantly. Success changed Nicholas's attitude to classroom activities and his class teacher commented that he constantly wanted to write his words. His parents have had the scheme explained to them and have agreed to help him practice his reading and spelling packs at home.

(Vallence, 2006)

His remedial teacher went on to use the scheme with other older dyslexic pupils, some by then two years behind peers and in the junior school stage. She reported that the multisensory mouth training element (Montgomery, 1984) was proving very helpful for a child with speech and language difficulties.

Vallance concluded that although the scheme was based on worksheets it was important that they were used for direct teaching in their entirety not left as copy work. Although the intervention was for two half hours per week she considered this to be the minimum and that for the early stage it would have been best to work with Nicholas every day to get him over the critical 'cracking the code' phase.

The outline format of a 'Beat Dyslexia' worksheet (Stone et al., 1993)

Worksheet 27: Letter D, *d*, d, *a consonant*

1   **Make the alphabet arc** (this means laying out the capital wooden letters in an arc, see Chapter 7).
2   **Pull out capital letter D and feel its shape**. Under this instruction is an arc of the letters and under that is a large cursive letter *d*. There are three lines in which the letter is written and the letter has a lead in line (1) on the bottom line and a lead out one on the down stroke (3) all numbered and with arrows to show how it is drawn. In the circle or body of the letter is a large dot.
3   **Say d. Air is trapped behind the tip of the tongue, then released.**
4   **Trace over the big d with your finger. Notice you start the same as for a.**
5   **Dot is the clueword because you go round the dot first when you write lower case *d*.**
6   **Trace round the big *d* above in green because *d* is a consonant.**
7   **Trace and copy.** A set of lines beginning with cursive *d* are provided to complete this task. The first set of three lines are wider.

At the bottom of the worksheet a set of 'd' type letters are given with example marks allocated from 0 to 5 with the instruction – **Give yourself a mark.**

Worksheet 28: More about letter d

The instruction is – Find it, Say it, Hear it, Write it.
    There then follows a series of tasks:

1   Put a ring round every letter that says 'd'. You should find four.
2   Write *d* under the pictures that begin with d.
3   Write *d* in the box if you hear d in the word (a cassette tape plays the
     words).
4   Trace over the letters, filling in 'd' to finish the word (e.g. *di_. san_ etc*).
5   Now use these words for reading, recording, hearing, speaking and
     writing (all shown in pictures).
6   Read and copy in your exercise book – *an ant stands in a sandpit.*
7   Practise your reading and spelling cards. Find and trace *d* on your record
     page.

The original schemes on which the above format is roughly based follow a
different pattern and are all by direct teaching. Only some of the games are in
a worksheet format.

1   Alphabet work.
2   Reading pack.
3   Spelling pack.
4   Dictation.
5   Games.

A typical lesson from an APSL programme for the letter 'd' is set out in
Chapter 5 for comparison.
    The 'Beat Dyslexia' order relegates the reading and spelling packs to the
end of the session and so can easily be missed out if the work goes slowly.
There is also no direct dictation work but an emphasis on tracing and copying.
It thus tries to bridge what teachers generally do with the Gillingham and
Stillman approach. Vallence used the ideas in Beat Dyslexia to help guide the
sessions but preserved the G and S order and direct teaching format.
    What we learn from Nicholas is the critical nature of the first experience
with print. A dyslexic needs to learn a useful letter and its sound and name,
all connected within the one learning encounter.
    However, what teachers generally do is introduce a sound and its clue word
or story often through Letterland for reading; teach the graphemes in shape
groups, e.g. 'c, a, o, d' for writing and then use copy writing of news for spelling.
All of these introduce different letters in the different contexts. Although it
works with most beginning learners who eventually grasp the ideas, dyslexics
cannot overcome their specific disability in this manner. It will be argued that
this lack of structure and integration of the three skills actually slows down the
development of literacy in all learners and we could have competent readers and
writers by the end of the infant years if this was attended to.

As Nicholas demonstrated, he needed a very specific and consistent approach that moved only at his speed until he had grasped the principle and his dissociation area had its function taken over by other cells/areas and learned the procedures. Overtraining in the initial stage is the essence of this procedure until the whole process speeds up. The younger the child the more plastic the brain areas are likely to be to do this.

The younger the child and the sooner this remediation takes place the less confusion will have set in and the less inappropriate learning and errors will have been consolidated and have to be overcome. Another problem that can develop with increasing age is loss of the will to try. Because dyslexics experience years of failure it is not surprising that they lose motivation. They usually become three-time failures by the time they receive a Statement of special need and obtain specialist help from someone considered to be an expert. They will have failed to learn to read and write in Reception, failed again with extra support in Year 1 and failed again with one-to-one tuition from within the school resources. They may even fail again or be failed by the expert brought in to work with them. All these experiences lead to a lowering of self-esteem unless the family and school are very supportive and find the child's other talents (Edwards, 1994).

How is it possible for such a bright child to fail to learn the sounds and names of the alphabet?

This was the question that began the story of this research when a six-year-old boy with an IQ of 147 on WISC despite extra help and phonics teaching just could not learn to read and write. When he was taught by the APSL method of Gillingham and Stillman (1956) using the TRTS programme (Cowdery et al., 1984) he quickly became proficient, like Nicholas.

This raised a further question:

How was it possible for normal learners to learn those sounds and their symbols implicitly whilst dyslexics fail? The answer to this critical question will be addressed in Chapter 5.

General strategies for dyslexia-friendly reading teaching

Nicholas has shown us that he can learn to read and write when he is given the highly structured teaching format of the APSL programme, first devised by Gillingham and Stillman with its five integrated components. By the time he entered into Year 3 he had become a good reader and writer and was in the advanced group for the next phase of Clare's research.

As his knowledge develops he will be able to tackle a wider reading and writing vocabulary than just those elements specifically taught in the APSL programme.

In addition to the APSL format other dyslexia-friendly strategies can be used after the i, t, p, n, s phase. Some reading teaching examples follow.

Hearing reading

It is also important to encourage rereading of sentences and paragraphs so that meaning can be captured at the second or third reading and questions about the content can be asked. Books with a controlled vocabulary will help them to decode more easily but books with interesting content are more motivating.

Taped reading – audio stories

Following text in a book while listening to it on audio can be supportive. This is especially so when the pupils read into the recorder and then follow the text as they listen to the recording. This is the ARROW (Aural – Read – Respond – Oral – Write) technique, found effective by Lane (1990).

Onset and rime

In the TRTS remedial sessions the teachers reported that pupils said it was easier to blend single syllabled words when the word was split in one way rather than another, e.g. they found 'c - at' an easier way to blend than 'ca - t'; or the traditional 'c-a-t'.

The 'c - at' split was termed the 'onset and rime' approach by Bryant and Bradley (1985) that they had found effective with early learners. An 'onset' might be a single letter, digraph or blend and the 'rime' was the ending letter group as in '-at' in cat and '-and' in sand. Despite this we still find schemes and government guidelines advocating c-a-t- and s-a-n-d or 's' / 'sa-'/ 'san-'/ sand' when teaching children to blend. Why onset and rime is more effective than these other blending techniques is explained in Chapter 5.

(**Phoneme awareness** for example is being able to tap the three separate sounds in c-a-t and the four in s-a-n-d. It will be argued we cannot do this correctly until we can spell the words.)

PAT – Phonological Awareness Training (Wilson, 1994) and the analogy strategy training

This work was based on the onset and rime approach of Bryant and Bradley (1985) and the research of Goswami (1994), who found early readers were capable of using these analogies for decoding words during reading. Wilson applied the onset and rime and analogy strategies to her work as an educational psychologist with a dyslexic ten year old and then in a research project. She had found that the dyslexics tried to sound out all unknown words and only seemed to have this one strategy in their repertoire.

The pupils in her research project were all referred by schools because of 'reading difficulties' (spelling not recorded) and were aged 8 to 12 years old. They were taught how to break words into their onsets and rimes and then how to word build by using different onsets with the same rime, e.g. c-at, mat, bat, hat, sat, fat; s-and, hand, band etc.

The 24 children receiving the PAT programme over 20 weeks had made significantly more progress than the 24 matched controls in both reading and spelling. The scheme was developed into graded placement exercises and worksheets and widely used in Buckinghamshire.

Dyslexics trained in the scheme have advised that once they have grasped the main principle the exercises can be boring, which means they can be kept on them too long and need another strategy to learn.

The Edith Norrie letter case (Norrie, 1973)

Edith Norrie was born in Denmark. She was dyslexic but at the age of 20 had taught herself to read and write by making a set of letters of the Danish alphabet which she ordered and systematised. Her motivation was to read the letters in 1917 from her fiancé who was engaged in the First World War.

In 1939 she founded the Word Blind Institute in Copenhagen. In 1973 an English version of her system was published by The Helen Arkell Centre as The Edith Norrie Letter Case. In the box there are several lower-case and two capitals of each letter. It includes a small mirror in which only the mouth can be viewed.

The box is divided into three compartments containing letters and consonant digraphs. The letters are grouped according to the place of articulation of the sound in the mouth most frequently associated with it. When the pupil attempts to spell a word it is necessary to work out how the sound is made in the mouth with the aid of the mirror. This increases the awareness of speech sounds and the relationship between phonemes and graphemes.

The vowel cards are coloured red and there is a clue card for them with drawings of an apple, egg, ink bottle, orange and umbrella. The colour helps reinforce the idea that every syllable must contain a (red) vowel.

The consonants are coloured black or green to help sort out those that are voiced and unvoiced. The pupils learn to word-build with the letter cards and find it enjoyable. Errors do not have to be erased and words can be worked on in a concrete way to arrive at the correct spelling. The approach thus emphasises articulation training, phonic skills (phonological awareness and segmentation) and word building for spelling and reading. Bradley (1981) used the technique of word building using alphabet letters and simultaneous oral spelling (Chapter 5) in a controlled study and found it an effective method for promoting reading skills in dyslexics.

Unfortunately the Norrie letter forms are in print rather than in cursive and this encourages pupils to copy the letters in print as well. A Letter Case with cursive letters would be an asset. Joy Pollack and Elizabeth Waller were originally tutors at the Helen Arkell Centre and describe their methods in their popular book *Day to Day Dyslexia* (Pollack and Waller, 2004).

Multisensory phonogram training

When children are taught the sound of a letter alongside its grapheme or symbol and then learn to write it, this is multisensory training. It is however only one component of the techniques that dyslexics need. It has caught on in the reading teaching realm and when teachers use it they believe that they are addressing dyslexics' needs. Multisensory training is necessary but not sufficient to meet dyslexics' needs.

Synthetic phonics and the Clackmannanshire study

The Clackmannanshire study (Johnson and Watson, 2005) compared spelling and reading progress at the end of Primary 2. 300 children were given 16 weeks training for 20 minutes each day in one of three programmes:

1   Synthetic phonics to blend letters for spelling words.
2   Analytic phonics to decode words for reading.
3   Analytic phonics and phonological awareness training.

The results were that at the end of the programme the synthetic phonics group were about seven months ahead of the other two groups and seven months ahead of their chronological age in reading. They were eight to nine months ahead of the others in spelling. Contrary to expectation the synthetic phonics group were also able to read irregular words better than the other groups, and was the only group that could read unfamiliar words by analogy. Thus during the synthetic phonics teaching they were learning and developing transferable skills that the other methods were not providing for their groups.

Phonographix research in Bristol schools (Dias and Juniper, 2002)

Phonographix (McGuinness and McGuinness, 1999) is a synthetic phonics approach in which 79 items need to be learnt instead of 1,493 separate onsets and rimes, e.g. instead of learning separate rimes as in '-and' and '-unch' for 'sand' and 'lunch' children learn to blend the already known sounds 'a- n- d' and 'u- n- ch'. (Note the running through the word blending, not the use of initial and end blends.)

The Phonographix takes 43 sounds of the English language and in careful stages teaches the various symbols (referred to as sound pictures) that are used to represent those sounds. For example: ship is made up of three sounds. The first sound is represented by /sh/, the second by /i/ and the third by /p/.

The method teaches pupils to listen to words and split them up into the sounds that make them up (auditory processing). For example: the words cat and sheep are both made up of three sounds. In a carefully sequenced way the pupils are then shown how to represent these sounds on paper.

The graphemes are taught as 'sound pictures' using letter cards which can contain one or more letters, e.g. digraphs ch, sh, th, ph and wh; oa, ea, ou contain two letters that make one sound in a word. It teaches 43 phonemes represented by 100 letter combinations. Letter names are not taught. There are three levels:

Teaching reading is divided into two main parts: basic code and advanced code.

Level one: The basic code covers 25 sounds and is taught, one letter one sound and no digraphs. The skills training is phoneme analysis, segmenting, blending, reading and spelling of three sound words such as cat, dog, sit and words with 'consonant clusters' bell, off, less and words with 'adjacent consonants', e.g. sand, lamp. The vocabulary is carefully chosen for one-to-one mapping.

Level two: The advanced code introduces consonant and vowel digraphs, phonemes with multiple spellings, e.g. 'ou' stands for five phonemes; and letter pictures that represent more than one sound, e.g. 'o' as in 'hot' and 'oe' as in 'most'.

Level three: This deals with polysyllabic words and syllabification for reading and spelling.

Children in the research control and experimental groups were all in the Reception year and baseline assessed in the first half term and then again in the following May. Their progress was compared on a) Phonographix, b) Jolly phonics, or c) the NLS programme. The result was that after seven months the Phonographix group was ahead of the rest on all measures and on entry to Year 1 none of them needed ALS (Additional Literacy Support), whereas the teachers identified 25–30 per cent of the rest as needing this help.

All the children developed phoneme code knowledge but the phonographix group had better skills knowledge and when segmenting and blending were also able to generalise and apply these skills in an unfamiliar situation such as non-word reading.

As can be seen the synthetics and phonics are different from the G and S format and the 'synthetic' phonics in Phonographix is not necessarily the most effective way of teaching. However the researchers pointed to the structured and cumulative approach of the scheme as the most likely successful factor and the fact that it cut down confusion and overload giving the children a sense of mastery. To this we can add the use of letter cards to build the words.

Phonographix has also been found to be an effective programme for use with students following an ESOL course (English for Speakers of Other Languages) (Campbell, 2003).

When it was piloted in Camden schools in London with children with reading difficulties, after 12 to 18 hours on the programme the children were generally making two and four years progress in their reading age (Camden LEA website August 2003).

Based on such evidence, synthetic phonics and 'phonics first' became the central platform in the government's literacy guidelines (DfES, 2006) and later the Early Years Foundation Programme (DfE, 2014).

TRUGS – Teaching Reading Using Games (Jeffery, 2016)

All the specialist G and S programmes use games to reinforce learning, particularly of phonics knowledge and this resource is a structured set of card games to enhance other phonics programmes designed by Joanne Jeffery, Principal of Dyslexia Access in Devon and Cornwall. It is constructed in 15 stages from basic words in Box 1 through to Higher education levels, Box 3. There are four different types of card games to play, graded according to difficulty. Each is numbered and colour coded. It is focused upon improving reading skills and has become popular with SENCOs.

Pattern recognition training in early reading (Montgomery, 1977, 1979)

Observation of five teachers in their Reception classes teaching reading over a period of two years raised the question about how children actually learn to read in a Look and Say environment.

Children were shown key words in the Rainbow Reading scheme, 'read' the picture books, moved on to the controlled vocabulary story books. They took home word tins with their words in to practise at home. After they had acquired a sight vocabulary of 50 words by a process of paired associate learning using the 'flash cards' they were introduced to some phonics work by learning the sounds of the letters. Each day they told the teachers their news and traced or copy wrote it until they were allowed to write it themselves.

Some of the children began to read very quickly and others did not but the question was how did anyone learn by this method of pairing written words and their sounds – association learning or 'paired associate learning'. Good readers would need to have good visual memories but how did the brain perform this feat without any guidance? How might the poor and the non-readers be helped?

In brief the answers were found in perception research and tank recognition studies. Perceptual studies showed that eye and brain perform a features analysis on any input. The tank recognition studies showed that naïve subjects after doing jigsaws of a range of tanks were able to identify them very easily and much better than subjects shown pictures and told the main features of the separate tanks.

This posed a series of problems about reading. What were the relevant features in children's visual learning of words and could they be taught by the jigsaw method to identify and learn them? What were the features that made up words and their letters?

Some of the early learners appeared to scan the words correctly from left to right but others did so from right to left. If they fixated on the last letter when the teacher said the word it would make it difficult to learn to read it. If they fixated, as some did, on a particular letter such as the 'k' within a word this would not help either, especially if they were expected to play the game 'I spy something beginning with - - -'. What was the 'beginning' of a word for them? Did they know the meaning of 'beginning'?

The analysis showed that the lower case print letters of the alphabet were made up of four main features: a circle, a stick, long or short and a curved stick. In fact, the letters a, b, d, g, i, j, k, l, o, p, q, t, v, w, x, y, z could be made with circles and/or 'long and short sticks'. The children were given 'dots and stick' patterns to copy with counters and sticks. This ensured they could be taught to start on the left and work across to the right. They were also given jigsaws of words to make and say the word they had formed. This involved a close observation by the child of the features of the word they were to make. It helped them learn the words in their tins more easily.

WEEK 1 On red (pink)				
A1	**A2**	**A3**	**A4**	**A5**
G G G G	OO O OO	R RR R	Y YY Y	GG B GG
ROROR	YOYOY	GYGYG	RORROR	YOYYOY
YYGGYY	RRYYRR	OOYYOO	GGYYGG	RROORR
RRRGGG	OOORRR	RRRGGG	OOOYYY	BBBYYY
OO GG OO	YY RR YY	GG RR GG	BB OO BB	YY OO YY

WEEK 2 On orange				
A1	**A2**	**A3**	**A4**	**A5**
B BB BB	Y YY YY	G GG GG	R RR RR	O OO OO
OR OR OR	YY OO YY	GO GO GO	BR BR BR	GB GB GB
GGG RRR	RRR OOO	GGG RRR	OOO BBB	YYY RRR
BGBGBG	RYRYRY	GBGBGB	RORORO	GYGYGY
RRRRR	GGGGG	RRRRR	YYYYY	RRRRR

Figure 1.1a A coloured dots sequences to copy

Figure 1.1b Black dots and sticks sequences

Week 3

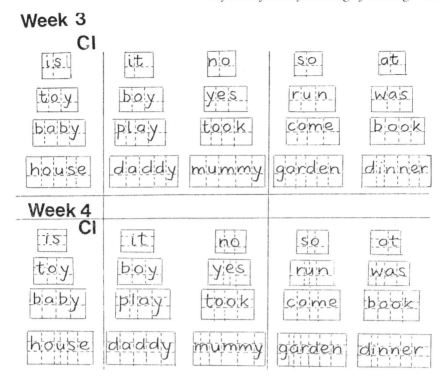

Figure 1.1c Jigsaw sequences with real words for the classroom, not the research
jigsaws
Source: Montgomery (1979), extracts from pages 22–24.

In a controlled study using 'dots and sticks' training patterns and non-word
jigsaws, those in the experimental training groups had moved ahead several
grades faster on the reading scheme than controls given paired associate
training. Those who had hitherto not begun reading had also moved forward
onto the scheme.

When pre-schoolers were also introduced to the 'dots and sticks' training
and word jigsaws they were able to enjoy them as informal approaches to
literacy work.

The manipulation of the 'dots and sticks' and jigsaw pieces enabled the
teacher to see which features the child was focusing on and which ones
needed to be modified. The handling of the pieces showed the readiness in
fine motor skills and the speed of the process. All of these aspects are important
in preschool and Reception learning not only of dyslexics and other poor
readers and writers but children in general and would support their literacy
learning. After the test development phase, pattern recognition training
materials were designed and tested. Case studies and 30 diagnostic points
were identified showing problems that early readers might have and how they
might be overcome.

Implicit learning

The power of implicit learning tends to be ignored in our education systems. However it is not only powerful in our lives but it is highly sustainable. Children who are born into a word-filled environment over their first 6 to 18 months learn to speak the language of their home. Implicitly they learn the names of important things – 'Mumma' and Dadda', 'doggy' – in their environment and key command words – 'want', 'go'. They move on to grammatically correct two-word utterances and then develop sentences. Some bright children may even speak in sentences at six to eight months and learn to read self taught at three to four years old.

Simultaneous bilinguals from birth are spoken to in one language by one parent and in another language by the other parent and they grow up speaking both languages fluently. Sequential bilinguals have a secure single home language (L1) but when they go to school are totally immersed in a second language (L2) and all the subjects are presented in L2. Some simultaneous bilinguals become multilingual by immersion in a third language at school. All this is acquired implicitly by ordinary learners, not necessarily those who have a particular talent for languages who may become polyglots.

Van de Craen (2016) showed a video-clip of a four-year-old Chinese boy who could not read, write or understand musical notation but who could play complex piano concertos – an example that implicit learning is not confined to languages and reading but that there are a wide range of skills and knowledge that can be acquired by this method. He went on to demonstrate through photographs of brain scans that the connectivity in the brains of bilinguals was greater than in monolinguals and discussed research that showed they were thus enabled to solve issues and problems faster, with greater ease and efficiency and less cognitive effort.

In the context of literacy teaching, implicit learning has an important place. It means that the school as well as the home must provide a reading-rich environment. Thus teachers tell stories to the children and they read to them as well as covering the walls with reading material and pictures. However it is often overlooked that beginners may not have the vocabulary and concepts contained in the story books. Children may never have travelled on a train but have flown abroad. They may never have spent a day at the seaside.

Good schools identify key experiences and fulfil the need. One primary school studied (Montgomery, 2009) took all 400 inner-city pupils for a day at the seaside. For all the children (and the accompanying parents) it was a hugely memorable outing and the literacy work that emerged from it was excellent. The school was the family for all of them.

The implications of all this are that classroom learning can be too sedentary and confined to the resources inside four walls but experiential learning outside the room with its capacity for wider, deeper and more sustainable implicit learning is a very important contribution to literacy.

It can be even more helpful if the outing is well-prepared in advance by giving clues and questions and ideas for things to look out for. A local studies walk up the high street of any small town in England can take the class through seven centuries of architecture. A cathedral or church may take them back 1,000 years, and local museums can enrich these experiences.

Experiential learning

It is important to ensure that children not only have a wide range of practical experiences but also that they are discussed and reflected upon before and after the event. When children engage in metacognition and reflection it enriches the learning and makes it deeper and sustainable. It enables it to be absorbed into existing cognitive structures and hierarchies of constructs.

Other useful supportive strategies in general use

- Pause – prompt – praise.
- Paired reading and shared reading.
- Language experience methods – the pupil writes/composes his or her own books with illustrations to read to friends, parents and the teacher.
- Older dyslexics write illustrated story books to read to children in the Early Years.
- Listening dogs – children read to real dogs trained to listen.

State-directed literacy teaching and learning

The National Literacy Strategy (DFEE, 1998) had not proved to be effective in raising the literacy achievements of pupils (Tymms, 2004). It moved too slowly for the most able. It was too rigid and too fast to meet the needs of the less able and it confused dyslexics. The Rose Review (Rose, 2006) was established to redress this situation and investigate what was found to be effective. It was concluded that this was 'phonics first' and 'synthetic phonics'. Unfortunately many teachers did not know the differences between basic, analytic and synthetic phonics, much less how to teach them because of the Look and Say system in which they themselves had been brought up and the lack of attention given to other than basic phonics in teacher training courses.

In teacher training and the National Curriculum, literacy became part of the English teacher's remit and this was a major error. Literacy teaching and learning is a complex subject in its own right not a lower order subset of English teaching. It is one of the most complex areas for investigation with a huge body of research and theory to encompass.

Just as one college had established literacy teaching as a four-year joint Honours programme with Learning Difficulties in the Early Years courses, it was swept away by giving all the main time to 'school subjects' defined in the National Curriculum – in this case English. Literacy was relegated to the professional studies strand in which 100 hours were shared between English, maths and science, with some PE and special needs inputs. So an Early Years 'specialist' might follow a full degree programme in academic geography and history but spend 30 hours on English with literacy included.

This English course would involve the selection of books suitable for stimulating reading and language in young children, inculcating the undergraduates into the National framework and its methods of teaching reading. They might spend an hour on spelling and often no time on handwriting. The rest had to be learned on the job, at first out in the schools on teaching practice 'sitting by Nellie' and then as a professional in a school following the latest National Guidelines, already the main college course diet.

It was not surprising that teachers and educators complained that the teacher's role had been reduced to technician status and involved following a set of prescriptions from the national guidelines that permitted no creative interpretation or differentiated input according to individual children's needs. Provision in schools was audited by Ofsted also following a set of prescriptions based on competency assessments and SATs outcomes ensuring that the national guidelines were followed and the teaching methods complied with current orthodoxy. Effective teaching as defined by the Teacher Education Agency and Ofsted was not necessarily what the research showed was 'good' teaching or effective methods for promoting it (Montgomery, 2009).

If the 'prescription' or any part of it was wrong the whole fabrication was set on a course to failure. Once again it was the children who suffered and the teachers were held to account, never the perpetrators. Although a move has been made to give teachers more autonomy in recent years there can be little change while Ofsted still follows in its same audit pathway – punitive, patriarchal, narrow and closed.

Aside from national prescriptions there are other problems that contribute to making the guidelines wrong. Frequently what is observable in the field and backed by research is not necessarily what should be going on or may be interpreted differently by another researcher. In the Clackmannanshire research Jolly Phonics (Lloyd, 1993) that was widely used in schools was not more effective than the NLS. Phonographix was effective by comparison but it is based on some unmerited doctrines.

Since that period what takes place in schools has become more and more centrally prescribed. It is important therefore to examine current doctrines such as in the Early Years Foundation Stage to find out what has to be overcome. This is because the government agents set the agenda and curriculum in schools and much of what they write seems almost in direct contrast to dyslexics' and early learners' needs.

National Primary Strategy (DfES, 2006, 2014)

The DFES (2007) guidelines referred to a 'running blend through words' such as s - a - n - d and s - t - r - ee - t. This is not the G and S system based upon what dyslexics (and other learners) find easiest for spelling/encoding, e.g. s - a - nd and str - ee - t and for reading (decoding s-and and str-eet). In the APSL programmes single letters' names and sounds are taught as well as initial and final blends as the spelling programme moves along. In reading for decoding the onset and rime strategy can also be taught.

Like multisensory training, synthetic phonics is necessary for dyslexics but not sufficient. They show a pupil how to use the sounds as they learn to build words for spelling or encoding. It must start as soon as they learn two sounds. Instead some teachers may still teach only basic phonics, that is, the sounds and their symbols expecting the pupils to transfer this knowledge to reading and writing. Others will teach analytic phonics that assist the pupil to decode during reading but they may even then wait until a sight vocabulary has been built. Synthetic phonics should show pupils how to build words for spelling. But, as will be seen, not enough time is given to this in the early stages.

Dyslexics need to learn analytic and synthetic phonics in a very systematic way because word building can be very problematic for them and must be directly taught, as was illustrated in the case of Nicholas.

The designers of the Early Years Foundation Stage (EYFS) below have clearly tried to move the teaching methods forwards but they come from a different perspective to the children arriving at it from an adult 'top down' perspective.

The EYFS (DfE, 2014) programme is divided into five phases (p. 50) as follows:

- **Phase One:** Identify sounds in the order in which they occur in words. We know from the research of Liberman et al. (1967) that this is not possible unless we can already spell them. A syllable cannot be split 'by ear' because the separate phonemes are shingled on top of each other in speech. Illiterate adults can clap syllable beats but not phonemes in a syllable. Dyslexics and controls were also unable to do this task correctly unless they could already spell the words (Montgomery, 1997a).
- **Phase Two**: Teach one set of letters per week in the order that make the most possible CV, VC and CVC words. Each set was to be learned in a week. (It took Omar six weeks to learn to write, and read the letter 'i'.)
  - Set 1: s, a, t, p
  - Set 2: i, n, m, d
  - Set 3: g, o, c, k
  - Set 4: ck, e, u, r
  - Set 5: h, j, f, ff, l, ss
  - 'Say a letter sound (with the mnemonic and action if necessary) ask the children to write it saying the letter formation pattern as they do so.'

This order of letters bears no relation to the difficulty children might have in constructing them, such as 's' and 'a', or the confusions between similar shaped letters 'n' and 'm' occurring together, and where in the mouth they can be felt for ease of identification 'l'. At least the vowels are more or less separated out. However there are no initial or final blends taught. Teachers complain that the four per week is too fast for most of the children.

Mnemonics are not an efficient way to teach phonemes, nor is just saying the letter pattern as they write the letter for dyslexics. They have a verbal processing problem and as they say the pattern so they delete the memory and become confused. They need 'in air' tracing practice following the teacher's model then writing it on paper – motor skills training while saying the sound, this will create less confusion. Some words do not make sense when spelled by sound, as already indicated.

- **Phase Three**: Teach the rest of the sounds and graphemes in 12 weeks and all the letter names if not already known.

  (This is not a structured and cumulative approach. Teaching the sounds and names in company with each other as in the APSL programmes so that words can be spelled out would help all learners.)

- **Phase Four**: In the last four weeks of Reception practise all the GPCs (Grapheme-Phoneme Correspondences) learned so far.

- **Phase Five**: Throughout Year 1 teach the last of the GPCs not yet taught and alternative spelling patterns for sounds.

  (There is no justification given for these so-called 'alternative' spelling patterns. It appears to be all about rote learning of different phonic patterns yet the English language is built upon both phonic and morphemics (meaning). There are also useful rules that govern a lot of spellings such as the L-F-S rule that links the doubling of ll, ff and ss. Children even in Reception enjoy thinking and problem solving more than rote learning and gain more from it. Examples of this cognitive approach are given in Chapter 5 under the heading of 'Developmental spelling' and for more advanced learners in Chapter 6 under the 'Spelling detective' approach.)

- **Phase Six**: Taught throughout Year 2 and beyond to increase fluency and blending. Some work is also given on spelling rules.)

  The DfES (2006) proudly announce 'Letters and Sounds, the Principles and Practice of High Quality Phonics' Primary National Strategy. What is high quality here?

  The DfES guidance also deals with letter formation and ligatures are recommended but no loops for joining. Each letter of the alphabet is shown with a dot at the point at which a letter should be started. There are several different starting points! This is completely unacceptable in motor skills terms for those with difficulties and leads on to poor writing in most children, as will be evidenced in Chapter 3. We are also told that there are four correct joins! Incorrect!

The major problem is how to correct such guidelines. The intentions are well meant but the guidance is wrong in many aspects yet again. It also allows for misinterpretation and adherence to old incorrect practices.

One teacher's creative response (Vallence, 2008)

After her learning experience with 'Nicholas', Clare decided for her MA dissertation to engage in an Action Research project in which she would put together a literacy curriculum for her school based on the APSL principles with other useful early years techniques and evaluate its effectiveness.

The opportunity arose because a new head had instigated a review of teaching and learning across the curriculum. The school was an independent primary school of 200 pupils aged from 3 to 16. As a newly appointed head of Infants Clare was tasked to undertake the review and the curriculum development for Key Stages 1 and 2. The focus was on language and literacy and the early identification of children 'at risk' from reading failure and methods that would help them overcome their difficulties. The new curriculum would be trialled in 2007 to 2008. After an analysis of theory and research and the materials and schemes in use in a variety of settings the following programme was devised and tested.

Her review found the following aspects needed changing:

- No consistent policy for reading, spelling and handwriting across the primary phase was in place.
- Phonics teaching was not systematic or cumulative, and lacking phonic knowledge was particularly noted in the juniors.
- Reading, spelling and handwriting were not taught with any particular reference to each other.
- Assessment for progression in reading, spelling and handwriting was not consistently in place. Teachers' understanding of how to teach reading, spelling and handwriting differed significantly across the primary phase most notably in the understanding of phonics.
- Sufficient time was not being given to the specific teaching of reading, spelling and handwriting skills.
- The teaching did not consistently take an approach that took into account the needs of all learners.

(Vallence, 2008: 92)

She found good language development provision, phoneme-grapheme correspondences taught across Key Stage 1, and cursive writing was taught from the outset. The staff were committed to providing an interactive and fun learning environment.

Eight core staff were involved from the outset and were able to present their own ideas and viewpoints on the findings of the review and the proposed new curriculum through interviews and a questionnaire. The results showed they were very interested and wanted to be involved in potential new ways of working but like all teachers were worried about the time factor.

They were given an INSET training day on phonics using the Hickey Multisensory Language Course and other materials. At the end of the session, the outline of the new curriculum was presented, e.g.:

- A pictogram system similar to Letterland (Wendon, 2003) would be devised that would allow teaching and learning to be interactive with characters and stories that reflected the ethos of their church school. The characters would all be human and be incorporated into print letters but cursive handwriting would be used in letter formation.
- The letter sounds would have actions to add to other kinaesthetic learning opportunities.
- Reading, spelling and handwriting would be taught together in a multisensory way using elements of HMLC, with spelling and handwriting taking a prominent place in the teaching.
- The teaching would follow the order of HMLC for teaching the sounds as well as syllabic and linguistic elements. And although the stories and learning through play activities would form part of the activities, a daily 20-minute or so session would concentrate directly on the reading, spelling and handwriting activities using many of the ideas in all the schemes.
- The children would be taught the common GPCs initially in Reception and then across Key Stage 1 with further GPCs added. These would be reinforced throughout Key Stage 2 using elements of 'advanced code' activities in Phonographix as well as syllabic and linguistic elements from HMLC. Cursive handwriting would be taught and linked to the spelling programme as part of the spelling programme at all stages.
- Continuous assessment would also form an essential part of the curriculum, both with reading and spelling assessment and also observational assessment so that those 'at risk' of failure could be identified as early as possible.
- Elements of Letterland, Jolly Phonics, Phonographix and HMLC were adapted to suit the particular school setting.

(Vallence, 2008: 108–109)

The Alphabet Kingdom

The system design was as follows, e.g. for i , t, p, n, s.:

- Impatient Indian Action: fold arms in front.
- Truthful Ted Action: move arm to the side like a train
- Prayerful Polly Action: pick peaches and pears from a tree.
- Noisy Nurse Action: nod head.
- Strong Samson Action: lift up a weight.

Each lower and upper case letter was colourfully illustrated, incorporating Indian, Ted and Polly etc. and produced on computer jpeg files so they could be used in all the materials. The first was an A5 story book of all the letters. These were followed by each character being given a story, an action and a song. The story book could be taken home by each child for the parents to read to them.

There were also characters for the short and long vowel sounds and vowel and consonant digraphs. The vowels were presented as twins, e.g. Amazing Acrobat and Amy; Ever-ready Ed and Eva; Impatient Indian and Iris; Ongoing Ollie and Opal; Underwater Ug and Unis.

A typical Alphabet Kingdom lesson had the following format:

- Read story, sing song, do action – look at the belongings of the character from their special bag of things that begin with that sound.
- Say the sound again and again so the children feel the sound with their mouth.
- While saying the sound, e.g. 't', the children write a large cursive 't' in the air and then on lined whiteboard, the children practise letter formation following HMLC.
- The children work in their scrap book using a textured cursive letter to trace over with their fingers.
- The children work in workbooks, again practising the single letter formation, each time saying the sound as they form it.
- The children then practise blending for reading and joining the letter 't' with 'i' the previously learned letter to make 'it', 'ti' for spelling on lined whiteboards or in handwriting books.
- Practise the sounds for reading and spelling using the cards.

Associated with this process other activities included sound bingo, sound spelling activities, craft activities and story-related roleplay and themes.

The cursive letter formation used was 'Handwriting for Windows CD' (Balcombe, 2004).

At the end of the pilot study period lasting six months, seven of the eight children in the Reception group (group 1) were able to give the letter sound, not just the character of the plain printed letters that had been taught. They were also able to blend it with other consonants and vowels to create VC, CV, CVC, CCVC and CVCC words.

The same seven children were able to write the correct cursive grapheme for a given sound and their free writing had improved.

Child number 8 had been taught capital letters for writing in her pre-school and was identified as struggling to keep up with the pace of the others in the group. Age four years six months she wrote:

I PLAW WUF rObUN (I played with Robin)

She did develop some phoneme–grapheme knowledge but had difficulties retaining what was learnt from one day to the next. Thus when the others were doing blending and encoding she worked with the teacher or teaching assistant (TA) using the HMLC programme in its entirety going at her own pace. This proved successful and she retained what she had learnt.

At five years 0 months she wrote:

> *I wet to The Bleech*
> (I went to the beach) This was written in cursive.

The programme was also implemented with Key Stage 1 and Key Stage 2 groups. They were put into mixed age groups and divided into: 1) an advanced group (reading a year or two above age level, spelling a month or two above); 2) an average skills group; and 3) a struggling skills group for teaching. The programme began at the level of their skills with revisions as appropriate.

At the end of the pilot in six months the advanced group (six children) had made from 10 to 16 months' progress in reading and from 6 to 12 months in spelling. In the middle group only one child out of the six had not made more than six months' progress in reading and spelling. Her progress was to be kept under review.

The strugglers in group 3 did not make more than the six months' progress expected and divided themselves into two groups – those who were progressing developmentally and those who would need further and more systematic intervention, however they were all now reading and writing at around their age level.

When the programme was implemented at Key Stage 2 (Years 3, 4, 5) with four mixed age groups similar results were obtained. Groups 1 and 2 were already reading and spelling one or two years above grade level. Group 4 were already receiving remedial provision including work on Alpha to Omega (Hornsby and Shear, 1993) for some.

The average increase in skills in six months:

- Year 3 was 9.1 months for reading and 8.6 months for spelling.
- Year 4 was 12.3 months for reading and 11.2 months for spelling.
- Year 5 was 10.2 months for reading and 9.8 months for spelling.

Although these are small numbers and a pilot study the staff, parents and the children were all very positive about the whole process and it does indicate the value of allowing teachers opportunities for creative research in their own classrooms. This study did make a positive difference to those children's lives and is a useful model for good practice. It should also be tested on a wider scale by teachers in their own classrooms.

The reading-friendly toolkit for teachers

- Integrate reading, spelling and handwriting teaching of sounds and symbols.
- Teach sounds in use order – i, t, p, n, s.
- Make sure pupils can feel the key features of the different consonant sounds in their mouths.
- Teach left to right scanning using 'dots and sticks' patterns.
- Teach onsets as single letters, consonant blends and digraphs.
- Play the 'I Spy something beginning with – ' game regularly.
- When hearing reading be explicit about the clues they can use, e.g. initial sounds, picture clues, syntax and semantics.
- Encourage rereading of sentences and paragraphs to aid fluency and comprehension.
- Teach the analogy strategy for rimes from the outset, e.g. p-it, t-it, n- it.
- Adapt schemes such as Letterland to show both print and cursive letter forms.
- Word build using letter cards.
- Use games to reinforce learning.

Conclusions

In this chapter a key issue has been identified: it is the problem of definition, the definition of dyslexia, the definition of reading and spelling and the definition of 'good' provision and effective processes to teach children and meet their needs. A lot of time and money appears to have been spent looking in the wrong places and following untested practices and prescriptions.

It was proposed that the teaching of reading is more effective and achieves more rapid results when it is fully integrated with the teaching of spelling and handwriting. A structured, cumulative and multisensory programme is required for all learners but with dyslexics initially needing a much slower, individualised support. They need reading and spelling pack work associated with alphabet training so that they achieve the mastery learning that other children acquire with normal methods.

The reasons why such integrated learning is not presented in the widely used commercial schemes and the government guidelines appear to be because of incomplete definitions of reading acquisition processes and what are effective methods of teaching reading.

There has been a lack of published data on the effectiveness of the learning outcomes of any of the early years schemes in operation and of what works with dyslexics. If a dyslexia programme gives an uplift of several months after a year of no progress this cannot be regarded as an effective intervention programme because at such a rate the pupil will never catch up even to grade level and will in fact regress over the years.

This chapter, with the help of Nicholas, has emphasised the uses of the HMLC programme and the critical problems that it addresses that the usual methods did not. In Chapter 5, data on the effectiveness of other APSL and non-APSL programmes is presented and discussed.

Other dyslexia-friendly reading approaches have been outlined. These are not replacement strategies for an APSL programme but can be added to the wider reading repertoire. They will also help the normal reader acquire literacy skills more easily and increase their reading skills.

The case of Nicholas is not unique. Over several decades hundreds of similar case reports have been collected. The authors developing the G and S programme in the 1920s, in particular the remedial teacher Bessie Stillman, and users in the decades since must have found the same problems because their programmes are working even now.

Initially it appears that the dyslexic fails to learn sound and symbol correspondence just like Nicholas. In most cases, as will be seen in later chapters, they are older than Nicholas and on average about seven years old before they are diagnosed. It also seems that at seven to eight years some dyslexics even without support do 'crack the alphabetic code' for themselves but by then they have missed out on three years of literacy learning and practice.

Because there appears to be a neurological dissociation that prevents implicit associations like other normal children from proprioceptive feedback during reading activities they need to be explicitly taught. However, normal teaching of phonics from the outset does not achieve this. Dyslexics need a specific highly systematic multisensory form of intervention linking sound-graphic symbol-articulatory feel-and motor writing skills connections.

The training on one symbol needs to continue until it is fully acquired and linked to all four VAKs aspects automatically. This may take a considerable time with some pupils.

The multisensory APSL programmes must then first address their sound-symbol problems because they have failed either to learn any sounds at all or have acquired sporadic phonic knowledge. Their cases and needs will be explored in Chapter 5 as alphabetic phase dyslexia.

Nicholas's dyslexia was identified in Reception and in Year 1 the HMLC remedial programme began to work for him. Such cases have raised the challenge that if we could identify dyslexia in Reception before the children fail to learn to read and bring some appropriate remediation to bear we might truly 'beat dyslexia'.

In the next chapter new research on the identification of dyslexia in the Reception year and logographic phase is detailed. It shows how, in the ordinary Reception class, the teacher as part of the daily routine work can intervene and prevent the onset of the early stage of dyslexia.

2 Identifying and remediating dyslexia in the logographic phase

Introduction

Dyslexia is regarded in the majority of cases as a verbal processing difficulty, with particular problems in the area of phonological processing (Vellutino, 1979; Frith, 1980; Brown and Ellis, 1994; Snowling, 2000). This is the problem that was illustrated in the case of Nicholas in Chapter 1. It is the problem that 90 per cent of dyslexics appear to present. For a review of the other theories and positions, see Montgomery (2007).

Frith (1980) described a three-stage progress in reading and spelling development and later (Frith, 1985) how they were divided into six steps with sometimes reading and sometimes spelling being the pacemakers. The phases or stages were termed logographic, alphabetic and orthographic. The logographic phase is the focus of this chapter.

The logographic phase is the beginning stage of literacy development and is the acquisition stage. It therefore can best be investigated in the Reception Year. It was after studying the key literacy activities in Reception classrooms such as speaking and listening, hearing reading, teaching phonics and writing it was found that children's free writing could reveal much of what they had been learning in their literacy periods about words. Free writing, sometimes called 'emergent' writing and 'creative spelling' (Read, 1986) is investigated here. The advantage is that the evidence free writing provides is concrete and records can easily be stored for later comparison.

Both Chomsky (1971) and Clay (1975) found that children's first impulse was to write not read. When asked to write a story they would settle down immediately and make marks on paper. When asked to read they would say they could not do so as they had not been taught yet.

Children's early marks on paper are more significant than might be supposed:

> The errors children make when they write are neither random nor thoughtless. When examined diagnostically they reveal systematic application of the child's level of understanding.
>
> (Rosencrans, 1998: 10)

This chapter will demonstrate the diagnostic approach to children's early writing and how it may be used to develop their literacy knowledge. It will also show how to diagnose potential dyslexia and engage in early intervention.

The logographic phase

In the cases of normal spellers Gentry (1981) identified two steps that occur within the logographic phase. The first was **precommunicative**, in which the children made scribbles and marks to represent their messages or as they told a story.

The next step was **prephonetic**. This was the creative or invented spelling stage where a single letter might represent a word or a group of letters.

The research with dyslexics from Chomsky, (1971) Liberman (1973), Bryant and Bradley (1985), Read, (1986) and onwards shows the same characteristics, that there was a failure of the potential dyslexic to move from the precommunicative scribble and marks into the prephonetic stage. This is illustrated in Figures 2.1 and 2.2 in the cases of Steven and Caroline and one wonders how it was possible for them to go through Reception and into Year 1 and beyond without learning some sound-symbol knowledge. Both were at least average in ability and both were receiving extra remedial help for reading.

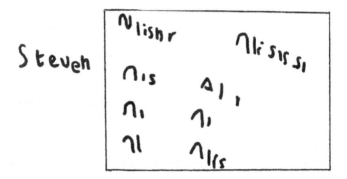

Figure 2.1 The precommunicative writing of Steven, aged six and a half years

As shown in Figure 2.1, Steven at six and a half can write his name correctly and has moved beyond scribble and marks. He uses some of the letters in his name to make word-like structures with spaces. He writes, 'I went out to play on my bike'. As can be seen there is no correspondence between his letter forms and the sounds of those letters. This was captured in a Look and Say reading regime prior to the introduction of the National Literacy strategy.

As shown in Figure 2.2, Caroline looks as though she has 'cracked the alphabetic code' because she inserts her name and words she has written hundreds of times during copy writing. She also uses part of her name to represent words as in NOLI, NON, NOO and NOI. She writes:

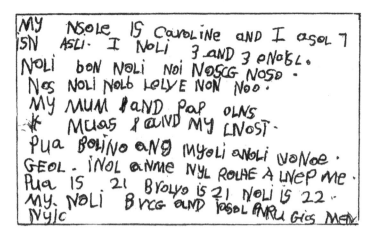

Figure 2.2 The work of Caroline, aged seven

> My name is Caroline and I have 3 brothers and 3 sisters. Some of them
> live at home and some of them do not. My mum and dad live at home
> and so do my goldfish.

She has not 'cracked the code' yet but could do so with some specific training
as with Nicholas beginning with i. t. and n in her case. She is so close and
must be desperate. In fact she was already becoming demotivated and
uncooperative in her remedial sessions. This is not surprising for she would
know that they were not working and they did not address her real need.

It is typical of many dyslexics that they usually do have the breakthrough
into phonics understanding at about the age of eight. It sometimes follows
after a highly structured and more specialised, remedial phonics intervention
programme has been introduced in a one-to-one setting but their knowledge
may still be sporadic. At that stage they also need help with word building
because although they know the sounds of some of their letters they seem,
like James in the preface, not to know how to put them together to make
new words.

The major problem is of course that at eight they are now three years
behind their peers and destined never to catch up without more help. This is
critical as they are now to enter the junior phase where the tuition depends
on developed literacy skills to learn rather than learning to acquire those skills
– reading to learn rather than learning to read.

What the early dyslexia researches showed (Liberman, 1973; Chomsky,
1971; Bryant and Bradley, 1985; Vellutino, 1979) was that the critical problem
in the earliest phase of dyslexia was a failure to develop the following skills:

- symbol to sound correspondence;
- alphabetic knowledge;

- appreciation of rhyme; and
- phonemic awareness.

When these are more closely examined it can be seen that they all relate to one main feature and this is the failure of the dyslexic to learn the sounds (and names) of the letters of the alphabet and then incorporate these into word building when writing (encoding) and to use them to help decode words when reading starting with initial sounds or onsets.

In the Look and Say regimes this knowledge is implicit and somehow has to be discovered by the pupil. Only after an initial sight vocabulary of some 50 or more words has been acquired some phonics may be introduced. This phonic knowledge was usually 'basic' phonics (single letter sounds taught in alphabetical order without letter names) and usually made explicit for reading but not for spelling. Despite this and the explicit teaching of phonics in the later remedial interventions the researches showed that dyslexics failed to acquire this knowledge until they were taught by the Gillingham and Stillman methods (Montgomery, 2007).

The failure of dyslexics to acquire the alphabetic and phonic knowledge are the reasons why dyslexics are said to lack 'phonological processing' skills. When they get letters in words muddled, especially in the middle of words, they are said to have 'sequencing' deficits and when they forget what they were taught the previous day they are regarded as having 'working memory deficits'. However, these difficulties are the result and not the cause of the dyslexic problem, the core of which is the failure to connect sounds with symbols because of a minor neurological dissociation problem (Geschwind, 1979) that does not respond to the normal methods used in Reception classes.

Since the National Literacy Strategy was introduced in 1998 it was expected that phonics teaching would accompany reading teaching. However, the ethos in Early Years teaching was slow to change and the following quote from Whitehead (2004) illustrates the prevailing orthodoxy:

> Increased experiences of reading add greatly to children's visual memories of many distinctive words, as well as commonly occurring digraphs. The work of Goswami and Bryant (1990) appears to confirm this view that school instruction in reading and writing alphabetic script helps children detect and recognise phonemes and this supports their early spelling strategies. It is only at a fairly late stage in spelling development that instruction will benefit children. This conclusion – that any formal teaching of spelling should be delayed until children have started reading and are able to evolve their own strategies for understanding the nature of writing and spelling – brings the implications of research evidence for school and classroom practice into sharp focus.
>
> (p. 186)

Thus the pervading belief in Early Years education was that spelling need not initially be taught because pupils would evolve the principles and practices naturally for themselves from their widening contact with print. However, what it did not take into account was the 40 per cent whose literacy development was deficient or slow and uneven and who left school after ten years unable to read and write adequately. The NLS did not work for them thus the guidelines were changed to include 'synthetic phonics' and 'phonics first' (DfE, 2007).

It is currently estimated that there are 6 million illiterate people in the UK and up to 10 per cent are still dyslexic in our schools (BDA, 2017). The implications of this are that 'phonics first' and 'synthetic phonics' have not worked either and a specific and different intervention is needed for them.

> It is hardly surprising that children who fail to learn by the normal methods need some specific form of help.
>
> (Blakemore and Frith **2006**)

Research cited in Chapter 1 has shown that when there is systematic and integrated teaching of reading, spelling and handwriting from the outset, normal acquisition is facilitated and literacy development is promoted. Those with dyslexia are helped begin literacy acquisition by very specific techniques.

The early warning signs of difficulties – avoidance and evasions

When children in Reception fail to learn easily what other children do no matter how hard they try they can become demotivated and may withdraw from any activity associated with literacy as much as they can so as not to be revealed. Others may act out their distress and become disruptive or they may take to riding on trucks outside, climbing under desks, tearing up other children's work and engage in all sorts of avoidance tactics whenever reading or writing tasks begin.

The child with coordination difficulties will experience similar frustrations despite perhaps being able to read as well as the rest. As soon as they try to write anything down they may manage a row of '*iiiii*', and '*tttttt*' but 'f' will stump them. For some reason they find they are unable to connect to the paper and push the pencil up and over and back to cross the line. Emily, in her first month in Reception, tried and tried to make 'f' and went red in the face, became tearful and ended by scribbling all over her page.

If dyslexics are good at drawing they will draw instead of write or they will learn to copy other children's writing even when they are sitting opposite as Nicholas did. Thus they can conceal their reading and spelling difficulties and avoid loss of esteem. In a busy classroom they may go unnoticed if they keep very quiet. They may even learn to write the same set of words from memory and learn the stories in the reading book and recite rather than read them.

Debbie from the age of four learned the stories in her books and recited them when her proud father showed off to friends and relatives how well she could read. At school she was fortunate, she did quickly learn to read and was not dyslexic.

By the time the dyslexic concealing his or her difficulties has been found out their specific learning difficulties have become complex and overlaid with years of mistakes and anxieties and misapplied interventions and misspellings.

We also know that the mistakes that dyslexics make once they do begin to learn to read and write are not indicative of a disordered system but follow the same pattern of development of normal but much younger pupils' misspellings and misreadings (Montgomery, 1997a). This has led some researchers, such as Elliott and Grigorenko (2014), to suggest that it is a problem that does not exist and dyslexics are just poor readers and writers.

However, this approach cannot be supported by the evidence from the dyslexics themselves, as will be shown in the subsequent pages. It has also been held by many that dyslexia cannot be reliably identified until the age of at least seven years when the dyslexic fails to learn to read and spell by the normal methods.

This position will be challenged as the analysis of the scripts of children in Reception are discussed.

Reception writers

Since 1990 the scripts of Reception class children have been collected and analysed for handwriting and spelling skills. From these analyses it was possible to determine a range of skills already present in some children on arrival at school and their absence in others and a failure to develop at the usual time. As the cases built in numbers it was possible to devise a rating scale to enable teachers to assess new entrants' beginning skills to determine the types of need and appropriate interventions. In 2012–2013 it became possible to test the instrument on several cohorts of Reception children and to evaluate its validity by reassessing them again when they entered Year 2.

The Writing Research Project 2012–15

The core task that most Reception children engage in on a regular basis is to write a story or their news in the form of copy writing. This was converted into a free writing opportunity. The writing was unaided and enabled the child to demonstrate his or her emergent writing skills.

Embodied in the assessment was the concept of early sound to symbol correspondence or knowledge of the sounds and/or names of alphabetic symbols. It was argued that potential dyslexics would demonstrate a failure to use simple 'phonics' knowledge in their emergent writing, just like Steven and Caroline.

Many children arrive at school with some of this knowledge that they have acquired from the environment, as they are being read to at home or in the nursery or playgroup without being directly taught. Other children without such opportunities but with some direct teaching, after a few weeks in the Reception class, begin to acquire this knowledge.

It is particularly helpful where they are also taught how to use the information to make words or use it to decode words in reading. This is seen in the use of initial sounds (onsets) during reading as well as picture and context clues to help read text. In writing they may use an initial sound to stand for a whole word. These skills can be facilitated by playing the 'I Spy' game – 'I spy something begnning with - - -'. In none of the classes was it noticeable from the scripts that word building had been taught in the early months in Reception.

It was possible to place scripts in an order of observed increasing spelling development and then the problem was to give each a relevant and informative title to communicate the assessment position consistently. When this was achieved the assessment was applied to the several cohorts of scripts from 175 children in eight Reception classes in four different infant schools. Another external assessor after 30 minutes training also used the scale so that inter-observer reliability scores could be calculated.

One middle range class (N=28) was selected for the test trial. The scripts were assessed using the rating scale and after the analysis some minor adjustments were made to the scale and the wording. The rest of the scripts were then analysed using the revised schedule and the original class scripts were reanalysed after this.

Emergent (free form) Spelling Assessment

Scripts with mainly correct and legible spelling score 10

10 Mainly correct spelling, legible, systematic word spaces.
 9 More correct spelling, skeletal phonics, meaning clear.
 8 Some correct words, phonics, phonetics, meaning generally clear.
 7 Skeletal phonics, phonetics, some words, meaning apparent.
 6 Some phonic skeletons, word bits and phones, some meaning.
 5 Word forms, letters, phone(s) evident.
 4 Letters, possible phones.
 3 Some letter shapes and letters, in a line.
 2 Marks, mandalas, occasional letters, possibly in lines.
 1 Scribble, marks in some order.
 0 Random marks.

The strategy is to identify the statement that most typifies the writing sample and award that 'score' or rank.

A score of five is pivotal in that it identifies those children who have just 'cracked the alphabetic code'. This is best seen in their attempts to make words using **'skeletal phonics'** such as 'wt' for 'went', 'ws' for 'was' 'goig' for 'going' and 'se' for 'she' etc. or the use of **phones** – single letter sounds to represent a word 'w' for 'was'. **Phonetics** would be represented by 'kwiz' for 'quiz', 'buk' for 'book' 'apl' 'nite', 'marster', 'berd', 'butiful'.

Correct spelling of common words such as 'I', 'the', 'and' and 'my' do not count as phonic achievement as they are so commonly used they can often be recalled visually rather than phonetically. It is also possible that acute and observant children may copy some words from notices on the walls. They may also write some words so frequently for their news that they recall them visually and write them from this image and motor memory rather than know how to construct them and by analogy spell similar words.

The assignment of the assessment marks is not an exact science but will give a reasonable idea of both individual levels and the level of the whole class at the outset and at intervals afterwards. What is critical is that potential dyslexics will be seen to fail to develop phones and skeletal phonics during the Reception year. This would then enable the teacher to institute remedial or a more appropriate training method to suit the dyslexics' needs. What these techniques are will be described in a later section of this chapter. The following assessments are two examples from the early developmental stages of the research.

Example analyses of emergent writing

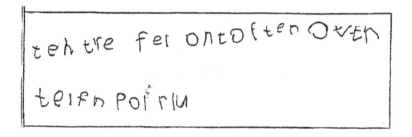

Figure 2.3 William, aged five years and two months

The tree fell on top of the telephone pole wire

On our ten-point scale this effort would score about seven for emergent writing.

Diagnostic points and developmental suggestions:

1   Handwriting: His handwriting and letter formation is of a reasonable size and pressure. He has been taught print script so the propensity for joining all except 't' and 'e' is poor. Without the use of lines he has little to guide his placement of letters in a straight line and nowhere to put descenders to increase the legibility.

2   Spelling: It is a readable sentence with some good phonetic equivalents.
There are also some spaces between words. 'The' is spelt 'teh' showing
William is using a visual strategy borrowed from reading. He needs to be
taught the 'th' digraph and to be helped to write this word as a whole
joined syllabic unit.

He omits the 'p' in 'top' and so when he rereads the sentence aloud his
pronunciation needs to be checked and he needs to be encouraged to write
the word in full correctly.

'Tree' might be corrected by explaining that the long 'e' sound is usually
signified by 'ee' especially in the middle of words. William might detect other
words with this 'ee' pattern in his storybook.

These three features would be enough to deal with until secured.

The use of 'riu' form for 'wire' is a common representation for this difficult
word and can be left for a later stage, as can long vowel 'o' in 'pole', signified
by silent 'e'. This can wait until short and long vowel work is systematically
undertaken even though the temptation to teach 'magic e' instantly may be
great. First the children would need some careful work on distinguishing
short and then long vowel sounds. This is the critical point of the c-v-c
exercise and leads to the four affixing rules and thousands of correct spellings.
This is too soon for William.

Figure 2.4 Kelly, aged five years and one month

Kelly B. 'She is in bed. She is sick. She has chickenpox.' On our emergent
writing scale Kelly would score about eight. Her handwriting is less under
control than William's but she has a little more spelling knowledge.

Both the above examples were collected after one month in the Reception
class. This was prior to the National Literacy Strategy (DfEE, 1998) when
print script was prominent with no ligatures and the classes were still engaged
in learning to read by the Look and Say methods.

In the research studies below, to develop the assessment scale the children were being taught reading in the 'phonics first' (DfES, 2007) regime.

In this research there were originally four schools participating and one of them was a private school (N=64). This school participated in the entry to Reception survey but withdrew from the follow-up study in March 2013. The management committee was very anxious about confidentiality issues despite all assurances given in formal letters.

The children were tested again on free writing in a ten-minute test on entry into Year 2. This time school B1 did not participate possibly because a new head teacher had just been appointed.

The catchment areas of schools A and B were in council estates and school C was set in an owner-occupier estate. School C children consistently obtained higher scores than the other two schools. This confirms the disadvantages associated with being poor found in The Sutton Trust Research (Jerrim, 2013). D1, D2 and D3 were in the private school.

In the present study the ratio of boys to girls 'at risk' was 1.4 to 1 respectively and 20.7 per cent of the whole cohort was at risk from potential literacy difficulties after five months in school.

These three schools were the feeder schools to the large secondary school C in an earlier Year 7 writing research project (Montgomery, 2008). In that research 18.6 per cent of the cohort had spelling difficulties that put them in the 'dyslexia zone'.

In all the four schools in the Reception survey, including the private school results the gender differences were very clear and in the predicted direction. Boys overall scored 3.51 (N=91) on the spelling scale on entry into the

Table 2.1 The numbers of children in five Reception classes and spelling scores on entry (F1) and after five months in school (F2)

Class	Nos	Free Writing 1	Free Writing 2	Nos 'at risk'
A1	17	2.33	7.12	3 + 2
A2	18	2.44	4.3	11+
B1	21	3.24	6.13	4 + 2
C1	28	6.11	6.76	0
C2	27	5.37	6.1	5
Totals	111	4.29	5.32	23 + 7 Borderline (scores 4)
Private school, initial results (F1)				
D1	21	3.57		
D2	22	3.5		
D3	21	4.05		
Totals	64	3.71		

Free writing F1 = October 2012 sample: **Free writing F2** = March 2013

Reception class. Girls scored 4.41 (N=86) showing they were more significantly advanced in spelling skills than boys and more were on the verge of literacy.

A score of five out of ten on this scale was critical for developing literacy skills showing that children have just 'cracked the alphabetic code'. In each class at this stage on entry only a handful of children might be expected to have achieved this. However, after five months it should be expected that all the children have achieved a score of at least five points but this was not the case. It is possible that many more could achieve this if the teaching strategies were slightly modified.

Boys' handwriting (Chapter 4) and spelling development compared with that of girls was significantly less advanced in both areas of writing. Thus from the beginning of school they are at a disadvantage and have an increased chance of underachieving across the curriculum.

The scores in Table 2.2 are from four schools with three different types of catchment area in increasing order of potential socio-economic advantage A to D. Looking at these results we can infer the effects that higher socio-economic advantage brings to both boys and girls so early in their educational careers.

The private school sample was in the Midlands whereas schools A, B and C were in the same coastal Essex area. The differences between schools D and C may illustrate differences between areas of the country or that the private school is taking in the whole social range not defined by ability but willingness to pay.

Girls have the advantage over boys in both areas of writing skill, handwriting (and spelling) so that it is not surprising that at 11 years the national SATs for boys' writing is significantly lower than that of girls. However, this need not be so if we intervene to bring them all up to standard well before the age of 11 and target the end of the infant phase for this. Growth spurts in the early teens that may affect boys more than girls can also be accommodated by good provision. Unfortunately handwriting teaching in English schools has been a much-neglected area (Medwell and Wray, 2007).

What is especially interesting is the 'teaching effect' seen in C-type school on the spelling skills. In one of the classes they were using lines to write on and a more systematic approach to writing than the rest as well as having interesting experiences to trigger writing such as a 'Bring your grandparents to school day'.

The writing samples in Figure 2.5a–f below show the range of skills with which the teachers had to deal.

Table 2.2 Initial socio-economic advantages in spelling scores

	Boys	*Girls*	*N*
A + B Social housing	2.38	3.03	56
C Owner occupier	4.52	6.81	55
D Private school	3.34	4.06	64

Figures 2.5a–f show emergent writing samples after one month in Reception (all half original size).

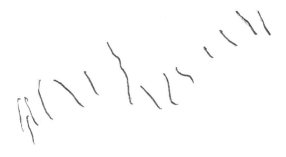

Figure 2.5a 'I went to the park'

These are random marks in a line across the page. Scores 1 for spelling because he has some idea of writing as marks across the page in a line with spaces. There may even be two words here.

Figure 2.5b 'My scooter goes ding a ling'

This is an organised scribble or drawing that shows he knows the marks must follow along the line and the words have strokes sticking up above it and bodies on it with spaces. Scores 2 for spelling.

Figure 2.5c 'I went oyster picking'

His script shows marks on paper that include roundels or 'mandalas' in lines. He scores 3 for spelling. Writes from right to left.

Figure 2.5d Millie writes, 'I went to nanny's'

This sample shows some distinct letter shapes but there are no phones. Capital 'I' commonly starts sentences at this stage and children learn the habit. She scores 4 for spelling.

Figure 2.5e Lana writes 'Little red hen makes the bread'

We can see the beginnings here of skeletal phonics. She scores 6. She writes from right to left then left to right indicating the importance of stressing starting points and providing coloured dots as clues on the left of the page.

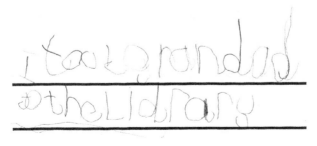

Figure 2.5f 'I took grandad to the lidrary'

He scores **9** for spelling. The spelling is almost correct, the meaning is clear but word spaces are not well defined yet. He appears to have some handwriting coordination difficulties.

Figure 2.6a–c shows some scored examples of spelling in one class after five months in Reception. They are writing about their space project.

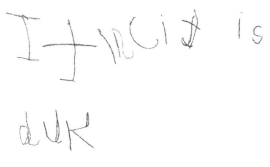

Figure 2.6a She writes: 'I finc it is duk'

This scores 6 for spelling

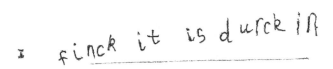

Figure 2.6b Amber writes 'I finck it is durck in (spia' space).

This scores 8.

Figure 2.6c 'I thinck theer is loabs of Planit in spais'

This scores 9.

If this teacher had given the children lines to write on it would have helped them organise the work better and they would not stand the 'p's on the line. They have been encouraged to make some ligatures but not shown their purpose, which is to use them to facilitate joining. This child is ready for joining but unfortunately the DfE guidelines do not endorse this at this stage.

Some schools introduce joining for the digraphs such as 'th', 'ch', 'sh','wh' and 'ph' but this is still only part of full cursive teaching.

The follow-up study, 2015

The children in the original Reception classes were followed up again when they entered Year 2. This time only two schools (A & C) agreed to join in and provide samples of their Year 2 children's writing in a ten-minute period. There were four Year 2 classes altogether, two classes with 35 subjects from School A and 58 subjects from School C who had participated in the original Reception year study.

The overall totals for the two schools in Year 2: the mean writing speed was 7.11 words per minute; and the spelling error rate was 12.85 per script.

The predictive capacity of the spelling scale (F1 + F2) used in the Reception year was tested against spelling error results in Year 2 (a); spelling errors with words per minute (b) and with words per minute (c) using Spearman's rho correlation test on each set of data.

Table 2.3 Writing speed and spelling results from Year 2

	Nos.	*W.P.M means*	*Sp errors means*	*Sp err %*	*Co/H diffs.*
School A1	18	5.57	13.41	22.4%	5
School A2	17	5.66	14.34	25.7%	
Totals	35	5.61	13.88	24.05%	
School C1	33	7.93	14.61	18.26%	14
School C2	25	7.76	9.28	12.67%	10
Totals	58	7.86	12.31	15.47%	

Table 2.4 Correlation values between literacy tasks in Reception and Spelling in Year 2

a) F1 + F2 and spelling errors		
School A	A1 = + 0.58 (N=18) **	A2 = –0.41 (N=18) *
School C	C1 = + 0.55 (N=33) **	C2 = + 0.51 (N=25) **
b) Spelling errors and w.p.m.		
School A	A1 = + 0.38 (N=18)	A2 = + 0.48 (N=18) *
School C	C1 = + 0.28 (N=33)	C2 = –0.05 (N=25)
c) F1 + F2 and w.p.m.		
School A	A1 = + 0.14 (N=18)	A2 = –0.12 (N=18)
School C	C1 = + 0.13 (N=33)	C2 = + 0.47 (N=25) *

In each class the level of significance is indicated by asterisks, * shows significance at the 0.05 level; ** indicates the 0.01 level. A correlation of +0.05 to +0.58 indicates that the initial spelling error scale accounts for 25 to 29 per cent of the variance seen in the spelling error count two years later and is a significant amount given all the intervening influences on a child's writing.

The strongest predictions were of course between the early free writing in Reception and later spelling errors counts not words per minute. The interesting difference is in the case of Class 2 in School A. The children's results from the outset have always been markedly different and started off as very low. This table shows that there was an inverse relationship between their Spelling scale in Reception and the later spelling error count. Instead there was a significant and positive correlation found between the number of words they wrote and the spelling errors. There was also a tendency shown in this direction in the other class in the school Class A1.

Class A2 was always much less advanced in skills in Reception than all the other classes. The strong relationship found between words per minute and spelling error suggests an approach to writing that values and reinforces correct spelling over encouraging children's emergent or creative spelling. It is possibly an idea held by the children themselves, that it is more important to get things right rather than to try and learn from error. It is an attitude that is disadvantaging in later years in any kind of problem solving and learning context. Can this be a consequence of teacher attitude or status rearing techniques?

Early identification of potential problems

It was hypothesised that the free writing test in Reception would indicate those children at risk in later years of literacy difficulties. The critical borderline of a score of five points was considered essential for becoming literate. A score of under ten points when the two free writing tasks in Reception were totalled was taken as the indication that the child would be likely still to have difficulties by Year 2 as illustrated by the percentage of spelling errors. Accordingly a Sign test was applied to the data for each of the four classes in the two schools (N=74).

Table 2.5 Showing the predictive power (+ve) of the free writing task

	+ve	-ve	Total	Sign. level
Class A1	15	2	17	0.002
Class A2	13	1	14	0.002
Class C1	25	7	32	0.001
Class C2	21	3	24	0.001

The emergent or free writing task in the Reception year was a significant predictor of later achievement or underachievement in spelling in Year 2, e.g. a high score of ten points or more in Reception predicted a low spelling error score of under 20 per cent in Year 2 and vice versa. The +ve sign indicates the number of cases in which the prediction was correct.

The wider research data already cited shows that in an ordinary cohort of 100 children it can be predicted that about 4 per cent would be dyslexic. In disadvantaged communities it can be as high as 10 per cent. When spelling difficulties without reading difficulties are added to this the incidence rose to nearly 20 per cent in the Year 7 studies earlier in this research. The three primary schools in these present studies (A, B and C) were feeder schools to the large comprehensive School C in the Year 7 research.

The Reception class data on entry indicates that there would be a significant number of children in the order of 20 per cent with dyslexic-type difficulties going forward. Even if the schools did engage in 'phonics first' there would still be at least a handful of children who by Year 2 had not begun to read and write more than a few words coherently and independently. An analysis of the number of problems found across the class groups was as follows.

An analysis of the numbers of writing problems in Year 2

There was a group of 94 children in the two schools in Year 2 who had taken part in the initial emergent writing study in Reception whose scripts could be analysed. There were 54 children identified with one or more problems out of the 94.

The criteria were:

- 26 out of the 54 scored 9 points or less on F1 + F2, free writing;
- 40 out of the 54 scored 20 per cent or more for spelling errors in Year 2;
- 23 out of 54 scored 5.1 or under on words per minute in Year 2; and
- 46 out of 54 showed coordination and/or legibility problems in the profile.

Table 2.6 The percentages of children with different levels of problems

Numbers	Out of 54	Out of 94
4 problems	24.08%	13.83%
3 problems	27.78%	15.95%
2 problems	25.93%	14.89%
1 problem	22.22%	12.77%

When all the children with spelling error counts of 30 per cent or more were totalled it came to 21 pupils of the 94 or 21.28 per cent of the cohort. These can be considered to be in the dyslexia 'at risk' zone and in Year 7 it can be predicted there will be little change and they will still be disadvantaged in composition by the number and range of their misspellings. If they also have coordination difficulties then they will be in serious difficulties by then. There were 17 children out of the 21 with spelling problems who had some coordination difficulty – that is 81 per cent. There were 43 per cent of the 'at risk' group of 21, or 9 children who wrote very slowly, that is under 5.1 words per minute when the expected speed is 7 to 8 words per minute.

All the children in the Year 2 follow-up were writing and spelling well enough to communicate some meaning except one boy who wrote four words, even so these were correctly spelled and he had not demonstrated difficulties in the Reception class (scored 6 on entry). Even those who initially showed many difficulties were writing something although some very slowly at a rate of 2.8 w.p.m. but by Year 2 they had all 'cracked the alphabetic code'.

This indicates that none of them are likely to be diagnosed as having dyslexia in the junior years because the skills they have do transfer to reading and they have four more years to develop. They are likely to still have spelling problems that may cause problems in the secondary phase.

The results are pleasing in a cohort of nearly 100 children. The prediction from dyslexia researches is that perhaps 10 per cent in this coastal area should already have observable dyslexic difficulties at this age in that they have not well-established sound to symbol correspondences and word-building skills.

The possible reason for the difference is that the writing research was also designed as an intervention study. After the first test the teachers were sent detailed reports on each child's handwriting and spelling status and were informed whether or not the child had 'cracked the code' or was on the verge of it and so on. Suggestions were then made on how each child might be helped to make progress and recommended an articulatory awareness training technique when teaching sounds linked to their symbols.

Example reports for one school

In the reports below the children had been given yellow words to trace over then copy write them or if they felt able they went straight to copy writing the message (their news).

Later in the week in October they were asked to write their own news in free form writing without any help or models. Emergent writing a) is the report on this and the score is in brackets.

In March they repeated the free form writing. On this occasion they wrote about space because they had been learning about it. The report on this is Emergent writing b) and the score is in brackets.

After the retest in the following March the teachers were sent another set of individual reports giving details of progress made and further suggestions on how to help them move forward.

1. Zainab: L Copy writing (0): Variation in size and pressure; wobble and shake; all words present, indistinct; spread within letters. May have mild coordination difficulty, or could just be developmental immaturity and lack of practice as yet. Observe accuracy and fluency of writing with the different hands. Reinforce the use of the hand that gives the best result even though this may not be the preferred hand for other activities.

Emergent writing a. (2): Makes marks, mandalas and occasional letters. Has not 'cracked the alphabetic code' as yet. Suggest lines for writing on to help locate place and position in space. Suggest focus upon teaching two easy letters to write and their sounds and names such as 'i' and 't' and show how simple words can be built using them. Can reinforce this with 'onsets' in reading and I-Spy games.

Emergent writing b. (6): 'It in citl is duk' No translation given but appears to refer to it being dark in space as other children write about the same topic. Z has cracked the alphabetic code and is using whole word forms and skeletal phonics as for dark – DUK.

Year 2: Wrote 12 words; 1.2 w.p.m. 4 misspellings – 33.3%. Coordination difficulties noted in a).

2. Kacey: Copy writing (0): Traces over the yellow letters; wavy scribble for the copying in lines, some wobble in tracing, probably due to developmental immaturity and lack of practice as yet. This will only resolve as he becomes more expert. It is important he transfers from tracing to copying or preferably to emergent writing. He needs some rhythm and pattern training to develop fluency.

Emergent writing a. (3): Makes two letters or letter shapes. Has not 'cracked the alphabetic code'. Lines for writing on will help locate place and position in space. Suggest focus upon teaching two easy letters to make and their sounds and names such as 'i' and 't' and show how words can be built using them. As he also makes 's' and 'p' shapes it may be possible to use these as well quite soon. Emphasise the articulatory feel in the mouth of the different consonants.

Emergent writing b. (4): 'ithf/syesu' 'It is colourful in space'. Letters and possible phones. The beginnings of phonic knowledge appear here as 'it' and 'hs' (the 's' has a bar on it making it also look like an 'f'. The 'su' could be a representation of 'space' giving a correct initial sound or maybe just partial visual recall. He also seems to be inserting letters from his name. Suggest initial sounds or 'onsets' are worked on during reading and writing so that he expands any basic knowledge that he already has.

Year 2: Wrote 52 words, 5.2 w.p.m.; made 25 misspellings – 48.08%. Left handed, coordination difficulties noted in a).

3. Luke: Copy writing (2): Traces well over the yellow letters, some wobble; firm writing for the copying. Omits 'e' in played, 'ith' after 'w' and 'my'. Writes the letters as one continuous writing unit which is good needs help with correct formation, again a line to write on would help resolve some of the errors with descenders and ascenders.

Emergent writing a. (2): Makes letters and letter shapes in own name and draws a picture of the new baby. Has not appeared to have 'cracked the alphabetic code' as yet, did not appear to understand the writing task or did not leave time to do it after drawing.

Emergent writing b. (8): 'I thinck it iz CKItFl in spas'. 'I think it is *terrible*? in space'. Some good phonetic equivalents, some word spaces and meaning clear. Joining of letters in small words such as 'it' and 'in' is necessary as his ligatures are becoming too big to affect later joining and will impede writing speed and fluency.

Year 2: Wrote 52 words, 5.2 w.p.m.; made 38 misspellings – 74.51%. Coordination difficulties noted in a).

4. Eesa: Copy writing (1): Traces over the yellow letters with some wobble and shake, has distinct difficulties with the 's' and 'm's. Copies 'I' correctly but 'w' looks like an 'n', the 'e' is drawn and the rest of the letters are 's' 'm' 'i' (very long) and below are some 'm' like letters. All these letters are variable in size and shakily drawn. He may have a mild coordination difficulty that pattern, rhythm and strengthening exercises can improve.

Emergent writing a. (2): Writes own name correctly in capitals but rest of 'writing' consists of scribbles and mandalas. A line to write on would focus his attention. He has not 'cracked the alphabetic code' yet nor grasped the nature of the writing task. Capitals are thought to be stored like drawings differently from phones and their graphemes. Parents or grandparents often teach them these capitals.

Emergent writing b. (8): 'i thigikit is drkand coald inspiays.' 'I think it is dark and cold in space.' Eesa has made a lot of progress and the message is easily readable with good phonic and phonetic equivalents. There are a few word spaces and a full stop. He exerts a lot of pressure on the letters, there is some wobble and has difficulty making the 's' and 'k' the right size so there is some coordination difficulty still apparent.

Year 2: Wrote 62 words, 6.2 w.p.m.; made 9 misspellings – 17.74%. Coordination difficulties noted in a) and b).

5. Georgia: Copy writing (5): Copies all the words, good sized writing cannot fit it all in quite. Uses capital A's and reverses form of 'y's. Brofeo for 'brother' indicates use of a phone so may have more in her repertoire if this can be explored. May just have cracked the code although emergent writing does not show this. Has two of the letters in her name 'G' and 'A' and some letter-like forms.

Emergent writing a. (3): Makes letters 'e' and 'o' as letter shapes. Has not 'cracked the code' here yet. Suggest focus upon teaching the two easy letters and their sounds and names such as 'i' and 't' making explicit the articulatory feel of the consonant. Show how words can be built using them, adding 'e' and 'o' soon to help with writing her name.

Emergent writing b. (9): 'I think it is kuld in spias.' The meaning is very clear. There are word spaces and she is using whole word knowledge plus good phonic skills. This suggests she has a good visual memory as well as phonic ability. Good clear writing of a reasonable size, suggest encourage joining now.

Year 2: Wrote 144 words, 14.4 w.p.m.; made six misspellings – 4.17%. No coordination difficulties recorded.

6. Josh: R/L Copy writing (4): First attempt – severe wobble and shake and looks scribbly but the words are just readable. The second attempt under the yellow line of writing has all words present, but some are indistinct, spreads within letter 'm's. Has mild coordination difficulty or a lack of practice with this hand.

Need to observe accuracy of writing with the different hands. The first attempt is the serious coordination difficulty problem area even though it may be the preferred hand for most other tasks. The second attempt under the yellow writing is readable with some spread and wobble. This hand needs to be encouraged for writing.

Suggest check handedness in other tasks such as eating, drawing and bead threading and foot for kicking and starting walking. Try to stabilise on the one best hand for writing.

Emergent writing a. (2): Makes marks, mandalas and occasional letters, 'J' and 'O'. in his name. The rest looks more like an overhead view of a maze. He tells a good story about it running to 11 lines! Has not 'cracked the alphabetic code' as yet. Suggest give lines for writing on to help locate place and position in space. To aid his coordination give him pattern and rhythm training and possibly finger-strengthening exercises. Again focus upon teaching two easy letters to make and their sounds and names such as 'i' and 't' and show how words can be built using them.

Emergent writing b. (7): 'ItIin it iz dorci zpioz.' 'It is dark in space.' The 'z's are reversed 's's and the 'c' is reversed in 'dark'. There are still signs of mild coordination difficulties in his writing so needs some more strengthening and fluency training. He is using phonic skeletons and phones to represent words and the meaning is roughly understandable.

Year 2: Wrote 33 words, 3.3 w.p.m.; made 12 misspellings – 36.35%. Coordination difficulties noted in a).

7. Sophie: Copy writing (9): 'I went dancing' is copied in a highly creditable manner. It is the same size as the model although without a line it waves up and down a bit. All the letters are clear and well formed and are made in one movement and not drawn. Spells Sophie with a reversed 'e'.

Emergent writing a. (3): Makes letters and letter shapes but has not 'cracked the alphabetic code' as yet. She makes four 'words' one below the other. The letters B i e h n p and o appear frequently in these 'words' in random order.

If she could master one 'phone' or even two as described previously she could soon be on her way to writing independently.

Emergent writing b. (9): 'I thincK theer iS loabs of Planit in SPais.' She has made excellent progress. There are word spaces and good spelling knowledge and strategies. Writing is a little too large on the difficult letters such as 's' and 'k'. If she had lines to write on now she would also be able to write 'p's correctly and bring the rest under control.

Year 2: Wrote 98 words, 9.8 w.p.m.; made seven misspellings – 7.14%. No coordination difficulties recorded.

8. Savannah: Copy writing (8): 'I played with some playdough' is copied correctly but jammed to the right on the first line and is well spread on the second line for 'playdough'. It is roughly the same size as the model although without a line it waves up and down and some letters are large. All the letters are clear, made in one movement and not drawn. Tails of 'y's and 'g's slash to the right.

Emergent writing a. (3): Makes letters and letter shapes but has not 'cracked the alphabetic code' as yet even though she can write her own name sometimes correctly at other times repeating middle area letters. Could be introduced to the first letters as above.

Emergent writing b. (8): 'Ispia finck it is durck in.' 'In space I think it is dark and/in.' Shows some useful phonic strategies and knowledge. Text is mostly readable and there are word spaces. Needs lines to write to improve the quality of the final product and begin the correct placing of ascenders and descenders.

Year 2: Wrote 59 words, 5.9 w.p.m.; made seven misspellings – 18.68%. No coordination difficulties recorded.

9. Chelby: Copy writing (3): Traces over the yellow letters quite well and with a firm consistent line and pressure. Firm writing for the copying but varies in pressure and size, sometimes wobbles on long strokes. Needs help with correct letter formation as some are upside down and drawings appear among them. Lack of one-to-one correspondence in the copying. Not enough room to make the letters.

Emergent writing a. (2): Makes two letters 'b' and 'n' and some mandalas. Draws and scribbles in colour all over the page. Does not understand the writing task and what it should look like. Could try giving smaller task units – two or three short words on a line with plenty of room for the copying and same for the emergent writing.

Emergent writing b. (9): 'Ifinctherare alyns in sbs.' 'I think there are aliens in space.' This is a very clearly written and readable message. Word spacing needs encouraging. There is very good phonetic and phonic knowledge apparent. She has made a lot of progress. Lines and joining need to be introduced, she is ready. Excellent drawing of a space alien suggests high (mental) ability on the Draw a Person Scale; the writing is also well coordinated.

Year 2: Wrote 22 words, 2.2 w.p.m.; made seven misspellings – 36.36%. Coordination difficulties noted in a).

10. Freddie: Copy writing (1): Traces over the yellow letters with variation in pressure and some wobble. Nearly manages to copy 'I went' but it deteriorates to a very shaky and faint 'w' and an 'e' upside down followed by 't' then 't' in 'to' and ends there (I went to the hospital). Shows coordination difficulties, so will need strengthening, rhythm and pattern training to support the writing skill.

Emergent writing a. (2): Makes one or two very large letters (F) and letter shapes in a line. Has not 'cracked the code' but did appear to understand the writing task.

Emergent writing b. (2–3): He makes some very large letter shapes (half a page long) that include 'i', 'F' and possibly 'n'. The marks are shaky but clear and in a line showing some development of motor skill and writing knowledge. However, coordination difficulties are still apparent and he needs some direct teaching to help him develop some basic phonic knowledge beginning with 'onsets' in reading and 'I spy' games.

His message is 'Daddy, granddad, Nana, mummy, Keith, Joshy, Benben, Leo – we all went on a holiday and took a picnic'. There is a sense of desperation here in that his message is long, coherent and interesting but his writing skills do not match it. This mismatch makes him a candidate for dyslexia if he cannot 'crack the code' soon. Try articulatory phonics with onsets.

Year 2: Wrote 52 words, 5.2 w.p.m.; made 14 misspellings – 25.93%. Coordination difficulties noted in a).

11. Hana: Copy writing (2): Traces over most parts of the yellow letters, some wobble. Starts with firm writing of her name, repeating 'h' s and 'a' s in a long line. Starts the copying above the letters but the shapes she makes have no one-to-one correspondence and only some are letters, the rest are letter shapes. There is a drawing of her on stage dancing!

Emergent writing a. (2): Writes her name correctly and draws a very good flower. Makes some very large letters and letter shapes in lines. Has not 'cracked the code' but does appear to understand the writing task and the letters in her name 'a' and 'n' that she can make could be targeted for word games and word making.

Emergent writing b. (10): 'I can see the star and moon fom the rocit.' Her message is clearly written and is interesting. There are word spaces, a full stop and correct spellings of the more common words with good phonetic equivalents for the rest. Could teach the 'fr' blend checking if she is actually articulating it. Needs some lines to guide her writing size and she could begin joining to help this. She needs help with the correct formation of her 'm's that are too open. Her drawings of three figures – possibly herself and two aliens – are good for her age (as on the Draw a Person Test) indicating ability above her chronological age level.

Year 2: Wrote 132 words, 13.2 w.p.m.; made nine misspellings – 12.12%. No coordination difficulties recorded.

So many assessments and demands are made on schools at present that anything outside their remit is probably impossible and so my thanks to the teachers and the children for their time in participating in the project. It is hoped they had time to read the reports and take action on at least the suggestions about 'phones'.

This has been exploratory field research with all its attendant control difficulties. Tentatively it can be suggested that addressing the key factor – explicit teaching of the use of phones in early spelling and using them in word-building during writing – may have played a role in the cohort's results after the reports had identified the problem.

In summary: On entry to Reception, 11.1 per cent of pupils had established 'phones'. Five months later (exit from the study), 56.6 per cent had established 'phones'

As can be seen all the three schools' SATs results (Table 2.7) have experienced a remarkable and sudden uplift in 2014 as the project children take SATs. This could be due in part to the interventions suggested in the project being taken up by staff in the schools and as the reports were passed on. The uplift was from an 8 to 30 per cent improvement.

It is now important that schools incorporate the articulatory phonogram technique into their Reception year work which will only need minor adjustments to what they ordinarily do. This will increase the numbers of children who develop 'phone' knowledge to use in reading and writing. The results will enable them to confirm or reject the process for themselves. Alternatively research needs to be funded to take the process forward. I favour the teacher–researcher approach in developing evidence-based practice as it has the potential for greater sustainability and improvement.

Table 2.7 Key Stage 1 SATs results Level 4 and above for the project schools, Yr 2

	2011	2012	2013	2014	2014		
					Reading	*Writing*	*Maths*
School A	35%	47%	48%	78%	85%	80%	66%
School B	37%	37%	50%	66%	76%	78%	46%
School C	77%	87%	88%	96%	95%	98%	96%

After a further 17 months, on entry into Year 2 the main factors affecting the cohort's achievements were residual coordination difficulties, legibility and orthographic spelling problems.

It is suggested that the specific articulatory spelling technique (multisensory mouth training) used to connect sounds and symbols is able to help these children overcome the early obstacles. If unaddressed these difficulties would pervade all their academic activities and cause them to underachieve not only in school but even at degree level.

The toolkit for teachers: logographic phase

- Every Reception class teacher should take a sample of each child's free form writing of news or story one month after entry into the class in October before half term.
- Every Reception teacher should give the following standard sentence for each child to do near point copying on a line beneath in the same October period:

'I like to play with my toys'

- Use the spelling scale to assess the skills displayed in the free form writing task and give each a rank and where necessary a comment.
- Compare notes and assessments with colleagues. This should enable the teacher to:
    - identify whether 'phones' are being used and by which pupils;
    - monitor progress and give specific help where needed;
    - teach the initial sounds and names of the first five letters in use order: i, t, p, n, s.
- Multisensory-articulatory phonogram training. Use the multisensory mouth-training technique linking articulation, grapheme, phoneme and handwriting movements.
- Teach the initial and end blends as they go along as in the APSL programmes: st-, sn- and sp and -st, -sp and -nt.
- Retest the children on the free writing task again in March of the following term before the Easter holiday. Any child who has not by then 'cracked the alphabetic code' and is not using phones should be placed on the early stage APSL programme.
- This involves one-to-one training using the spelling and reading packs and alphabet training as Nicholas was.
- A trained teaching assistant might be able to take over this APSL task for the summer term so that no child enters Year One without some basic sound to symbol correspondence knowledge, can word build using it for spelling and use it for decoding in reading.

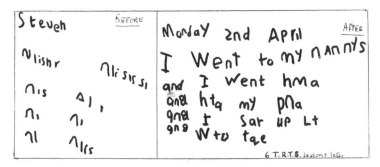

Figure 2.7 Steven's progress after 6 × 20-minute sessions of TRTS
(The school did not permit cursive writing until the Junior stage)

David (see Figure 2.8) is in Year 6, aged 11 years. He was set to write about his favourite subject for ten minutes in 2002 after four years of the NLS and one year after the Code of Practice (DfEE, 2001). He has written 74 'words' at a speed of 3.7 words per minute. How was it possible that his needs were ignored?

Figure 2.8 The logographic phase writing of David, age 11 in Year 6

Summary and conclusions

This chapter has examined the nature of the potential difficulties in the Reception year and how these relate to theories about the origin and nature of dyslexia in the logographic phase. The overt sign of the logographic phase dyslexia was that sound–symbol correspondence did not develop in free writing and was termed 'phone failure'.

Based upon the dissociative theory of the origin of dyslexia a field research study in intervention was set up and the results have shown all the children in the cohort now have some alphabetic and sound-symbol correspondence knowledge on entry into Year 2 and are using it in their spelling. A follow-up study is planned for their entry into Year 7.

In a previous cohort study in Kingston upon Thames (N=114, Montgomery 1997a), in a school of middle socioeconomic status, four children were identified at the end of the Reception year with lack of articulatory awareness potentially leading to 'phone failure'. In the present study 20 children were identified with 'phone failure' after five months in Reception so that on entry to Year 1 it could be expected that at least ten children might still be struggling to write any message using phones. On entry to Year 2, that 10 per cent could be expected to be identified as dyslexic but this was not the case. Some of the children still had problems and these were observed in the high number of spelling errors, low word counts and handwriting difficulties.

The Key Stage 1 SATs results for reading and writing in all three schools showed a big uplift in 2014 in comparison with previous years, e.g. from 8 per cent in the already high standard school and up to 30 per cent in the lower standard schools.

One of the factors that emerged very strongly was the problem the children encountered in handwriting to support their spelling knowledge. It was evident that the handwriting teaching techniques needed to be adjusted on a much broader scale than the intervention on 'phones'. In fact, the writing techniques in use were frequently acting against the best practice for ergonomics and motor skills development. Unfortunately bad handwriting habits are known to be very resistant to change. How these issues can be addressed will be discussed and exemplified in the next two chapters. This is because of the importance of handwriting in the multisensory triangle.

Since the writing research field project and casework in Reception classes was completed, new research from Germany has confirmed the importance of the association between handwriting and spelling in the acquisition and development of reading.

Suggate et al. (2016b) tested 144 German preschoolers (kindergartners) age 6.1 years before reading instruction took place. They were tested on a wide range of cognitive and skills items. These included Fine Motor Skills (bead-threading; coin slotting and tracing through a maze); Grapho-motor skill – a Greek letter copying task; and Writing – they wrote their names and were read seven letter names to write.

Emergent literacy was tested using expressive and receptive vocabulary tests; phonemic awareness – rhyming, word-building from two phonemes; segmenting spoken words into phonemes, identifying the presence of a specified phoneme in a word; letter knowledge – letter or sound of letter lists; Reading skill – non words and real word reading suitable for the age range.

They found that the best predictor of decoding (reading) was the ability to copy letters, grapho-motor skill not the broader FMS. The study demonstrated that children who could write not only could read better but that early reading goes hand in hand with writing. In an earlier study (Suggate et al., 2016a) writing letters was shown to be more effective in literacy acquisition than pointing at letters, confirming that implicit transfer from reading to spelling is lower than from spelling to reading.

In Chapter 3 types of handwriting assessment will be examined across the age ranges and in Chapter 4 new neurological insights into handwriting's contribution to reading will be discussed. The Reception cohorts' writing will be reassessed in terms of motor skills competencies and the interventions they require. Handwriting problems across the age ranges will be identified, with remedial strategies detailed.

Despite the accumulated knowledge the picture seen through this research in these English classrooms is that of a prevailing orthodoxy in literacy acquisition and development from the Look and Say era with mild modifications. The teaching of reading is still largely through visual methods, tracing and copy writing predominate, sounds are now taught alongside this in alphabetic order without using them in word-building, and any spelling teaching involves drills. Consonant and vowel digraphs are now taught and some schools ensure they are joined. Only a small number of schools teach cursive from the outset.

The evidence shows that handwriting with spelling must be given an equal platform with reading if real progress is to be made in literacy development.

3 How to assess and use handwriting samples to diagnose difficulties across the age ranges

Introduction

> Handwriting has a low status and profile in literacy education in England and in recent years has attracted little attention from teachers, policy-makers or researchers into mainstream educational processes.
>
> (Medwell and Wray, 2007: 10)

Ten years later little has changed except that there has been more interest in the subject in the research field but the findings have, as yet, been ignored in many classrooms.

The advantage of collecting handwriting samples is that the analysis of each script reveals a range of features that can contribute to understanding and developing writing skill. Six handwriting factors such as speed, style, form, fluency, legibility and coordination can be examined and in addition the number and nature of any spelling errors can be captured. This makes any writing sample an important piece of output from the learner. Spelling and handwriting are called the 'lower order' writing skills with composition being the 'higher order' skill that includes grammar, genre, deep and surface meaning and so on. In underachievement it is composition and how to motivate learners to write that have received the most attention. It is now time to show how lower order skills or lack of them and automaticity undermine achievement on a wide scale in recording, responding, composition and examinations.

The question of whether just one sample can reveal any or all of these features must be raised and it is surprising how little variation there is in a range of scripts produced in good faith under the prescribed conditions. Perhaps the most variable is the style of handwriting that individuals can adopt if they are skilled. The variation is less as the skill level declines.

The major early influence on writing is of course the teaching and learning activities used in particular classrooms. This can be determined by tradition or custom and practice; directed by outside agencies such as governments or changed by innovative theory and research confirmed in practice.

Handwriting teaching features strongly in the curricula of some countries, such as France (Thomas, 1998), just as it once did in the UK in the early years of the twentieth century. In that period all British children learned a joined 'civil service' hand that was a simplified form of copperplate writing from the nineteenth century. Children had 'copy books' in which they practised their joined-up writing.

Copy writing is still a mainstream activity in the Reception class 100 years later but a joined script is not. Even after the government guidelines (DfES, 2007) insisted that children were taught to write letters with ligatures, 'flick ups' to assist later joining, this has not necessarily been adopted in some classrooms. Children are now expected to join their letters by the time they are in Year 2 (DfE, 2014) not from the outset, although a number of schools in the researches to be cited teach a fully joined script from the outset in Reception. This seems to be more popular in the independent schools.

In the remedial dyslexia field it has been part of the programmes to teach a fully joined hand with lead-in and lead-out strokes from the outset (Gillingham and Stillman, 1940, 1956; Hickey, 1977, 1991; Cowdery et al., 1984–7, 1994). When the Gillingham and Stillman system was introduced into the UK in the 1970s it clashed with the custom and practice in primary and secondary schools where print, an unjoined form was favoured and so the pupils learned to join in the remedial classes then unjoin in the general classroom. It could be a very damaging and distressing process.

Fernald (1943) developed a system of 'tracing in the air' in the practice of writing cursive forms before the child wrote them from memory on the page and this was found supportive to the remedial approach as well as to the developing writer. Neither cursive nor tracing in the air were adopted in mainstream classrooms in the UK as they did not fit with the perceived 'good' practice at the time and this is still the state of affairs today in most schools.

There appear to be three different levels of teaching wisdom in operation. The most common and widespread is:

1   The basic 'custom and practice' passed on from one teaching generation to the next. It is a system that is not questioned, 'We do it this way here, because we've always done it this way'; 'It's what teachers do'.
2   At the second level we can see 'good practice'. This is what observers of education and researchers identify as the more and most successful practices being used by teachers that give the required results. This is the most favoured method of governments, finding out what good teachers do and then implementing policies based upon this. The problem with this is that best practice may not be the best there is and what teachers are doing may not be what they should be doing.
3   At the third level and the most rare, the top of the pyramid, there is 'evidence-based practice'. This provides the rationale for the theoretical and practice research that shows the relative effectiveness of different

techniques. It also finds what ought to be in operation even when it is not and can suggest new or old directions for development.

However, the methods of identifying evidence-based practice may miss this level of teaching wisdom because of the strategies researchers use to try to find them. If they are not widely involved in practice and in the theory and research they must rely on 'key words' searches to identify the research and then use RCTs (Randomised Control Trials) as the criterion for effectiveness of that research. RCTs are a poor device for investigating the fuzzy contexts of classroom interventions. Their single variable manipulations in experimental contexts can never afford the insights that experience of many classrooms reveal. RCTs omit theory developing research as well as case and field work that is more often recorded in books.

In this book evidence-based practice is presented in which the whole research process has been followed – from observation in a wide of range of field settings to determine patterns of successful practice; then theory and research-based interventions have followed and their effects have been evaluated to develop more coherent theories and practices to test in real-world settings, there are few RCTs.

Most recently, it has been reported that the GCSE scripts for external marking have been copied and uploaded to send them to markers' computers. There have been complaints that this has made many scripts more difficult to read. It can be predicted that this will lead schools and markers to demand that the pupils use a more 'decipherable' style such as print, which is more similar to the style we see in books. If so, this will set back cursive writing development once again and disadvantage many learners.

In 2013, 45 states in the US removed handwriting teaching from the curriculum. Word processing or keyboarding remained. It will be important to track the effects of this decision on the literacy of their populations. The majority of US schools teach D'Nealian cursive – a more upright version than the ovoid form illustrated in Chapter 4.

Tests

A test or assessment is just one set of observations often made in a given timespan. Its purpose is to provide a sample of observable behaviours for analysis. This may lead to grading individual results for access to different treatments or programmes, using them to prepare curricular inputs, or using them for the diagnosis of particular needs and interventions. A considerable impact is created by having an appropriate and correct definition of what is to be tested and in the case of dyslexia much of the research and practice does not use such a one.

In dealing with handwriting there is less controversy over its definition but a great deal of disagreement about the best method for its acquisition and development and the ultimate purposes or goals towards which it is directed.

What can be assessed in handwriting?

Assessments are either formal tests with norms for comparison or informal tests where clinical expertise, individual experience and preferences may play a part. As with many behavioural outputs an experienced clinician can learn much from a sample of such behaviour. Currently the six aspects of handwriting outputs that can be assessed by teachers are speed, style, form, fluency, legibility and coordination difficulties, spelling skills plus grammar and compositional qualities. It is now also possible for neurological and motor skills that initiate and control the handwriting to be recorded and analysed in the laboratory but these techniques are not available or necessary in the classroom.

Of the six variables in handwriting, speed is the easiest to measure under timed conditions and in different tasks. The tasks may be free writing, copy writing – near or far point (from the board), fast, best or neatest writing. The assessments are usually in words per minute, letters per minute or sentences per minute.

The main task used in this book is free writing as fast as possible in 10 or 20 minutes. This is because it reveals the most about handwriting and spelling. The other formats can be used to gain additional information. For example, near and far point copying can be checked in individual cases. In Reception, many children find far point copying too difficult as it involves holding a letter or a set of letters in the memory and then transcribing it or them correctly. As the learner may not be able to write the letter from memory anyway, copying from the board is very difficult at this stage.

Children engaged in near-point copying where the teacher writes their 'news' then the children copy this underneath may initially be seen 'drawing' the letters. Instead of forming a letter with a single line they will draw bits of it and try to join them together. The question arises as to whether they should spend time drawing in this manner when they should be learning to write the letter. It is this problem that Fernald's tracing in the air method seeks to dispel because once a motor programme has been established by drawing or tracing it is difficult to erase and so making the right moves from the start is desirable.

For example, tracing over letters and dotted letters to guide the tracing that are gradually faded out are all common techniques in Reception. New neurological research discussed in Chapter 4 shows why these practices should be discontinued and Fernald's technique used instead.

The Reception learner in Figure 3.1 has been given no lines to copy on and the copy words are small and faint and so have to be widely spaced. There are no ligatures on some of the copy letters. 'Park' is written with a capital providing a poor model. This illustrates how important it is for the teacher and classroom assistant to be trained in teaching writing, not leaving it to chance even for copy writing.

Questions must be raised about the practice of allowing children to copy letters like below in any way they can rather than to be taught to write their letters 'free form' and place them on the paper. Handwriting teaching is more important than this child's teacher imagines.

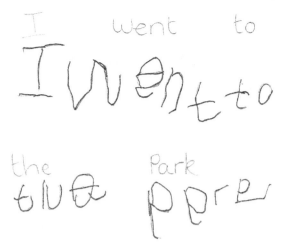

Figure 3.1 A Reception learner's drawing of letters

Handwriting assessments in general use

1. The classic sentence test of Speed and Form

'The quick brown fox jumps over the lazy dog'

All the letters of the alphabet are included in this sentence and it can either be copied or written from memory. Remedial teachers often use it to check for correct letter formation and joining. Wallen et al. (1996) in Australia standardised it for 8–9 year olds and above but Medwell, Strand and Wray (2008) used it in England with Year 2 and Year 6 children. The English schoolchildren had to copy the sentence for three minutes. The scores were in Letters Per Minute (LPM). Year 2 children wrote from 9 to 79 LPM with a mean of 33.7 and Year 6 children wrote 1 to 113 LPM with a mean of 64.2. Converted to words per minute the speeds were 8 w.p.m. in Year 2; and 13 w.p.m. in Year 6 approximately.

2. Lyth's sentence test: Sentence speed

Using MIDYIS (Middle Years Information Survey) Lyth (2004) found that when the pupils (N=10,000) in Yr 8 were set to write:

I can write clearly and quickly all day long

for one minute, one sentence per line and only one line each, the mean speed was 29 wpm. Boys wrote 5.4 lines per minute; girls wrote 5.7 lines. Pupils from independent schools wrote more – boys wrote 6.1 lines per minute and girls wrote 6.3.

Copy writing as in the 'fox sentence' is easier than free writing and writing for one minute rather than for ten enables a faster speed to be recorded.

3. The alphabet test: Speed

Berninger and Graham (1998) devised a test in which the subject wrote as many letters of the alphabet as possible in order from memory for one minute. After 15 seconds there was a ping and a mark was made and only letters to this point were counted and analysed. Christenson and Jones (2000) used a modified version for whole classes so that when they completed 26 letters they continued writing them in upper case. Letters per minute were scored.

Both research groups found speed of writing the alphabet highly predictable of later levels of composition in the later stages of education. The test involved two elements – alphabet knowledge related to spelling and reading, and handwriting or fine motor coordination skills. As dyslexics' alphabet knowledge is insecure they will perform poorly on this test as will those with handwriting coordination difficulties.

4. DASH – Detailed Analysis of Speed of Handwriting (Barnett et al., 2008)

DASH has five tasks:

1 Copy best –'the quick brown fox – for 2 minutes';
2 Alphabet writing – lower case for one minute;
3 Copy fast – 'the quick brown fox' fast in two minutes';
4 Graphic speed – Optional item – draw Xs in wide circles for one minute;
5 Free writing – about 'My Life' for ten minutes. The test is standardised for pupils from 9.0 to 16 years 11 months.

It therefore contains a range of speed items but not a range of diagnostic indicators of writing skill.

5. The ten-minute free writing test: Speed (Roaf, 1998)

Pupils in a large secondary school were asked to write as rapidly as possible on a topic of interest 'my favourite-- - -' for ten minutes. She found that pupils writing at a speed slower than 15 words per minute were failing in all areas of the curriculum and poor handwriting skill and lack of legibility contributed to low self-esteem and UAch. 25 per cent of her school population from Year 7 to Year 11 (N=1273) were writing at a slow speed, under 15 words per minute. 12 per cent of the population had motor coordination difficulties and 2–3 per cent had severe difficulties.

6a. The 20-minute free writing test: Speed (Allcock, 2001)

This was similar to Roaf's test but pupils (N=2701) in a sample of secondary schools had to write on their favourite subject as rapidly as possible for 20 minutes. Allcock designed the task to match the length of writing tasks that secondary school pupils are required to do. This provided a set of norms to indicate speeds at which pupils were writing and identified difficulties when they were slower than 25 per cent and 40 per cent below the means for the age group Those writing 25 per cent more slowly she concluded needed 25 per cent extra time in examinations and those writing at a speed of 40 per cent slower needed an amanuensis.

Table 3.1 Mean writing speeds across age ranges, Allcock (2001, N=2071)

	Year 7	Year 8	Year 9	Year 10	Year 11
	13.9 wpm	14.6	15.7	16.3	16.3
25% lower	10.4	10.9	11.8	12.2	12.7
40% lower	8.3	8.8	9.4	9.9	10.1

The mean for each year was roughly one word more than the chronological age of the pupils.

Year 9 speeds were sampled in two cohort intakes (2007 and 2008) in a specialist Arts school in Hampshire (Montgomery, 2008). This data was markedly different from Allcock's because of the higher socioeconomic status in the area and the Arts specialism that attracted these particular cohorts.

Table 3.2 Mean writing speeds in two Year 9 cohorts using the 20-minute test

	w.p.m.
Year 9 2007 N = 88 20.74	Nos. writing in cursive N=15; semi-joined 26; print 47
Year 9 2008 N = 91 18.12	Nos. writing in cursive N=16; semi-joined 38; print 37

In a period when government guidelines required pupils to have achieved a fluent joined hand by the Year 6 SATs it is surprising that so few in a specialist Arts school have achieved this. The forces that act against it must be strong. These forces are likely to be the original training bias in which most children are taught print with some ligatures. They may or may not be taught to join at a later stage but just urged to close up the letters in the words.

At the same time there is a strong pressure for neatness and legibility and this is often interpreted as print that looks like the textbooks. Print is especially used in project work unless it is word processed and semi-joined for the rest because the initial teaching formats did not permit joining.

6b. The 20-minute writing test: Speed, form, coordination, legibility, spelling and composition (Montgomery 2008)

Using the 20-minute test it was found that the speeds varied among schools in Year 7, with slower speeds from the schools in lower socioeconomic areas. There were also consistent gender differences with boys' scores poorer than girls'.

Table 3.3 Writing speeds in Year 7 in three secondary schools (N=536)

	School A (N=125)	School B (N=160)	School C (N=251)
Cohort speeds			
Boys	11.84 (N=75)	12.89 (N=61)	11.14 (N=123)
Girls	14.32 (N=50)	14.77 (N=99)	13.69 (N=127)
Mean	12.78	14.05	12.44

Allcock's samples were mainly of schools in the south east and the Midlands. The three in the above table came from different socioeconomic areas in the south and east. The lowest status areas had the slowest speeds. Girls consistently wrote faster than boys in all three schools by roughly two words per minute. Where girls outnumbered boys this also inflated the overall means for the school (School B) and vice versa in School A.

The advantage of the 20-minute test for the secondary pupils is that it is more challenging in terms of composition writing and allows fatigue effects to set in and masked difficulties or old problems to emerge as the writing skills become challenged. A more detailed analysis of scripts in School C showed that approximately one third had some coordination difficulties and just under one third had spelling problems.

Similar results were found for Year 5 pupils (Montgomery, 2015) in relation to socioeconomic status and gender. The free writing test was reduced to a ten-minute test for these younger pupils.

Table 3.4 Writing speeds in Year 5 in three different schools (N=197); 10-minute test

SES	Numbers	w.p.m.	Coord diffs
School X Church Sch	N=85	10.04	7.0%
School Y Rural Sch	N=60	8.05	20.83%
School Z Coastal Sch	N=52	7.81	36.54%
Mean	(N= 197)	8.84	

Following the 'rule of thumb' only the children in school X were writing at a speed consistent with their age group circa 10–11 words per minute.

Table 3.5 Writing speed at the beginning of Years 2, 3 and 4; 10-minute test

		Numbers	w.p.m.	Age
Mixed SES	Year 2 Four classes	94	6.78	7 +
Mixed SES	Year 3 One class	21	7.5	8 +
Middle SES	Year 4 Three classes	84	9.95	9 +

In the Year 2 group School A was in a low socioeconomic area (N=36; w.p.m. = 5.61) and school C was in a middle socioeconomic area in a coastal region (N=58, w.p.m. = 7.86). Overall, at the age of just seven years, the mean writing speed of the group was about seven words per minute and can be expected to rise over the year to about eight words per minute as seen in the Year 3 data and then rise again as in the Year 4 data.

Once again the words per minute appear to be just about one number above the age of the group, pupils in low socioeconomic status areas having lower writing speeds than those in higher ones. The conclusion is that schools must work to address the needs of children in these lower SES areas so that they are not disadvantaged before they begin their learning journey.

Assessing style

Assessing form or style is a relatively straightforward task. In the UK there are three main style categories. These are print, semi-joined and cursive. However, there are different standards and qualities within the three categories and some are perceived as controversial.

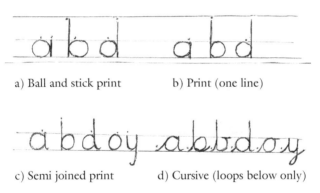

a) Ball and stick print   b) Print (one line)

c) Semi joined print   d) Cursive (loops below only)

Figure 3.2 The three main categories or styles in school scripts

The dots indicate the various starting points of different letters. In cursive they begin on the line for separate letters. The cursive style may stand upright as in 'd' above or it may have ovoid bodies and slant forward or backwards. Left handers tend to favour the backward slope because they pull the letters to the midline, right handers push from the midline to the right side of the paper.

Children often incorporate other styles into their handwriting as they grow older. An early one, even in infant classrooms is to incorporate Oxford 'i's. This is the inclusion of a small circular 'o' on top of the letter 'i' and sometimes 'j' instead of the dot. It is mostly affected by girls and is not to be encouraged in fast writing because of its slowing effects. Boys tend to incorporate features from 'gothic' style, which is more angular and with small capital e's in order to be a little different. They copy it from comics and graphic novels.

In France a fast flowing, joined form of handwriting is taught from the outset (Thomas, 1998). It is regarded as a fundamental skill that once mastered frees the mind. The teaching process begins at the age of three and goes on to age eight or nine years and it takes precedence over reading because it is more demanding.

In English schools the government guidelines now suggest letter formation begins with letters with ligatures to prepare for later joining, which should be introduced by Year 2 (!) and by the end of the junior stage should lead to a fast and fluent joined hand when assessed in SATs at the end of Year 6. However, not all the letter forms encourage joining, e.g. the semi-joined style that is the DfE recommended form does not encourage joining for 'b' because there is no ligature, 'o' is without a lead-out stroke, 'y' is without a loop below the line. In Figure 3.2d – cursive – all the letters begin on the line with the lead-in stroke and all the letters have lead-out strokes. There are also variations in forms allowed for whichever the children find easiest or prefer. This applies in particular to 'b', 'p' and 's'.

Table 3.6 The proportions of different writing styles in Year 7 (N=441) in 2008

	Print	Semi-joined	Cursive
All Pupils	27%	42.8%	25.5%
Boys	24.5%	41%	34.5%
Girls	28%	53%	19%

In earlier decades custom and practice dictated that children were taught a print script like that in their reading books with no ligatures. Teaching of joining was not begun until they entered the junior school at age seven or eight. It is evident from scripts illustrated in Chapters 2 and 4 that even now some teachers have found it difficult to adopt the ligature system.

Research, however, has moved on, showing that there need to be changes in both custom and practice and the government guidelines. The current perceived 'best' practice' is fundamentally wrong. This research and necessary changes will be discussed in the next chapter but, in summary, we should return to joining from the outset.

Assessing legibility: Test of Handwriting Form and Legibility (T-HFL)

In the wider frame there are no tests for legibility. This is possibly because legibility may be differently regarded by different markers. The perception of illegibility is influenced by various eye conditions, the style preference, how much practice in reading difficult scripts has been experienced and so on. However, over time and study some general guidelines have emerged that can be used to assess and improve legibility. It does not involve scoring as any of the 12 criteria set out below in Figure 3.3 may result in a score of e.g. five that was attained on completely different items.

It is important to work on legibility even after writing speed and fluency have developed. In the earlier stages it has been shown that fluency and form are more important than speed and that writing becomes legible as fluency grows. In the case of the learner with legibility problems it is necessary to concentrate on a speedy, fluent style for class and homework. The pupils must realise that the work is for an audience of at least one, the overworked teacher.

The best way of using T-HFL is to ask the pupil to read the list with a mentor and then look at a page of his or her writing and see how many errors can be found. Allowing the child to lead is the best style, with prompting where necessary.

Some features in combination may make the script more or less illegible. The T-HFL Figure 3.3 below can easily be used by pupils and teachers to evaluate handwriting and find the errors in letter construction and form and then just TWO interventions after that will improve legibility. These interventions are on i) body size and ii) letter slope and they have been identified over time with pupils needing help as the most effective for transforming writing and achieving legibility.

An additional problem may arise if the letters are malformed in the first place and then the correct formation needs to be practised. This is difficult and involves careful and regular practice in forming the individual letters correctly. It is best practice to teach correct formation in the first place.

Explaining to pupils that handwriting has several purposes can help, e.g. there are four types of handwriting:

1   a fast running hand for personal notes;
2   a fluent speedy style for teacher audiences, exams, SATs etc.;
3   a slow careful script in semi-print for form-filling;
4   calligraphy or 'beautiful writing' for posters and exhibitions, possibly using Italic or Gothic style.

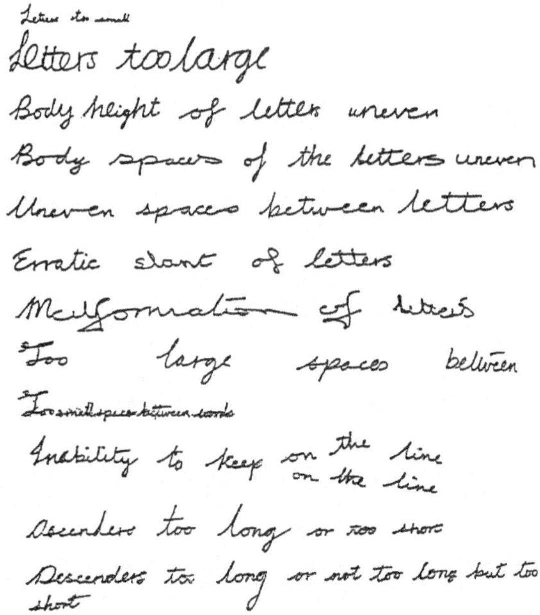

Figure 3.3 Test of Handwriting Form and Legibility, T-HFL
Source: Montgomery (1990) based upon an idea by Elizabeth Waller.

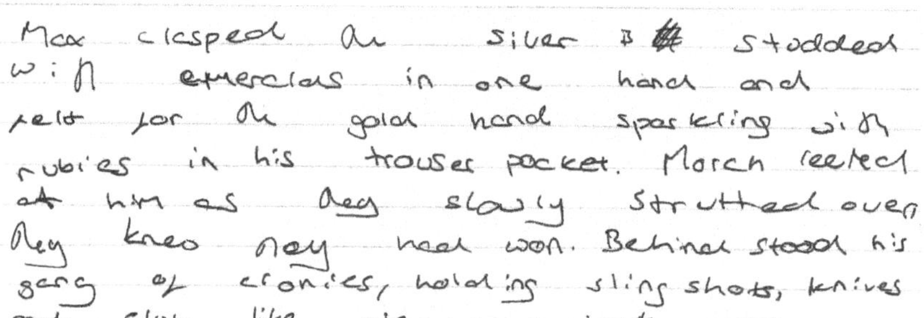

Figure 3.4 Leah, 12 years 10 months (half size)

Using T-HFL to analyse Leah's script shows the writing is of a suitable size, spacing between words is large and rivers of space run down the page. She uses a mainly unjoined print script. Ascenders ('sticks') are frequently too short but descenders ('tails') are adequate for some letters such as 'p' and 'y'. The 'tails' and 'sticks' tend to slope in different directions. There is a tendency to drag words below the line. The body size of letters varies and there are uneven spaces between them; some letters are malformed such as open 'd's; 'th' looks like a large lower case 'n'. These factors indicate a mild coordination difficulty and lack of systematic teaching of correct letter forms in the early years.

Leah's writing style is what we call a fast running hand for personal use but it is not good for exams. In exams she will be under pressure to write at speed and this is when the poor construction will disadvantage her and be at its worst when externals try to read what she has written. She needs handwriting form and fluency training; examples are given in the next chapter.

Assessing fluency

Fluency is a more difficult assessment to make as it depends on the combination of several factors. A fluent script shows correct letter formation and easy joining. It is legible and speedy. A lack of fluency may arise from minor coordination and style errors and other features such as an awkward pencil hold or grip and wrong paper position. A lack of handwriting practice may also result in lack of fluency in a particular age group.

Alex's script in Figure 3.5 below is an example of a lack of fluency based upon a semi-joined, variable letter size and pressure and some coordination difficulties.

Alex is writing at a good speed for his age but much more slowly than we might expect from his high ability. He says he does not enjoy changing to cursive 'squiggles' now. In this section of 68 words he makes 10 misspellings. This is also high for his ability although not unexpected in the age group.

His writing is relatively legible, semi-joined but not fluent. The body size is large and heights of letters are uneven; the spaces between words varies; the slant is erratic; ascenders are frequently too short. Overall the script has a cramped appearance.

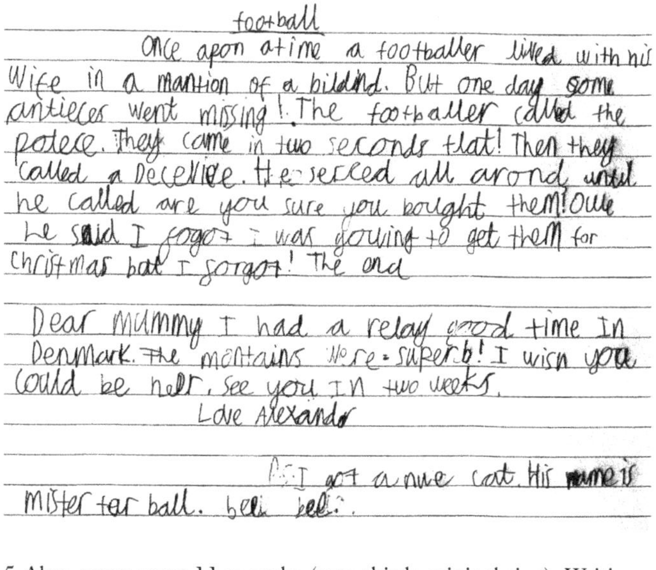

Figure 3.5 Alex, seven years 11 months (two thirds original size). Writing speed 11.1 w.p.m. IQ 137. Rigid tripod grip

There is variation in pressure seen in the darker and lighter words and letters and other indicators of some coordination difficulties. At speed under pressure this script is likely to deteriorate and become less legible. He also needs fluency training (described in Chapter 4).

Assessing coordination difficulties

Coordination difficulties may become confused with legibility issues because poor coordination can result in malformed letters and problems in positioning letters and words on the lines. There are, however, distinct indicators of coordination difficulties that observation of children writing and the scripts produced can reveal. A list of indicators is as follows:

- Script drags in from the margin.
- Rivers of space run down the page.
- The script is very faint.
- The script is spiky.
- Words wave about above the lines and drag below them.
- There is a variation in pressure seen in darker and lighter letters and words.
- Pressure may be so strong ridges appear on the reverse of the paper.
- Script may be very large and faint.
- The writer may complain of pain after a few minutes.
- Particular lower case letters may look like capitals, e.g. S, K, W, F because they are more difficult to form precisely and small.
- Ts appear as capitals because the cross bar cannot added precisely enough down the upright
- Other letters such as U and M and N may randomly be formed extra large as the coordination control is lost.
- There may be holes in and ink blots on the paper.

Figure 3.6a Tamina's dysgraphic handwriting on entry into Year 2

Tamina's writing is very faint and shaky, spidery and has taken considerable effort to produce this much in ten minutes.

Coordination difficulties make some pupils write much more slowly and with considerable effort. Others with coordination difficulties may write very rapidly but the script is large and faint and becomes increasingly illegible during extended periods of writing, especially in the 20-minute test.

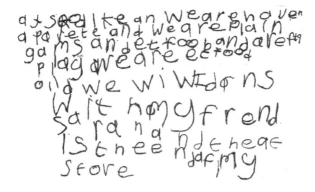

Figure 3.6b Sarah's Christmas story, aged seven years six months

This story took Sarah three-quarters of an hour to write. The script drags in from the margin; rivers of space appear as fatigue sets in halfway down and the writing becomes fainter and more spread out; the words do not maintain regular lines; letters such as 's', 'w' and 'k' are the size of capitals; there is variation in pressure. The script is an unjoined style and many letters are poorly formed and vary in size in words.

Her reading age was seven years two months and her spelling age was six years nine months and indicates the deleterious effect that poor handwriting skills can have particularly on spelling but also that it impinges on reading. The neurological evidence of these links will be discussed in Chapter 4.

Harry, in Figure 3.6.c, writes about the day his tooth came out in the back garden and he cannot find it. It is a typical example of the writing of a child with dysgraphia. It is very faint, does not maintain the lines; the letters are incompletely or poorly formed; they vary in size and there is some shake; the words drag away from the margin and then back to the left of the page.

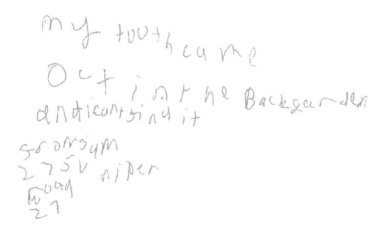

Figure 3.6c Harry's writing aged seven years

Figure 3.7a The Star Tracking Task – a simulation game for teachers

The Star Task:

- Photocopy a larger version of the star – about twice the size.
- Sit in front of a large mirror with the star on the table in front of you so it can be clearly seen in the mirror.
- With the non-preferred hand hold an A4 piece of card over the star on the desk so you can only see the star in the mirror not when you look down.
- Draw round the star in the track under the card by only looking in the mirror.
- Do not cheat!

Reflect on the emotions and sensations that are experienced or better still share them with a friend who could hold the card for you.

Repeat the procedure with the non-preferred hand and compare the results. Think why they are different in most cases. Why might one or two adults be unable to do the task with either hand? A few adults will be able to do this task relatively well. Consider why this might be so.

A child with coordination difficulties can experience these same challenges when learning to write and often cannot move the pen in any direction at all like Emily described earlier.

Much simpler tracking tasks are given to young children than the above in Figure 3.7 to practise pencil control and develop finger strength. This star track is used to simulate developmental coordination difficulties in adults and give some idea of what it feels like when the brain has difficulty controlling the pen.

a.

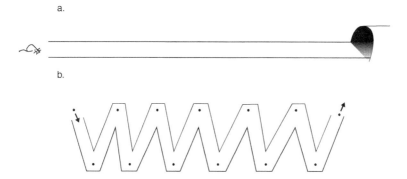

b.

Figure 3.7b Example of simple tracking tasks for young children

Assessing pen or pencil grip

There is a range of grips that may be used but the standard one is the **flexible tripod grip** (see Figure 3.8) for right and left hands. Left handers should hold the pen a little further from the point so that they can see the letters as they write. The second most popular grip is the **rigid tripod grip** with two fingers – index and middle on top of the pen. Writers may switch to it during long periods of writing or it may be their typical grip adopted to gain better control of the pen in the earlier years. This may be because of lack of finger strength at that time, bendy reflexed joints or long finger lengths.

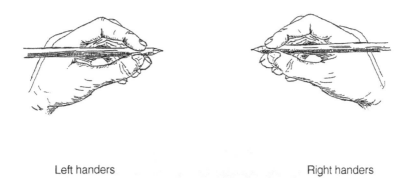

Left handers   Right handers

Figure 3.8 The standard flexible tripod grip

A tripod grip in which the pen rests between the index and the middle finger resting on the third finger is also adopted by some pupils during long writing periods.

In addition to the two main tripod grips there are others that are less common: the 'thumb over' or **quadruped grip** and variations on this wrap-around type and the **'hooker'** or a palm-up grip. The 'hooker' is thought to be adopted when the child has some neurological difficulty so that the writing hand has to be switched to the left hand in the right-handed or to the left in the right-handed. In the Reception class children not used to holding implements may use the most immature grip with the pencil held in the full fist or 'stab' grip. The next level of development is that in which the pen is held like a fork with the index finger pointing along it and the rest of the hand wrapped round it on top of the pencil or crayon.

Figure 3.9a Thumb over grip of a young child, almost a fist grip. Year 7

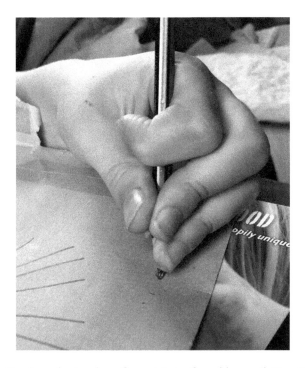

Figure 3.9b Quadruped grip – long finger joints of an older pupil, Year 7

A judgement has to be made about whether or not to try to change a well-established pen or pencil grip. It is possible to select a sample of fatter or thinner pens for the child to try to gain a firmer grip. Adjusting the nearness of the fingers to the pencil point may help, especially if they are too close to it. Plastic moulds that increase the girth and guide the grip to tripod can also be purchased and some companies have built these features into the pens themselves.

An alternative may be that the grip is weak and finger-strengthening exercises are the best option. All such interventions need to be taken only with the willingness of the learner to try the techniques and to persevere for long enough to gain some effects where these are possible.

Change is not always possible in cases of severe coordination difficulties and alternatives such as word processing and speech activation technology or scribes may be required. Even word processing may not be a good alternative for some pupils because they may have difficulties with that as well as with handwriting.

Some research may suggest that there is no advantage in using the tripod grip rather than the quadruped grip but the test tasks are short and the effects of fatigue and pain over time are not recorded.

Assessing paper position and needs of left handers

The furniture is a consideration in all of this. Make sure both feet are firmly on the floor and the seat and desk top are the right size for the writer. A desk top about ten inches below the eyes of the writer should be the comfortable distance. Short sightedness will cause the pupil to bring the head down closer to the paper. Some may even write best with one eye closed by head on arm. This is fairly rare and eye tests are advised.

The position of the paper should be differently angled for right and left-handers. It is never straight in line with the desk edge as some inexperienced tutors may insist upon. The wrong paper position can radically affect the handwriting ease and fluency. Children with coordination difficulties may find a slightly sloping desk easier to write on than a flat one. Before any investment is made in such adjustments the effect can be simulated by an empty hard-back file to find if it helps.

More slope for left-handers than for right enables them to see the tip of the pen. There are a few writers, very often 'hookers' who write with the page horizontal. The paper is placed at right angles to the desk and as they write they pull down the page. It enables them to see the words as they write, not cover them.

When writing, the elbow is in a locked position so that the forearm swings across the page from right to left in right-handers and dictates the exact slope the paper needs to be. For left-handers the left elbow is locked and the forearm swings in towards the midline from left to right.

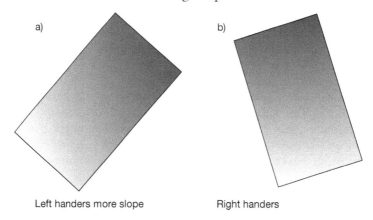

Figure 3.10 Paper position for left (a) and right handers (b)

The non-dominant hand should hold the paper firm on the desk. It is important that left-handers should sit on the left of peers so that their handwriting arm is free to move and not be hampered in any way. They also need to be taught to write letters by the teacher modelling the process with the left hand. It can be expected that 12 per cent of any class will be left-handed, which is three or four children in every classroom.

Motor skills in formation: assessment criteria for Reception handwriting samples

In the early years the general guidelines expect that by the age of five years a child should have good control over large and small movements, move confidently in a range of ways and handle equipment and tools effectively including pencils for writing. Between three to five years a teacher should be able to expect a child to have:

- established hand dominance;
- circle anti-clockwise and clockwise;
- make vertical strokes;
- form letters correctly;
- copy some letters; and
- use one-handed tools.

As will be seen in the following examples the widest range of these skills may be observed in Reception classrooms where the youngest children are just four years old. Age, however, does not fully determine the level of skill maturity – some of the youngest may be the most skilled in pencil control. The important factor is whether the skill observed in any individual Reception learner is fit for purpose in the learning environment that has been constructed and the curriculum on offer.

The assessments discussed in the previous sections apply to the scripts of pupils who are already writing. There were no similar assessments of children's handwriting skills as they are developing. However, in a series of research studies Reception children's writing was used to develop the ten-point scale below (N=470 scripts).

Scoring 'first marks on paper' for copy writing and free writing:

10 Letters all the same moderate size on a line.
9   With clear ascenders and descenders.
8   Spaces between words.
7   With appropriate capitals.
6   Bodies sit on the line, real or imaginary.
5   Letters formed in a single fluid movement.
4   Distinct letter shapes.
3   Drawn letters.
2   Mandalas and letter-like shapes in a line.
1   Some letter-type marks in a line across the paper.
0   Random scribble and faint marks.

Figures 3.11a–f show emergent (free) writing samples after one month in Reception (all half original size).

Figure 3.11a A page of scribble scores 0

In the first sample (Figure 3.11a) we see a page of scribble, rather faint and shaky. This child's work needs careful monitoring. He is already showing a weak grasp and poor pencil skills without any connection to the print he is seeing in the early story books. He will need motricity training and finger-strengthening exercises with colouring and drawing activities to support writing movement training.

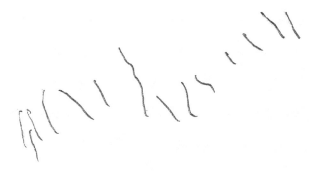

Figure 3.11b 'I went to the park'

He makes some wavy strokes with a firm hand, a good sign. The strokes march across the page with gaps between them showing he has absorbed the basic structure in the line of words he is copying. A line to write on would help him keep to the horizontal. He starts on the right side of the paper. Scores 1.

Figure 3.11c 'My scooter goes ding a ling'

This writer tries to follow the line and make letter-forms but the pencil control is poor. The writing is spiky and shaky, indicating a potential coordination difficulty. Scores 2 but needs skills monitoring and finger strength and fluency training.

Figure 3.11d 'I went oyster picking'

This script shows marks on paper that include roundels or 'mandalas'. Interestingly they are oyster shapes indicating familiarity with them and possibly advertisements for them. The 'I' is formed correctly and is where he started the sentence. He also needs lines to write on and to learn to start on the left of the page not the right. He leaves spaces between his 'words' showing more advanced knowledge than 3.11.c. He makes small, relatively firm marks showing good developing pencil control. Scores 3.

Figure 3.11e 'I went to nanny's'

This sample shows 'distinct letter shapes' (4) 'formed in one fluid movement' (5) that all 'sit on the line' (6). She has good coordination skills but has not yet cracked the alphabetic code to begin spelling. Scores 6 for motor skills and 3/4 for spelling.

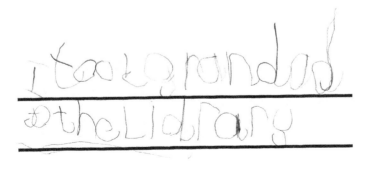

Figure 3.11f 'I took grandad to the lidrary'

Table 3.7 The results of the Handwriting Skill Assessment on Reception Scripts

School/classes	SES	Nos	Boys	Girls	Mean scores	Word count
Schools A1/2 & B1	Council estate	58	3.19	4.2	3.52	6.91
School C1/2	Owner occ. estate	55	4.00	5.95	4.98	5.74
School D1/2/3	Private prep.	64	5.43	6.82	5.86	9.5
Totals		177	4.21	5.67	4.79	

In Figure 3.11f he already has a good command of writing but the faintness suggests a mild coordination difficulty with the wobble and change in pressure of the letters. The letters are mainly formed with single lines and float above the lines. There are no spaces between the words yet. The 'g' and 'y' sit above the line with no descenders. Capital 'I' is correct.

Although there are ligatures on some of the letters they are not used for joining and some of the letters such as 'k' and the final 'y' are drawn in two parts not as a full flowing letter as in the Fernald method and full cursive. Scores 7 for motor skills and 9 for spelling.

Table 3.7 results shows that girls' motor skills in copywriting at the beginning of the Reception year are significantly more advanced than those of boys and that the skills of children from more affluent homes are also higher than the rest. As expected, the children in the prep school were the most verbose (word count).

It will be argued in the next chapter that motor coordination skills and handwriting, if appropriately encouraged and trained, can improve the situation for boys and all the children, enabling them to learn to write more easily and fluently. This will enhance reading and spelling development and lift achievement.

Handwriting toolkit for teachers

- An explanation of the four different purposes of handwriting.
- The ten-minute free writing test.
- Norms for Year groups. Pupils should count the number of words they have written and compare this to the norms for their age group. Explain why speed is important to them.
- Pen/pencil grip pictures and photographs.
- A supply of pen/pencil grips and moulds.
- Paper position. Check that pupils' papers are correctly angled for their personal use and explain the need.
- Copies of the T-HFL and image on the whiteboard.
- Pupils should ring errors, pairs discuss and assess their relative legibility.

- Legibility training focusing on two key issues: a) make body sizes all the same size; and b) make all ascenders and descenders slope in the same direction. Institute daily practice for five minutes for those who need it.
- Use the 'Lazy fox sentence' to check for correct letter formation.
- Reception teachers should use the scripts of learners to monitor progress and plan interventions, teaching cursive from the outset.
- Motricity training for those who need it.
- There is a wide range of resources available to support handwriting and a list of some of these and their sources may be found after the reference section.

Conclusions

The study of children's handwriting has suggested that it is much more important than current educational practice acknowledges. Six factors have been identified in handwriting that contribute to success or failure in later academic activities such as composition and narrative writing. In secondary schools up to 80 per cent of the time may be taken up in writing so that any difficulties will be very stressful and disadvantaging for the learner. For those with coordination difficulties it can be very demotivating and they will seek to avoid writing.

Across the age groups and different schools it was confirmed that girls had more advanced writing skills than boys of the same age and this of course is reflected in the results collected in the national SATs and GCSEs, up to A-levels.

Research using the assessments found that a much larger proportion of the school population was at risk from handwriting difficulties than schools may realise. This was in the order of one third of all the learners. Research in gifted education and now in a wide range of education contexts shows this is a major contributor to underachievement across the age and ability ranges. Boys were more vulnerable to this than girls. Whether this is necessary and if learning trajectories can be changed will be addressed in the next chapter.

4 The contribution of handwriting to literacy development and how handwriting difficulties can be overcome

Introduction

For some considerable time handwriting difficulties have been identified as one of the major causes of underachievement among gifted pupils (Whitmore, 1982; Silverman, 1989, 2002; Montgomery, 2000). However, such writing difficulties are not limited to the gifted. Roaf (1998) found that pupils in her secondary school who were writing at a speed slower than 15 words per minute in a 10-minute, free writing test were underachieving in all areas of the curriculum and 25 per cent of the school were writing at this speed or below. Slow and poor handwriting was also associated with lower perceptions of self-worth.

Bravar (2005) found that 70 per cent of Italian children referred for underachievement had writing difficulties. Of these, 47 per cent had poor handwriting and the writing of 23 per cent was illegible but only 6 per cent had actually been referred for their writing problems.

Pre-term children have also been found to be a population at risk from handwriting difficulties. Feder et al. (2005) found that full-term controls wrote at a higher speed and with greater legibility at six or seven years than pre-term children.

In Chapter 3, six factors in handwriting were identified for assessment and they can also prove problematic. They are speed, style, form, legibility, fluency and coordination. They are not independent of each other for poorly taught letter forms may make for slow and dysfluent writing just as poor pencil grip or a weak grip can result in poor letter form and legibility problems and so on.

Cohort analysis of pupils in Year 7 in three English non-selective state schools found that 32 per cent of the 536 pupils had handwriting difficulties of some kind that would affect their school achievement (Montgomery, 2008). Only one pupil in 536 was writing at a speed of 25 words per minute in Year 7 in the 20-minute test. 1.5 per cent of pupils were writing at a speed of 15 to 20 w.p.m. Girls were writing 2.5 words per minute faster than boys at this age. Overall the mean writing speed was 12.4 words per minute, considerably slower than in Roaf's school but in a longer test.

The slower speeds would prevent them from writing their ideas down easily and fully in examinations and if they have coordination difficulties this will affect legibility and may cause pain when writing at length.

The fact that almost one third of these pupils at 12 years of age had some kind of handwriting difficulty is very concerning and seems disproportionate when we consider the nature of the task. Almost all children, except the 1 or 2 per cent with severe difficulties and perhaps the 5–10 per cent with DCD (Barnett et al., 2008), can be expected to learn to write fluently and well. In the cohort study we therefore have 20 per cent who are being failed in some way by the writing curriculum.

This is not an isolated result. It seems that all the writing research studies in the UK show this kind of decrement from the Reception year onwards. It is likely to be due to the failure of handwriting to have a proper place in the curriculum as Medwell and Wray (2007) reported.

Is handwriting still needed?

With the arrival of computers and laptops some people suggest that handwriting is no longer needed but recent research using fMRI scanning has shown that handwriting is much more important in literacy development, especially in reading, than has previously been thought.

For example, Berninger (2015) followed children in grades two through to five and her study showed that printing, cursive writing and typing on a keyboard were all associated with distinct and separate brain areas. The children had all learned by the separate modes from the outset, e.g. always using keyboarding, print or cursive.

When the children composed text by hand, they not only consistently produced more words more quickly than those using a keyboard but expressed more ideas. In the oldest subjects brain imaging suggested that the connection between writing and idea generation went even further. When the children were asked to come up with ideas for a composition, the ones with better handwriting exhibited greater neural activation in areas associated with working memory and increased overall activation in the reading and writing networks.

Mueller and Oppenheimer (2014) found that in both laboratory settings and real-world classrooms, students learned better when they took notes by hand than when they typed on a keyboard. This suggests that writing by hand allows pupils and older students to process a lesson or lecture content and reframe it. This process of reflection and manipulation leads to better understanding and memory encoding than keyboarding or cutting and pasting.

Preliterate five-year-old children printed, typed, or traced letters and shapes, then were shown images of these stimuli while undergoing fMRI scanning (James and Engelhardt, 2012). A previously documented 'reading circuit' was recruited during letter perception **only after handwriting** not after typing or tracing experiences. The researchers found that the initial duplication process mattered a great deal. When children had drawn a letter freehand, they exhibited increased activity in three areas of the brain that are activated in adults when they read and write. These were the left fusiform gyrus, the inferior frontal gyrus and the posterior parietal cortex.

By contrast, children who typed or traced the letter or shape showed no such effects. The researchers attributed the differences to the messiness inherent in free-form handwriting. This is because not only must we first plan and execute the action in a way that is not required when we have a traceable outline, but we are also likely to produce a result that is highly variable. The variability may itself be a learning tool for different forms of the same letter. We might also hypothesise that freeform writing not only activates the spelling-writing areas but also connects them to the reading-meaning areas as we use all our skills and concentration on the task in hand.

Such research has strong implications for the early years writing and reading curriculum. In other words, to produce good readers more quickly we need to teach handwriting by free form writing of letters and not allow children to copy or trace them. This means that Early Years training and teaching needs to be changed.

When children trace or copy letters as they are learning to write they can often be observed drawing them, as shown in Chapter 3, Figure 3.1, and the representation for this is found in a different area of the brain from writing (Seton, 2012). Children frequently chat while copy writing and thus their brains cannot be engaged in making the grapheme–phoneme linkage. Even when they are not talking their concentration in tracing and copying is not necessarily linking the graphemes to the phonemes or the 'motoremes'.

Research by Marin, La Voie and Montisinos (2012) showed that those taught cursive from the outset made more progress in speedy writing of words followed by semi-joined and slowest were those taught print. They advocated teaching cursive from the outset as switching was too hard for most children. Other researchers specifically recommend *not* allowing children to trace letters because doing so delays memorisation of letter-forms (Overvelde and Hulstijn, 2012). Not tracing or copying runs against the custom and practice in most English Reception classrooms. It would appear that this practice has been wrong for over 70 years.

When cursive from the outset was introduced in 16 schools in the Kingston cursive project lead by Paula Morse, almost all the children were reaching Level 4 in writing by the end of the infant phase (Low, 1990). Other such initiatives in Kent, Portsmouth and Avon supported these findings. The results have implications for current early years handwriting and spelling teaching and for supplementary learning support at the later stages. Unfortunately, as the leaders of the cursive movement in the schools move on, the practice reverts once again to teaching print first (personal communications from Kingston and Portsmouth head teachers).

Why cursive?

A fast running hand is the ultimate purpose of handwriting teaching. There are also a number of other reasons for encouraging children to learn cursive even when they have been taught print or semi-joined scripts. It is especially important as a remedial support in dyslexia and dyspraxia. Wedell (1973) concluded from his research that it was essential for children with coordination difficulties to learn cursive from the outset.

The reasons for teaching cursive are because it:

- aids left to right movement through words across the page;
- eliminates reversals and inversions of letters;
- eliminates the need to relearn a whole new set of motor programmes after the infant years;
- induces greater fluency in writing which enables greater speed to be developed without loss of legibility;
- the motor programmes for spelling whole words and syllables are stored together and so improve spelling accuracy;
- space between letters and between words is orderly and automatic;
- all words and single letters begin in the same place, on the line;
- all letters are made with a continuous line from one starting point, not four different ones;
- a more efficient, fluent and personal style can be developed;
- it reinforces multisensory learning linking spelling, reading and speaking;
- pupils with mild handwriting co ordination difficulties experience less pain and difficulty; and
- it improves the legibility of those with coordination difficulties unless they have severe problems when alternative support is needed.

Criticisms of cursive

It is argued by Webb (2015) and Sassoon (2015) for example, members of the National Handwriting Association, that the child needs a simple uncluttered visual form of letters to establish the target for writing. This should not be the ball and stick version but a monoline form with a small lead-out ligature on most letters. This may well be true but the purpose of posters illustrating the basic letter shape in monoline should provide this as well as exposure to the print in children's early reading books.

The second major criticism is that for many children, starting all letters on the line causes confusion (see Figure 4.1).

These errors and confusions certainly occur with some writers but it is the method of teaching employed that creates them. For example, if letters are all taught singly and in family patterns this problem will occur especially where there are many drills and few discussions about the process and the desired products. In one project school (Caunt, 2004) the teachers actually believed

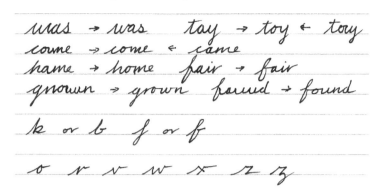

Figure 4.1 Potential confusions when letter joining

that always returning to the line no matter what was the correct interpretation of cursive joining.

When letters are taught so that as soon as two are known they are used to build words then the most efficient joins are demonstrated and practised. This means that the correct form is laid down in the motor memory in the first place not incorrect ones that are difficult to correct later.

Handwriting in Reception

Case studies (Montgomery, 2015) of 175 Reception class children's writing in four different schools illustrated the effects of different teaching methods and some of their shortcomings. After one month in Reception the children did a copy writing then a free writing task for ten minutes. They were followed up after five months in Reception and then again on entry to Year 2. Each follow-up involved a free writing test for ten minutes.

The copy writing and free writing scores showed the same effects of socioeconomic status on literacy achievement and teaching methods as for the older pupils. By the end of the first five months the children from the lower socioeconomic status schools, the poorest children, were already five months behind the rest and had not caught up when they were retested in Year 2. The research with the Year 7 cohorts showed that approximately one third of pupils at that age had handwriting difficulties that lowered their potential achievements. The three state primary schools in the Reception class studies outlined above were feeder schools into the large comprehensive where 32 per cent had handwriting difficulties.

The analysis of the scripts showed that the eight Reception teachers involved:

- did not teach cursive from the outset;
- all taught ligatures on some of the letters but the Teaching Assistants did not always follow this practice;
- no teacher taught joining ligatured letters even when a child was ready;

- only one teacher gave the children lines to write on;
- only one teacher engaged in emergent writing (and no copy writing); and
- no teacher engaged in developmental spelling.

The Reception teacher's toolkit

The evidence from the research showed that in the Reception Year the handwriting development programme should:

1 Give 'motricity' training to prepare the developmentally immature to write and reinforce the skills of those arriving in Reception already writing.
2 Provide finger-strengthening activities such as drawing and finger painting; using tools especially knives and forks; work with dough and building blocks; sand and water play; dressing up play and cooking etc.
3 Teach letter shapes by 'in air' tracing and free forming them large on whiteboard, in sand and on paper.
4 There should be no tracing over or copying of letters. No copying of news.
5 All writing paper should have wide lines to put the letters on.
6 Each letter should be formed with one continuous line like a piece of string.
7 Freeform letters should have ligatures so that sets of them can be linked.
8 Training in pencil hold should be given to show the flexible tripod grip so that the pupils know the final goal even if they need adaptations at first.
9 A range of pencils of different thickness and length together with plastic moulds should be provided to help those with a weaker grip to achieve the tripod format.
10 Handwriting teaching should be in cursive from the outset.
11 Handwriting teaching should be linked to teaching to spell from the outset.
12 Letters for writing should be introduced in use order and frequency not alphabetically or by shape groups. The order should be e.g. i, t, p, n, s, d, a, as used in remedial programmes.
13 As soon as two letters can be written freely they should be joined to build a word.
14 Useful common words can be taught as a whole writing unit once initial progress is made e.g. ***the, and, said***.
15 Teaching initial sounds for reading words, decoding and alphabetical order should be linked to what has been learned from writing. They should be shown in cursive and in print script.
16 Examples of the letter forms in print and cursive should be displayed around the classroom.

The children's 'in air' movements for writing have to be carefully monitored to ensure they are correct. The teacher needs to model them with her back to the children and then watch them form their 'in air' letters with the help of any assistants and the other children.

An important factor is to give the writing programme as much time as the reading programme. All the usual methods can apply in reading such as teaching the value of 'onsets' or initial sounds to begin to decode words using context and picture clues and analogies with known words to help decoding. The alphabet system using pictograms can be taught with its print script as used in story books. The eye and brain are very adept at learning by features analysis that a letter in print is the same as that one in cursive without necessarily being specifically taught. But it is helpful to point out that the different forms are really the same letter.

When we write, the difference is that we need to develop a fluid motor programme that will draw out the correct spellings, a recall skill whereas when we read the spellings are already present and there is a visual pattern recognition skill to learn.

Establishing correct spellings in a personal lexicon so that they can later be recalled is a much more difficult task than recognising the word already formed by a set of letters in a story book. Using reading and copy writing and tracing is not the most efficient method for building a spelling lexicon (word memory store). When we rely more on reading to establish the spelling lexicon the features often become stored in the wrong order, e.g. 'form' for 'from', especially the middle letters are muddled.

Eyes have to be trained to work from left to right in English writing systems just as hands have to learn to do so when making spellings. About 50 per cent of pupils may arrive at school with a preference for eye movements scanning in the left to right direction but others may have a preference for right to left or randomly right and left. A left to right scanning habit has to be established otherwise some children will use the final letters of a word as the onset. Coloured starting dots and the 'dots and sticks' pattern recognition training can help reorientate this scanning activity before it leads to confusion.

Once motor habits are well established they are difficult to change – 'old habits die hard'. Thus spending time in establishing good habits in Reception is the better plan. It is surprising that the national curriculum gives such little attention to it. This lack of attention in the early stages can lead to a lot of extra work and distress in schools in the junior and secondary years and causes much unnecessary underachievement. In the following sections a number of interventions are exemplified to show the diagnosis that can be made, what can work and the range of techniques that might be needed.

One of the most important factors in teaching, developing or changing motor skills is to ensure that the learner has the appropriate cognitive goal and knows what is to be achieved and why. It has been known for a long time that skilled performance increases not only after practice but especially after cognitive rehearsal of the skill. For example, skilled performers such as divers and darts players mentally rehearse the dive or the throw as they present themselves for the act and novices have been shown to improve if they do so even when they only mentally rehearse.

Thus when teachers demonstrate the writing movement of a letter the children need to mentally rehearse it and then try to follow it in their own continuous writing in-air free form movement.

Early Years interventions

'Motricity'

Many children arrive at school in the Reception class with less well-developed skills than they need for literacy work. They may not know how to hold and use a pencil, dress themselves without help and walk, run or hop fluidly. At the other extreme some will arrive already writing and reading. Some will have had play school or nursery school education. There is thus a vast range in skill with which the teacher is confronted.

Identifying the different levels of skill and the particular needs is an important part of the teaching process. Different activity corners and opportunities enable the teacher to do this. Free play areas with access to the outside and larger play apparatus and vehicles can provide evidence of gross motor coordination or lack of it when children continually bump into things or fall off them, or cannot build and manipulate blocks and toys, engage in sand and water play, undress for PE or put on their coats and scarves to go home.

Other more skilled children and those with preschool education can view these activities as tedious and childish and not consistent with their concept of learning now. They can learn to help the more immature children but not by dressing them, instead by practising their communication skills. Trying to tell the other child the next step to take, e.g.

- Are the shoes on the right feet? How do we know? Are they comfortable?
- Next step pull the laces tight.
- Cross the laces over once.
- Make a loop in one lace.

At this point the adult may need a while to complete the task for the child. Parents aware of the problem usually buy wrap-over fixings but this deprives the children of a useful learning experience. The same with zips as opposed to buttons, although even zips are problematic for some children.

Diagnosing individual levels of ability in Reception

The child:

- Responds correctly to the teacher's instruction to sit down, to listen, to be quiet, to put away toys, to stand still and so on.
- Participates satisfactorily in the movement songs and games such as 'The wheels on the bus go round and round'. If these are not known then the

rapidity with which the child can learn to join in is also important information.

- Moves in harmony with the rhythm of songs and music.
- Sings and moves in harmony together.
- Develops awareness of position in space through development of skills in PE and Games; undressing and dressing skills, buttoning and zipping.
- Engages in a wide range of strengthening and fine skills development activities, e.g. finger strengthening by working with clay and dough; using tools and various implements; cooking activities; using eating utensils in imaginary and real situations; finger painting; weighing and measuring; threading beads; building with bricks and Lego etc. and working on jigsaws.
- Engages in a range of more general motor skills activities such as climbing in and out of toy constructions and on climbing frames; riding tricycles and trucks; walking, running, playing football and handball, hopping and eventually skipping.

One of the key features is when the parent's and then the teacher's verbal instruction directs the child's behaviour. At about 18 months, when a child is placing rings on a stick, if she is told to stop she puts them on faster. Later she learns to stop and will even take them off again. Some children from disorganised families arrive at school without such control. They continue talking when told to stop. They run about the room when told to stop and stand still then come and sit down on the mat and so on. These children need to be taught to respond to simple verbal instructions before they can learn properly. In extreme cases they will need a Nurture Group setting to be taught these things (Boxall, 2002).

What children can all engage in together is motor skills development in PE and Games and especially importantly work in Dance. It can incorporate Music and Movement and more formal structured co-operative dance. During these activities it is important that the movements that are made in writing are modelled with the whole body in circles and rings and forwards and backwards to music and without it, but keeping a rhythm.

The traditional singing and movement games are also important. Instead of following a writing lesson for relaxation they need to precede it so that the round movements made by the arms can be repeated with hand work such as finger painting or pencil work making the round and round letter forms. Using Fernald's (1943) in air tracing of letters becomes essential work preparatory to writing them on paper.

The only copy writing they might engage in is to try to copy their own names. Even this can be made into a problem to solve by covering the written name and the child tries to write the first letter from memory, then checks the result. This can move on to trying to write the whole name using the Look – Cover – Write – Check strategy. They can then be shown how to hold the pencil and where to start the copying; red dots on the left of the line by the margin can help with this.

Each child needs to learn the initial sound and structure of the first letter of his or her own name. They can be grouped for this if need be and tuition given. Difficulties can easily be observed in this small group setting and plans can be laid to help overcome them. These may be more finger-strengthening activities with dough and clay or pencil hold moulds selected to assist weak grips. Different sizes of writing tools need to be made available to help children select the most comfortable for them.

Drawing and colouring and finger-painting activities can also be used to diagnose levels of skill and readiness for writing and provide rhythm and strengthening activities. Colouring too can be an enjoyable activity as children learn to colour within the borders of a figure smoothly and without scribbling. Colouring to a rhythm, a beat or to music can provide different experiences and challenges and show developmental progression when results are kept in a personal folder.

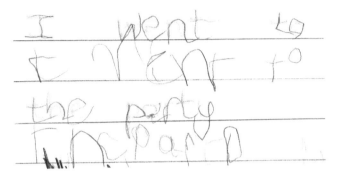

Figure 4.2a Gary's copy writing, five years one month: 'I went to the party'

The news here is written by a helper who has not been well trained to form the letters correctly and clearly for Gary to trace over first then to copy. The good feature is that he does have lines to write on. His copy writing is faint and letters vary in size, they are generally made with one continuous line and mostly with ligatures, 'w' is inverted as an 'm', 'y' is unmanageable. He needs finger-strengthening exercises with letter formation teaching. He appears to have a mild coordination difficulty.

His free writing shows knowledge of some letter forms but they do not relate to words or sounds. This time there are no lines for guidance but he does write the letters across the page resembling words in books. However he has obviously made no connection between what he copies and traces with letter sounds.

If he had been taught to trace two letters in the air and give their associated sounds we would expect to see them in his emergent writing within a week. Then we could show him how they can be used in reading to help decode text.

Figure 4.2b Gary's free form writing

Free form writing promotes connectivity between symbol and sound whereas tracing and copying keeps them separated, sometimes indefinitely as in dyslexia.

Handwriting case work across the age ranges

When members of Potential Plus UK, the former National Association for Gifted Children, an organisation supporting parents of potentially gifted children gave samples of their children's handwriting, 40 example cases from Reception to Year 7 were collected and 32 showed handwriting and/or spelling difficulties and a further 7 needed help with legibility issues. Each was given a detailed analysis of handwriting and spelling skills and suggestions for intervention were made. Some examples follow in the case list below.

Although the PPUK samples were from volunteers they represented about 4 per cent of the total PPUK group, not all those with concerns or time to join the project. This could mean that perhaps 10 per cent of a gifted group also had barriers to learning arising from handwriting that could have been removed by handwriting intervention or supplementary support.

In the following sections various scripts will be analysed and suggested developmental intervention strategies will be outlined.

Case work diagnosis and intervention advice

1. Emilie: six years – speed, legibility and dysgraphia

She writes, '*dear Grandma thank you for my lovely Pecil set i am loads of fun Sketching and Drawing You will Really Love the Pictures i've drawn*'.

She would benefit from having lines to write on to fix the location of where to start the letters. The paper needs to be sloped more to the right so that the script runs horizontally. Some initial letters are joined by ligatures but she

Figure 4.3 Emilie's thank you letter aged six years

quickly reverts to unjoined form with no ligatures. Some letters are not formed with a single continuous line. The script was faint and variable. Letters vary in size with short or no 'tails' or no 'sticks'. The 'p's stand above the line with difficult letters appearing large to look like capitals. The space between letters and words varies and the letters grow larger at the end as fatigue develops. All these indicators suggest a mild coordination difficulty – dysgraphia that needs immediate attention. Her spelling is good.

She needs to be taught a joined script with lead-in lines and be given double lines to guide the size of the bodies of the letters and make appropriate 'tails' and 'sticks'. Many of her letters are not well formed so the cursive style will assist with this.

2. Elliott: six years ten months – dysgraphia

(Left-handed rigid tripod grip, a thick support tube round the pencil.)

The writing is large and very faint. It increases in size with each A4 page and fills each one. The spelling is good. It illustrates a case of dysgraphia without dyslexia.

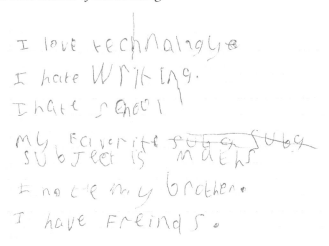

Figure 4.4 Elliot's handwriting under control filling page 1

Transcript:

> Page 1
> *I love technology. I hate writing.*
> *I hate school. My favorite ~~subg subg~~ subJect is maths.*
> *I hate my brother. I have Freinds.*
> *My brother is a idiot.*
> *Christmas*
> *Santa does not excist*
> *Santa doesn't give you presants that we ask for.*
>
> Page 2 filling page 2
> *building*
> *building is boring and you don't know*
> *where your food is.*
>
> Page 3 filling page 3
> A line of scribble and crossings through.
> *Princesses are stupid*
> *History Dinosaurs excist*
> *School teachers do work*

The diagnosis of dysgraphia is important so that he may have voice recognition technology to support him or a scribe to write what he requires. Using a laptop will also be useful but he may not be able to use it at the speed he requires. Meanwhile he is trying to write smaller and in cursive within the double lines (see page 126 for his first effort). He needs direct guidance on the cursive form now because he is just working from a copy.

Many schools do not permit such young children to use laptops, insisting they will need to handwrite in exams so must start practising now. Others only permit the use of the school laptops, which are in a secure store and the keys have to be fetched and the device returned at the end of the lesson. These laptops are not always in working order or in rooms where they can easily be connected to the electricity supply or the batteries run out.

Some schools and local authorities delay the process of Statementing of the need so that the expense is reduced. But this is at the expense of the young learner and raises yet another barrier to their learning.

3. Harry: seven years – dysgraphia

Harry aged seven years (see Figure 4.5a) writes about the day his tooth came out in the back garden and he cannot find it. It is a typical example of the writing of a child with dysgraphia. It is very faint (in the original), does not maintain the lines; the letters are incompletely or poorly formed; they vary in size and there is some shake; the words drag away from the margin and then back to the left of the page.

In Figure 4.5b we can see that Harry is left-handed and has an incorrect and weak grip, the pen is the wrong type for such a grip, he holds it too close to the point, and the paper is in the wrong position for him. His actual script also shows that he has coordination difficulties.

Paper position: Left-handers like Harry should have the paper sloped to the left side by about 40 degrees from the vertical, or more if necessary to get the writing to flow easily across the page in a straight line. In the picture we can see his writing is moving upwards across the paper. He needs to experiment to get the paper in the right position for him. He needs lines to write on to guide spatial position and lead the writing horizontally.

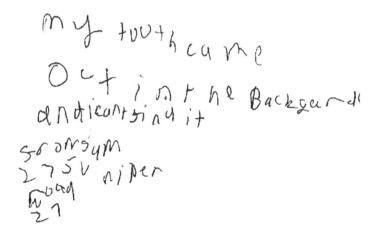

Figure 4.5a Harry's dysgraphic writing aged seven years

Figure 4.5b Photograph of Harry's pen grip

What we see in the picture is a grip that has been lacking in strength early on. The index finger is backwardly flexed, as the joint has not yet developed fully. His whole thumb has been used to increase early control over the pen and needs to be more flexed. A special tripod grip is required to support him until his fingers and thumb strengthen.

The whiteness at the index finger joint and the flush at the finger and thumb ends show that a large amount of pressure and effort have to be exerted; this means that fatigue quickly builds up and the writing deteriorates. Fluency training will help overcome this to some extent and ease the pain that can arise.

4. Loretta: seven years eight months – dysgraphia, Example report

Right handed for writing, some 'cross dominance' in using knife and fork. Tripod grip using Stabilo EasyBall triangular grip pen.

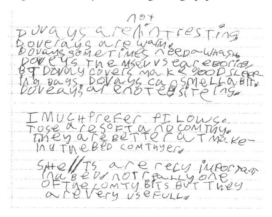

Figure 4.6 Loretta's handwriting (reduced to one third of original size)

> *Duvays are not interesting. Doveiays are warm.*
> *Dovays sometimes neeD a whasH*
> *Dovays the mservvsear eBoring*
> *Bt Dovay covers ma ke gooD sleep*
> *ing Bags. Dovays can smell a Bit.*
> *Doveya ar enot eesite ing.*
> *I MucH PreFer PILows.*
> *Tose are SoFT anD comThy.*
> *They are Better a T maKe-*
> *ing The BeD comthyer.*
> *Sheets - - - //*

Writing skill:
55 words in 10 minutes. 5.5 words per minute is a significantly slow speed for 7.7 years. The writing style is print with some ligatures. There are capitals for B and D suggesting earlier problems in identifying the lower case versions. Other capitals appear inside words as a result of fluctuations in pencil control, e.g. T, S, K, W, M. This is typical in cases of coordination difficulties. L looks like V in one word.

After the first paragraph the words begin to drag towards the mid-line; this is also typical in coordination difficulties. Spaces between words also vary and sometimes there is none. Some letters with descenders stand on the lines and ascenders are frequently too short.

Spelling skill:
This is generally good for the common words. The exceptions are for more difficult or less frequent words such as: duvet, dovay etc. comfy/comthy; exciting/eesiteing; pilow/pillow. Check for clear articulation for these words and encourage syllabification for spelling. Teach the short vowel sound and doubling rule for suffixing.

Suggested interventions on handwriting:
Although Loretta has been given lines to write on and this is essential for her, these lines are far too close together for her current need. It is preventing her from forming letters correctly and making some of it difficult to read.

My suggestion is to draw or find some practice sheets first of all with three lines matching the 'body' size of her current letters, e.g.

The body of the letter should fill the space between the lower two lines. Letters with ascenders should nearly touch the top line – except 't', which is a small letter.

Descenders should hang below the line not stand on it.

Give Loretta four sets of three lines to work on. Choose a useful short word and place it at the beginning of the line and then ask her to repeat that form across the page, leaving the space of an 'o' between the words.

The purpose is for Loretta to gain cognitive control as well as develop motor fluency. All the words should use the ligatures to join them up. The lead-in lines are helpful to find the position in space where the words begin. If Loretta does not like lead-in lines then use 'ghost' ones. Using cursive is essential in cases of coordination difficulties; see example of the LDRP ovoid cursive (Figure 4.8 below).

On the second day let Loretta choose the words she wishes to write. Analyse the effects together after several days practice for any progress or lack of it. Make any modifications and resume practice. Do not continue after a fortnight and do not give tasks longer than four sets at a time unless Loretta wishes to do so. When crossing 't's and dotting 'i's and 'j's do this after writing the whole word.

The apparent capitals such as P should be sorted by showing the lower case form must have a descender with the 'body' sitting on the line. As fluency and speed grow the other 'capitals' should come under control and reduce in size.

5. Zara: eight years two months – speed and legibility, Example report

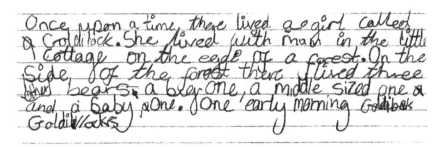

Figure 4.7 Zara's handwriting: left handed, tripod grip

Transcript:

> *Once upon a time there lived a e girl called g Goldilock. She lived with mum in the little cottage on the egde of a forest. On the side of the forest there lived three bther bears. A big one, a middle sized one a and a baby p One. One early morning Goldtok Goldi// locks*

Writing skills:
Zara is writing at a speed of 5.4 words per minute and 20.9 letters per minute. This is a significantly slower speed than the average at her age and suggests there are some problems and one of the reasons she does not enjoy writing. The average speed is 9 to 10 words per minute and many of the ablest pupils write at a speed of 15 words per minute at her age.

Her writing form is a large, semi-joined script without lead-in strokes. The descenders, 'tails' are very long on 'g' and 'y'. The letters slope forward and back. The bodies of the letters vary in size within words and sometimes are as large as capital letters. Letters such as 's' and 'z' that are more complex to make are often too large and look like capital letters. Spaces between words vary. The overall appearance of the MS is that it is cramped. All of these features make the script less legible than it should be and suggest a mild coordination difficulty and lack of fluency.

There is only one misspelling – 'egde'. She is spelling all the standard vocabulary well for her age.

Suggested intervention on handwriting:
The most problematic area is Zara's handwriting coordination in relation to fluency and speed. The interventions suggested are similar to those for Loretta.

- Find some fatter pens and pencils for Zara to try. She might find one that suits her best.
- Draw some three-lined paper to practice for fluency. Only draw half a page of lines. Practice for motor skills should be little and often – not more than about five minutes per day.
- She must try to make the bodies of her letters sit on the bottom line and touch the line above.
- All the 'sticks' and 'tails' should slope in the same direction either forward or back or upright.
- The sticks should touch or nearly touch the top line.
- Note that 't' is a small letter and its 'stick' does not touch the top line.

Ask her to write three common words such as 'and' and 'the' and 'why' in the top line and discuss how well she can do this.

- Next ask her to write a whole line of each of the words as fluidly and speedily as she can *and and and and and and*
  the the the the the the the
- Repeat the exercise several times more over the next few days and then after that with different words such as 'come', 'home', 'long', etc.

The LDRP model below is a fully joined (cursive) with lead-in strokes. The lead-in lines enable all words to begin in the same place on the line which is helpful for children with difficulties. As Zara does not use lead-in lines she does not need to change but use 'ghost-in' lines instead. Do not bother her with single letter practice.

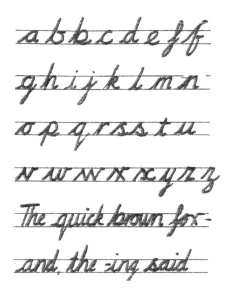

Figure 4.8 LDRP ovoid cursive

Keep the daily practice up for a fortnight with a day of rest in between each week and then review her writing with her. Does it look better and please her more? What does she find difficult? What are her thoughts on the process? etc.

She should now begin to try to use the strategies in her schoolwork.

At weekly intervals after this encourage her to have a practice session for speed. Then at the beginning and end of each half term she should write the 'fox' sentence as many times as possible in **one minute** to see if she is speeding up, e.g.:

The quick brown fox jumps over the lazy dog.

All the letters of the alphabet are contained in it.

The point of the regular discussion is to enable her to gain cognitive control over the skill and know what she needs to do even though she may relapse at times.

Other things to check are for her left-handedness, e.g.:

• Left handers should hold the pen a little further from the point than right handers so they can see the tip of the pen and the words they are writing.
• They should sit on the left of peers in the classroom to have enough free left elbow room.

- The paper for writing should be slanted more to the left (40–45 degrees) than right handers need to the right (20–30 degrees).
- Some left-handers write with palm upwards (hookers) even with the tripod grip and may need to have their paper placed horizontally.

One final point is the adoption by Zara of the Oxford 'i's. These are the little circles or rings she uses instead of dots. She should know that it is a habit that will slow down her writing speed and she should try not to use it especially when she needs to write later for SATs.

She may find this hard to give up so she might try thinking of using it only in classwork and not in homework so that both styles become fluent and she can switch from one mode to the other when required.

6. Thomas: ten years four months – Example report

Formally diagnosed as dyslexic, being home educated. Dysgraphia and dyslexia.

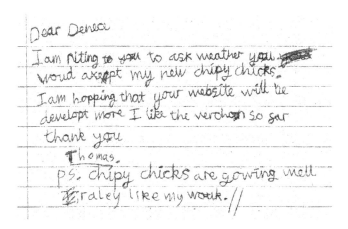

Figure 4.9a Thomas's handwriting in ten minutes (half original size)

Analysis: First sample
Writing skills:
- 47 words in 10 minutes: Speed: 4.7 words per minute. The average writing speed for this age group is 11 to 12 words per minute.
- His writing drags towards the middle line.
- The words sit between the lines not touching the lower line.
- There are no 'capitals' within words – this is good.
- There is some variation in size of letters in words.
- The script is mainly joined – this is good. It is cursive with no lead-in strokes.

Spelling skills:
Thomas makes 12 misspellings – hopping, weather, woud, chipy, developt, gowing, raley, wouk, verchon, riting, axept, Denece

- The spelling shows a good grasp of basic phonics.
- There is also good use of skeletal phonics and GFEs (good phonic equivalents) for difficult and unknown words: 'Denece', verchon', 'riting', 'axept', etc.
- The writing shows that he is now at the orthographic dyslexia level and needs a more cognitive-based approach (see Chapter 6).

Suggested starting strategies:
Writing skills:
His slowness will make it difficult for him to cope with the secondary school curriculum so he needs some help now with speed and fluency. There are signs that he has some mild coordination difficulties with writing that should disappear with fluency practice and it will also improve legibility.

It is important to discuss the reasons for the activities with Thomas so that he can gain cognitive control even if the motor skills are slower in developing.

First draw or find some practice sheets with three lines matching the 'body' size of his current letters.

The body of the letter should fill the space between the lower two lines. Letters with ascenders should nearly touch the top line, except 't' which is a small letter.

Descenders should hang below the line **not stand on it**.

Give Thomas four sets of lines to work on. Choose a useful short word **'and'** place it at the beginning of the first line and then ask him to repeat that form in cursive across the page leaving the space of an **'o'** between the words. Next write a cursive 'the' for him to copy. After this write 'why' and next 'write', point out the silent 'w'. Discuss 'write' with silent 'w' and 'written work' with 'w's to remind him reinforce with the cursive writing line. Discuss the meanings of the words 'write' and 'rite'.

The purpose is for Thomas to gain cognitive control as well as develop motor fluency. All the words should use the ligatures to join them up, even the 'M' which he misses. The lead-in lines are helpful to find the position in space where the words begin. If he does not like lead-in lines then use 'ghost' ones. Using cursive is essential in cases of coordination difficulties and dyslexia.

On the second day let Thomas choose the words he wishes to write. He must make sure each new line starts at the margin. Draw a margin on the left if the paper has none.

Analyse the effects together after several days' practice for any progress or lack of it. Make any modifications and resume practice. Do not continue after a fortnight and do not give tasks longer than four sets at a time unless Thomas wishes.

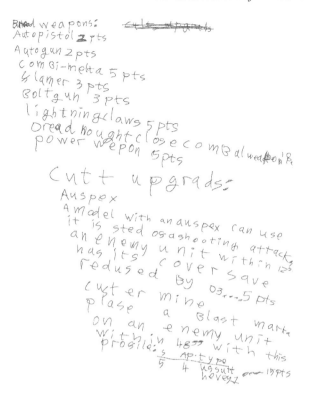

Figure 4.9b Thomas's writing at ten years ten months, six months later (half original size)

He can time his lines of writing to see if he is speeding up.

When crossing 't's and dotting 'i's and 'j's do this after writing the whole word.

The apparent capital such as P should be sorted by showing that lower case 'p' must have a descender with the 'body' sitting **on the line** and the descender hanging below, e.g. in f, g, j, p, q, y.

Feedback from parent: 'Thomas enjoyed trying the spelling strategies. He particularly liked the suffixing rules "double" and "drop" and quickly started applying them.'

His initial script sample looks as though he had been given some remedial help using cursive writing for his dyslexia but it has not 'stuck'. In the piece of spontaneous writing above he has reverted to his original style that clearly shows he also has handwriting coordination difficulties. It also indicates he himself does not perceive the relevance yet of the cursive style. A second report emphasised the need for this yet again.

Report on Paul (Mensa member) ten years, ten months – right-handed tripod

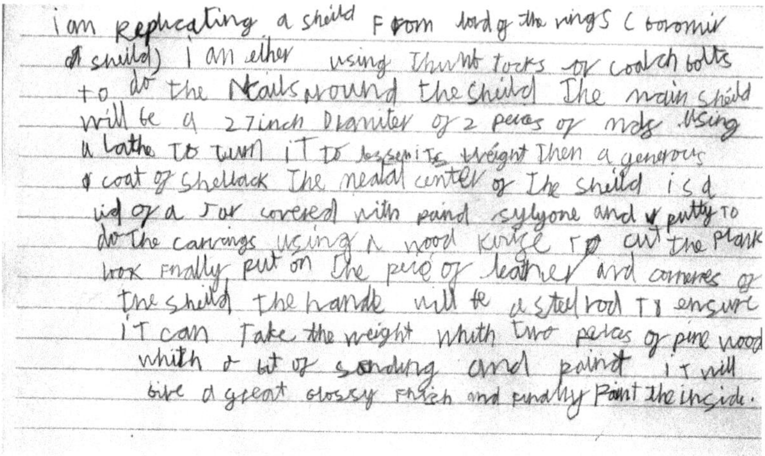

Figure 4.10a Paul's writing, age ten years ten months (half original size)

Transcript:

> i am Replicating a shield From lord of the rings (boromir x shield) i am either using Tbumb tocks or coalch bolts to do the Ntails around the shield The main shield will be a 27 inch Diamter of 2 pieces of mdf using lathe to turn it to lessen its weight then a generous x coat of shellack The meatal center of the shield is a lid of a Jar covered with pand sylyone and v putty to do the carvings using a wood Knife to cut the plask look fnally put on the peice of leather and correnes of the shield the handle will be a steel rod t8 (to) ensure it can take the weight whith two peices of pine wood whith a bit of sanding and paint it will Give a great glossy Fnish and Finally Paint the inside.

Writing skills:
Paul is writing at a speed of 14.3 words per minute and 43.7 letters per minute. At his age this is slightly above the average speed but much slower than we might expect from a pupil of high learning potential. The writing sits above the lines in places. The script is mainly joined but there is a problem connecting and forming 't'. Overall there is a variation in size of letters in words. The writing drags in from the margin and there are some rivers of space running down the page and some large spaces between the words.

There is some variation in pressure at the outset, in the middle and at the end that appears more clearly in the photograph. These problems suggest some difficulty in coordination of the handwriting and a lack of fluency in its formation.

The pencil grip in the photograph appears to be a weak rather than a precise tripod grip.

Spelling skills:

Paul makes five spelling errors and gives no punctuation except for a final full stop. Some letters appear as capitals (Finally, Knife) because of a writing difficulty and some capitals are inserted at incorrect points (Replication, Diameter) and omitted at others as in the case of names (Boromir, Lord of the Rings and i x2).

Figure 4.10b Paul's pencil hold

Check pen and paper slope:

1   If the grip is weaker than usual it would be useful to give Paul a fatter pen to use or buy some plastic pencil moulds that fit over pen or pencil and guide the fingers into the tripod grip (the school may have some of these). Let him try writing with several different sizes and weights to find which he prefers.
2   Check that the paper is sloped to the right when he is writing to about 30 degrees. It must not be vertical. Let him find the most comfortable paper position.

Although Paul may find these activities difficult at first his brain will grasp the idea and begin to guide his hand more over the long term. As the fluency in form increases it will speed up the writing and he will be able to explain his ideas better and be more comfortable writing.

It is important to use joined (cursive) writing because it is faster and increases automaticity so the brain can concentrate on the message. It will also reduce fatigue and pain over time. Exercises on the three-lined paper were suggested as in the other case suited to his age group.

In September 2016, four months later, his mother e-mailed the following update:

(a) We took him through some of the exercises you had provided. Going back to using the lined paper was very helpful. He didn't seem to mind doing the exercises either.

(b) We bought some different extra grip pens and this was immediately beneficial, in terms of his comfort while writing and also his will to write. Uncannily, he found the perfect pen very quickly from the choice we offered.

(c) Throughout the holidays, we were on the move quite a lot and we converted to handwriting practice by getting Paul to fill out forms and write 'to do' or shopping lists. He did this, sometimes happily, sometimes reluctantly.

(d) He has just started secondary school and his first task was to copy a timetable from computer to handbook. There is no doubt he was daunted as the handbook had very small spaces. He was very reluctant. After some encouragement to at least approach the task, he went for abbreviation and achieved 3/4 of the timetable by hand in one evening. Much, much more than we expected.

Overall, I think his confidence has improved a little, his grip is definitely more comfortable. There is some improvement in legibility and length of application but he is by no means at essay writing stage – more like paragraph but we are not unhappy with this progress – we were never pushing him to improve overnight.

It will be interesting to see how he goes in this first half term of secondary school. We will stick with the same extra grip pens which seem to suit very well. We will ease off the writing exercises. And we will get back to you on how he goes with the new handwriting challenges at secondary school where he has a different set of peers, expectations and challenges.

Our new school is very appreciative of your guidelines, which we provided them with. Their SENCo person had lunch with Paul yesterday and they discussed how the handwriting was going so they are also keeping an eye on it. If they give me any feedback, I will also pass this on to you for your research.

7. Charlie: 14 years one month – Yr 8 legibility

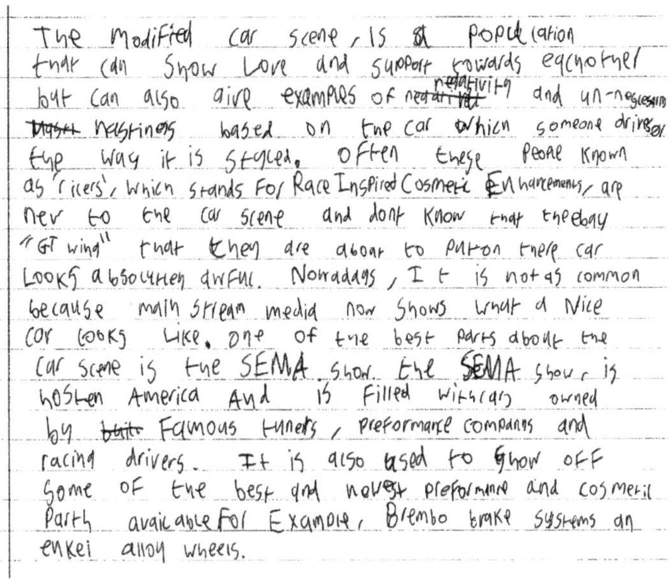

Figure 4.11 Charlie's writing (half original size), handedness and pen grip not given

Transcript:

> The Modified car scene , is a Population that can Show Love and support
> towards eachother but can also give examples of relativity realative and
> un- nescessra nash nastiness based on the car which someone drives or
> the way it is styled. Often these people Known as 'ricers', which stands
> for Race Inspired Cosmetic Environments, are new to the car scene and
> don't know that the ebay 'GT wind' that they are about to puton there
> car Looks absolutely awful. Nowadays, I t is not as common because
> main stream media now shows what a Nice car looks Like . One of the
> best Parts about the car scene is the SEMA show the SEMA show , is
> hoSten America And is Filled with cars owned by Famous tuners,
> performance companys and racing drivers. It is also used to show oFF
> Some of the best and newest performance and cosmetic Partly available
> For Example, Brembo brake systems an enkoi alloy wheels.

Writing skill:
Charlie is writing at 16.3 words per minute and 72.8 letters per minute. This
is an average speed for his age group but significantly slower than pupils of
the same age with high learning potential. His speed should be in the area of
25 words per minute.

Capital letters are used inappropriately in places and in many other places the
letters are lower case but written so large they appear to be capital letters

especially F, K and S. The letter P's often stand on the line so that they look like capital letters. Many letters are incompletely formed and the style is an unjoined print script without ligatures. The bodies of the letters vary in size in words and among words. All of these features suggest a handwriting difficulty in form and style and early incorrect habits being allowed to continue, or there may have been a lack of any teaching guidance in the early years. There appears to have been some resistance to change to acquire a more mature style as there has been no significant development over time. There is a problem with fluency and legibility making it likely that the work will be downgraded by examiners.

There is one misspelling of a plural 'companys' for 'companies'. However the writing form is such that at first there appear to be several misspellings and some undecipherable words. The scattering of capitals will also be likely to be regarded as errors in spelling and punctuation and lead to downgrading in literacy terms.

Suggested handwriting interventions:
They should be addressed in this order:

1   Check pencil grip.
2   Check paper position.
3   Work on writing style.
4   Give legibility training.
5   Give speed-up fluency training.

Each was then detailed.

8. Ralph: 14 years 11 months – legibility and style, example report

'His hand and arm started aching after 5 minutes.'

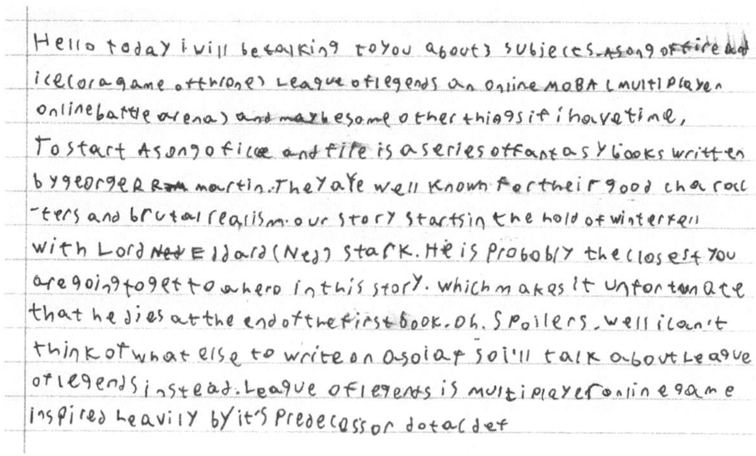

Figure 4.12 Ralph's writing: right handed, tripod grip

> Hello today I will be talkin9 to you about 3subjects.As ason9oftiread
> ice(oragame ottrrione) league oflegends anonline moBA Lmultiplayer-
> online battlearena) and mazbesome other thingif i have time,
> tostart Asan9ofice and tite is series offantasYbooks written
> by 9eor9e RR martin.TheYaYe well known fer theirgood charac
> -ters and brutalrealiSm. our story startsin the hold of wintertell
> with LordNed Eddard (Ned) Stark. He is Probobly theclosestyou
> are9oin9togettoahero in this story. whichmakes it unfortunate
> that hediesattheendofthefirstbook.Oh. Spoilers. well ican't
> thinkofwhatelse to writeonasoiat soi'll talk about lea9ue
> ofle9endsinstead.League ofle9endsismultiplayer onlin9ame
> inspired heavily bY it'sPredecessor dotaldef

Writing skills:

Ralph is writing at a speed of 15 words per minute and 64.1 letters per minute. This is relatively slow for his age group and ability. He writes in a tiny unjoined print script with very few spaces between the words. This makes it difficult to read. There are some full stops but these are not always followed by a capital letter. Apostrophe 's' is correctly used.

His letters are often incompletely formed and so can be mistaken for misspellings. There are no letters with descenders they all stand on the lines and so appear as capitals or 9s in the case of 'g'.

The effort in writing in such a tiny and precise form with all the letters separate is tiring and it is not surprising that he should develop an aching hand and arm after five minutes.

There is a serious problem of legibility given all these features that will not enable him to achieve well in written examinations. It appears that what he learned/was allowed to do in Reception has stayed with him and not changed except to reduce the size of his writing and gain in pencil control. It is suggestive of a rigidity in behaviour that is unusual and he may have other Asperger-like features that it may be useful to investigate.

Spelling skills: His spelling is good as far as can be deciphered and there appears to be only one misspelling – probobly. Again this may be an error in his letter construction. To correct it I suggest he uses a Cue Articulation strategy emphasising the error section 'prob – **able**' 'prob – **ab** – ly'.

Suggested handwriting interventions:

At the outset of the MS Ralph does an open larger joined scribble set of letter symbols as in a word. This suggests that he is capable of writing differently and in a legible freer format if he chooses and I think that it is important to check if this is possible first.

The following sentence is often used in tests to check speed and legibility as it contains all the letters of the alphabet: ***The quick brown fox jumps over the lazy dog***

Ralph should try to write the 'fox' sentence from memory in the lines.

- Each word must be separate from the other words by a space of an O.
- Each word's letters must be fully joined – a lead-in line need not be used.
- All the bodies of the letters must be between the two bottom lines.
- All the descenders' 'tails' must hang below the bottom line.
- All the ascenders' 'sticks' must rise towards the top line or touch it.
- 't' is a 'small' letter.

He should try to fit one sentence into each set of three lines.

Ralph's script may please him and be used as a personal note-taking style but it is not fit for audience purposes. If he cannot change his style then special measures will need to be requested for him for exams/SATs.

For example:

1   He may need to be allowed to word process all his examination papers but this depends on whether he can put spaces between his words and whether he can word process or type at a speed faster than his current writing speed – circa 20–25 words per minute.
2   Alternatively he may need to be allowed a scribe or voice recognition system; both take some time to learn to use.
3   His writing speed and word processing speed need to be monitored in case he needs to be given extra time in examinations if using them.
4   The school SENCO will be able to give details for the formal arrangements for extra time in exams.

If he is determined, it would be possible for him to write in a readable form with a short daily practice session within several months. It will be slow at first but will speed up as he persists. It will also cause him to experience less pain as his efforts become more fluent.

If he decides to try the writing change strategy he will lose nothing and it will provide evidence that all possible alternatives have been explored before extra arrangements have to be requested.

It is puzzling to understand why he has not been given writing support to change his style much earlier than this. Some of his errors appear to have developed in Reception as such errors are common then. Has this style been a recent development/acquisition?

What the above reports show

The example reports above show how the six different handwriting factors – speed, style, fluency, form, legibility and coordination – are interlinked. They show how two main intervention strategies involving body size of letters and slope of ascenders and descenders can be used with different combinations and procedures. The other factors that also come into play and need to be addressed are pen/pencil hold, paper position and furniture suitability. Moving them to cursive writing form where possible and being careful to maintain the motivation are the important targets.

Once children are writing freely the two strategies can be used at intervals to help them develop their writing speed, form, style and fluency. This will improve legibility and help overcome the milder coordination difficulty effects. In more severe cases it is essential for a diagnosis to be made as soon as possible so that supplementary or compensatory steps may be taken so that the difficulty does not become a barrier to learning and cause distress.

In the most severe cases of DCD an amanuensis or voice recognition system needs to be employed. Some pupils may be able to overcome their difficulties if allowed to use their own laptops at all times from Reception but word-processing skills may also be too difficult for others to acquire.

Some earlier examples of the results of interventions

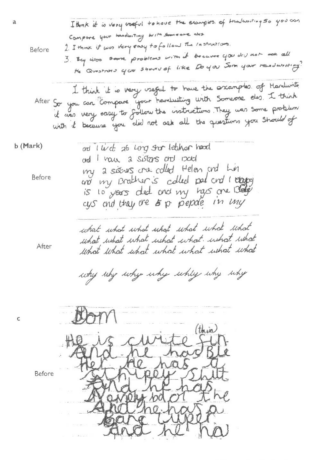

Figure 4.13a Examples of ealier interventions (1) (half original size)

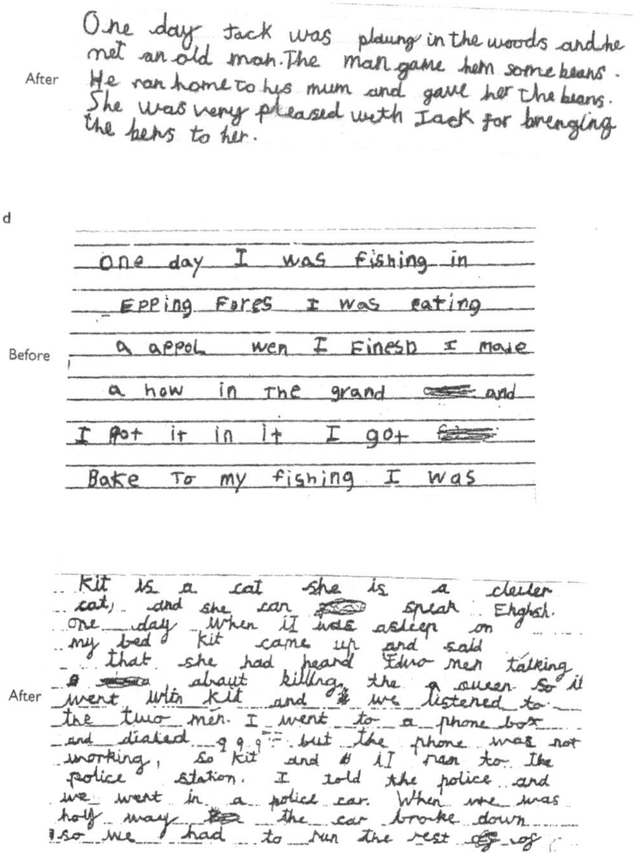

After

> One day Jack was plauing in the woods and he met an old man. The man gave hem some beans. He ran home to his mum and gave her the beans. She was very pleased with Jack for brenging the behs to her.

d

Before

> one day I was fishing in
> EPPing Fores I was eating
> a appol wen I Finesb I mave
> a how in the grand ~~and~~ and
> I pot it in it I got ~~c~~
> Bake To my fishing I was

After

> Kit is a cat she is a cleiter cat, and she can ~~speak~~ speak Engish. One day when it was asleep on my bed kit came up and said that she had heard two men talking about killing the a queen so it went wltn kit and we listened to the two men. I went to a phone box and dialed 9 9 9 - but the phone was not working, so kit and I ran to the police station. I told the police and we went in a police car. When we was holf way the car broke down so me had to run the rest of

Figure 4.13b Examples of earlier interventions (2) (half original size)

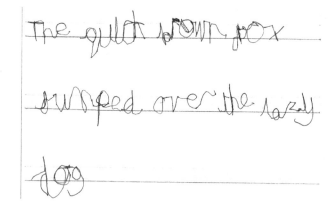

The quiot brown fox jumped over the lazy dog

Figure 4.14 Elliott's twelfth day effort. It is not so easy if you have dysgraphia (half original size)

Handwriting repair toolkit for teachers

- Card containing the model 'fox' sentence in cursive.
- Wall posters showing the individual cursive letter forms to be used.
- Teach in-air letter movements.
- Observe every child's writing movements on paper and penhold.
- An individual cursive writing model on a card such as the LDRP format.
- A selection of three-lined paper in various widths to fit the body size of the letters.
- A range of pencil/pen grips – plastic, clay moulds, or special pens.
- A supply of pens and pencils of different dimensions.
- Drawings and photographs of the tripod grip for right- and left-handers.
- Remedial PE programmes in consultation with PE staff.
- Copies of the T-HFL for addressing form to use with pupils.
- Motricity training games for younger pupils.
- Tracking games for younger pupils.
- Electric and electronic tracking games devised as design projects by older pupils for younger ones.
- Dance, and music and movement lessons linked to writing movements – see Write–Dance programme (Ousseren Voors, 2001).
- A set of spelling intervention strategies to link with the handwriting training (see Chapter 5).
- Two intervention strategies – body size and slant.
- Spaced practice sessions – daily for about five minutes.
- Remember letters that look like capitals mid sentence indicate coordination difficulties, not a need for teaching about full stops.
- See resource source list after the references.

Conclusions

The important principle in handwriting is that you must start as you mean to go on. This was Marion Richardson's (1935) advice to teachers teaching writing. In other words, teaching print or semi-print first and then changing to cursive later was not a good idea. Her view is now backed by research as well as experience.

Reception teachers in particular must give more time to handwriting teaching and use lines for the children to form their letters upon. The lines should be wide at first and then narrow down as the letter forms become smaller and more fluent. They must observe each child's pen hold and help adjust it to the correct tripod grip using the techniques described in the chapter and offer different sizes of implements and supportive grips.

Joining letters from the outset should be taught as soon as two letters can be written free-form. In remedial tuition with older pupils the development of speed, fluency and legibility become more important. If the letter forms themselves are made incorrectly these also need to be addressed.

All later attempts to change or improve handwriting skills need to be made carefully because they take time to implement and personal choice and motivation are very much involved. This is why it is so important to start in writing teaching in the form that is the ultimate goal.

Cursive writing from the outset is especially important for any pupils with coordination difficulties as they have so much difficulty in the original acquisition stage. Having acquired some skill they also find it very difficult to change. Cursive has a number of inbuilt advantages for them that print or semi print denies them and make it more difficult to write in the first place.

The two most effective remedial interventions should be undertaken first. The focus should be on a) making body sizes the same, and b) making the slope of the letters all go in the same direction.

5 Remediating dyslexia in the alphabetic phase

Introduction

Dyslexia in the alphabetic stage is observable as very poor reading and spelling, well below the pupil's age and ability and a lack of progress despite extra support. The school will refer the pupil to the educational psychology services for a diagnosis. This will involve testing using an individual IQ test – usually the latest version of the Wechsler Intelligence Scale for Children (WISC–IV) and associated reading and spelling tests and any further tests considered necessary. In administrative terms the decrement has to be 20 per cent between the literacy skills and IQ with literacy the poorer in order to qualify for Statementing and specialist dyslexia tuition.

This whole procedure demands investigation and is challenged in the next section.

In terms of actual skills the pupil in the alphabetic phase will have acquired some phonic and some whole word knowledge but the knowledge is insecure and incomplete. The pupil often does not know the sounds and names of all the 26 alphabet letters, may have problems with alphabetical order, remembering the days of the week, months of the year and naming left and right side.

In comparison with peers, the skills at six or seven years are at the level of a Reception learner just beyond the logographic phase. At ten years the skills may be at the level of a seven or eight year old. Reading accuracy will be lower than reading comprehension scores on the Neale Analysis of Reading Ability – NARA (Neale, 1997), an indication of the potential higher ability.

Spelling will generally be at a lower level than reading and attempts at word building may not succeed beyond the regular CVC level. In attempts to spell more difficult words they resort to simple phonetics which can be distorted by their mispronunciations or dialect patterns.

Dyslexics with very good visual memories may read at grade level but have very poor spelling. These were termed 'dysorthographics' and present special challenges for the school diagnostic and Statementing system.

Poor spellers, in their attempts to learn spelling lists for their weekly tests, may spend a lot of time on the task only to become muddled and score poorly however hard they try. It can be very disheartening and stressful, leading to psychosomatic illnesses and truancy in some severe cases.

In a spelling test Gavin wrote 'box' for 'parcel', a semantic substitution showing the lengths to which a pupil will go to try to do what is asked. In free writing dyslexics report selecting words they know they can spell rather than the word they really want to use and this of course slows down the writing process and the extra cognitive processing can interfere with compositional abilities and quality.

Poor handwriting skills or any tendency towards coordination difficulties will create further problems for the dyslexic not only in acquisition in the logographic stage but also later. It will cause them to avoid writing whenever possible and lose opportunities for developing automaticity and learning more spellings.

Why does dyslexia arise?

This question was raised in Chapter 1. It asked how it was possible for normal learners to learn sounds and their symbols without being explicitly taught and then use this knowledge to build their reading and writing skills while dyslexics could not? What was the mechanism? The research was showing that it was a verbal processing problem not a visual one (Vellutino, 1979).

The critical question then was how was the clever alphabet system of writing first invented? Presumably a dyslexic could not have done it. Researching writing systems showed that the alphabet system was invented only once in history and by the Phoenicians. They spoke a Semitic consonantal language (Gelb, 1963). It had 22 consonants and this was the breakthrough, the key! Consonants have a distinct articulatory pattern or feel in the mouth. Their order in a syllable can be detected whereas we cannot hear the sequence (Liberman et al., 1967).

The hypothesis therefore was that dyslexics would have an articulation awareness problem whereas normal learners would not. A series of pilot studies (Montgomery, 1981, 1984) showed there was some evidence for this and the hypothesis was tested and the results are shown below in Table 5.1 (Montgomery, 1997a).

Table 5.1 Mean scores on phoneme segmentation (PS) and articulation awareness (AA)

	Nos	Reading age	Spelling age	PS (15)	AA (10)	IQ	Chron age
Controls	84	8.61	8.02	11.94	7.75	110.03	7.94
Dyslexics on TRTS	114	7.95	7.62	10.27	4.31	110.43	12.90
Dyslexics Waiting	30	6.71	6.0	4.13	5.87	112.67	8.97

Key: PS Phoneme Segmentation (sing minus 's' gives 'ing' etc.) a 15 items test.
    AA Articulation Awareness. Test of 10 items

The table shows that dyslexics already on the TRTS programme have good scores on the phoneme segmentation test of 15 items of increasing difficulty in comparison with those on the waiting list and close to the scores of much younger controls with similar reading ages. The dyslexics' scores on the articulation awareness test were significantly lower both in the dyslexic group on the programme and on the waiting list. It was odd to discover that when making e.g. the 'l' sound many of them could not say where the tip of their tongue was touching or if the mouth was open or closed.

In a follow-up study in the same project 134 Reception learners were tested on the AA test and it was found that four of them had no awareness of where in the mouth their tongue was touching, or whether their lips were open or shut etc. The AA test was added to an LEA infant screening survey (Forsyth, 1988) and was found to be the only test in the set that had good predictive capacity for poor reading results at seven years.

Neurological research by Geschwind (1979) indicated that a dissociation problem in the left angular gyrus could interfere with the process of associating sounds with symbols during reading acquisition in dyslexics.

More recently, Waldie et al. (2013) showed over-activation in the right hemisphere regions of the putamen and precentral gyrus during both regular and pseudo-word lexical decision-making. No specific specialisation has been attributed to the putamen but it is involved in regulating movement and is thought to have a role in implicit learning which plays an important role in normal Reception class literacy learning.

The precentral gyrus is also associated with initiating the onset of movements and Waldie et al. suggest it is likely that this activity reflects increased reliance on silent articulatory processes.

Another recent study provided empirical support for the view that a letter-speech sound-binding deficit is a key factor in dyslexia (Aavena et al., 2013). These studies may indicate that in the remedial process the intact right hemisphere areas are activated and support or take on the functions of the left in the alphabetic phase.

What dyslexia looks like in the alphabetic phase

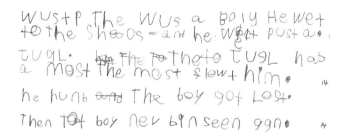

Figure 5.1a Hisham on entry into Year 2: dyslexia in the early alphabetic phase or very slow development of skill? 2014

Figure 5.1b Martin's writing late alphabetic stage aged ten in Year 5 (half original size), December 2007

He writes 78 words. 41 words are spelt correctly but these are the common words and those with regular CVC structure, e.g. Beth, the, in, she, went, into, put, them, bag. Thus no other words are spelled correctly. Many are roughly phonetic. The only help he gets is to be shown some of the correct spellings down the side of the paper. Learning support is not working for him or addressing his needs. His writing also shows difficulties in coordination, legibility and form. His writing speed was 7.5 words per minute, too slow for his age group.

Figure 5.1c Kelly's writing aged ten years two months. She is a diagnosed dyslexic now needing transfer to an orthographic phase programme (half original size)

The system breaks dyslexics?

The Statementing procedure and the Code of Practice endorsed a system that had grown up from the 1970s. It was one in which it was assumed that any child who was delayed in reading during the infant years would eventually catch up if someone gave them extra reading practice and some phonics.

When this did not work, in some areas and some schools they were relegated to the slow learner classes and groups and left to languish. James's mother (Preface) even in the 1990s had to fight hard to keep him out of the slow learner classes in secondary school. In other areas they were referred for psychological assessment and when they were not found to be slower learners they were put on a waiting list for extra reading support.

Today what we still see is dyslexics waiting, waiting and waiting for help. The wait can last three or more years to obtain a Statement. It is very specific help that they need as Nicholas and Steven showed and they should have it at the latest after two terms in Reception. They do not need to be referred for testing and diagnosis to an overworked educational psychology service. Let us intervene immediately with MAPT educational provision at the logographic phase.

When we find them in the alphabetic phase in infant or junior school we still do not need to refer them onwards and upwards. The class teacher, with the aid of the SENCo, can give them an individual reading test such as NARA, a spelling test, an alphabet sounds and names test, and collect a sample of the free writing to check speed and coordination. If needed, the British Picture Vocabulary Test (Dunn and Dunn, 1997) can give an indication of ability and vocabulary.

When a reading comprehension test as well as an accuracy test is involved as in NARA the dyslexic will score higher on comprehension than accuracy. This indicates the nature of the problem. Fiona was a bright child, verbally adept and good at problem solving. At eight years of age her reading accuracy was at the seven or eight year old level but her comprehension was at the nine or ten year old level. This indicated that she was indeed bright and potentially had an IQ in the region of 120 IQ or even 130 when 10 points are added for the depressing effect of the disability on IQ test items (Silverman, 2002).

Only if the case is complex might a psychologist be needed. Unfortunately, as the child grows older and fails to read and write as easily as peers the stress and loss of self-esteem induced may provoke 'acting out' such as behaviour problems and overactivity (seen as hyperactivity), or 'acting in' – withdrawal and depression. As will be seen in Pawley's (2007) research (see Table 5.1), the effect of giving a successful dyslexia intervention reduces the behaviour problems significantly. Thus specific dyslexia remedial intervention needs to be undertaken to find if it modifies the problem behaviour as well as improving the reading and spelling.

The only useful point is that if a dyslexic pupil becomes disruptive they are likely to be referred faster than the rest and this led to boys being referred a year sooner than girls in an earlier study (Montgomery, 1997a).

Even when dyslexic pupils have been referred on for psychological assessment teachers find that it only tells them what they already knew with some numbers attached.

Does the discrepancy really have to be 20 per cent?

Of course not. It is an arbitrary cut-off point for administrative purposes so that every child with a bit of a reading problem is not referred. However a decrement is a useful construct but it depends on how much. A decrement of 10 per cent at seven may become 30 per cent at ten years. Pupils may regress as well as progress. Reading skill on average should be expected to be within a few months of age level and rise above it when the ability rises. Some gifted children, for example, may read at five years above the grade level and have a reading age of 14 at 9 years old. Spelling may be less advanced.

When chronological age has been the criterion against which the reading decrement is measured then many able and gifted dyslexics are missed. This is because, like Fiona, they are reading at around grade level or perhaps 10 per cent below it when they should be reading well above the grade level in line with their ability.

A well-graded spelling accuracy test is an important diagnostic tool in the mix. This is because it can inform about the level of phonic knowledge as well as higher order spelling skills. A poor score on spelling in the presence of good or adequate reading will identify those hidden dyslexics with dysorthographia. Cohort studies detailed later suggest that there are at least 10 per cent of the population in this category in addition to those with dyslexia.

Can slow learners be dyslexic?

Because researchers have used an IQ of 90 to 100 or above as the criterion for including dyslexics in their research samples to cut down on extra variables this has suggested that slower learners cannot be dyslexic, they are just poor readers. This is incorrect. For example, a ten year old with an IQ of an eight year old and a reading age of a six or seven year old is dyslexic. He or she is not reading at the level consistent or slightly above the mental age and makes the same types of spelling and reading errors (Montgomery, 1990). They need an APSL programme but not in a remedial withdrawal setting. Their programme needs to go at a slower pace and be integrated into all their daily learning activities so they get the maximum opportunity for reinforcement and consolidation. They also need more language development work and are more prone to writing coordination difficulties.

It would be far more efficient and less expensive if schools could diagnose the dyslexia in-house and secure the funds for tuition immediately. They could then buy in the specialist or train up their own specialist to give tuition three times a week with a review after one semester to check progress. If there is insufficient progress (under one year in six months) the tuition should be terminated and the child referred on to the psychological services. They could always be put on a provisional waiting list for this in case.

We must break a way through the system not break the dyslexic and damage young lives.

What prevented us from getting on with the job? The back story

For more than 50 years conflicting ideologies concerning teaching provision for the dyslexic have prevented them from having their needs met. The conflict arises over the appropriate manner in which literacy acquisition and development should be addressed. The conflict emerged when the Gillingham and Stillman programme with its precise methodology was introduced into the UK in the early 1970s as a remedial programme.

A group of interested people, which included Kathleen Hickey, had attended a lecture on dyslexia provision by Sally Childs in 1969 about a programme being used in the US at the Scottish Rites Hospital that was proving effective. It was the Gillingham and Stillman (1956) version of the original Gillingham, Stillman and Orton (1940) programme.

The Bath Dyslexia Association raised funds so that Miss Hickey could go to the US to see the programme in operation and on her return could set about trying to introduce it into the UK. Miss Hickey, as she was always known, came back to the UK, shared her findings with colleagues and developed her anglicised version of the programme and began to test it out with dyslexics. By 1972 her successes encouraged her to offer training programmes for teachers who wanted to become remedial teachers or who were already working in the field.

This training programme also became very successful and she needed to find a location to establish a training centre. It was during this search for premises and demonstrations that I was able to observe her at work. Because she used a wheelchair it proved impossible for us to give her the regular access to suitable rooms and finally she found them at Staines in Surrey.

In 1977 she published her programme, the Hickey Multisensory Language Course (HMLC). It was her wish, carried out by her executor, that in any later publication the original design and method with its underpinning rationale should not be changed in any way and subsequent trainers at her Dyslexia Centre complied with this. Thus it is that the second edition, edited by Augur and Briggs (1991), is true to the original.

Later versions and variants have updated the theory and added phonological training. Miss Hickey would not have approved. Her original manual still forms the basis of the current Dyslexia Institute's approach and training materials to which phonological training and study skills have been added.

Adding phonological training although widely popular is not necessary in the specialist dyslexia programmes, as will be discussed later.

Among those trained by Miss Hickey were the designers of the Teaching Reading Through Spelling Programme (TRTS) by Cowdery et al. (1983–1987, 1994). They were already experienced remedial teachers and early converts to the system. Many of the games they designed for their coursework were included in the original HMLC manual.

It was as part of a year-long in-service training project run by the author in one of the Learning Difficulties Research Projects that each Friday afternoon the TRTS team discussed and wrote down their methods and variations on the basic theme. Most memorable was the whole afternoon spent on finding agreement on the best place for the -c, -ck and -k rules.

The differences from Hickey were the insistence that the children should write their own spelling and reading packs under the guidance of the tutor as well as draw their own keyword pictures. The order of the introduction of the synthetic phonics programme varied and the rules were tailored to their experiences of pupils' needs and knowledge. In the later stages there was more cognitive input in the form of linguistic rules based on the work of Cox and Waites (1972) and Childs (1966) and this is seen in *The Spelling Notebook* (Cowdery, 1987, 1994).

Alpha to Omega (Hornsby and Shear, 1976) was developed and published in the same era and became even more widely known and available. It differed from the Hickey programme and TRTS in that it was more based on a linguistic approach from Hornsby's speech therapy background and so had a different emphasis. Cursive was optional to fit with school practices. It is a phonetic–linguistic programme, the order of introduction of key sounds is different and the five vowels were introduced as a group. This is why it is more effective after the logographic phase or Level One intervention (see Rigehalgh's research below).

It was this latter aspect that the TRTS team found particularly problematic for dyslexics and why the vowels are separated out during acquisition in the G and S programmes. Their insistence upon the importance of cursive writing training was also in opposition to the prevailing custom and practice but consistent with the original programme. It inevitably caused problems, for back in the schools at the time cursive was often forbidden until the pupil entered the junior phase or was able to write neatly (Montgomery, 1998).

A more recent variant that became popular was *Beat Dyslexia* (Stone, Franks and Nicholson, 1993) mainly because it set out in worksheets daily tasks based upon the Hickey format requiring little diagnostic input from the teacher who might not be familiar with the programme.

Covering ground and knowledge already known is particularly problematic for dyslexics and many complain about this as each new tutor makes them go back over what they may already know or know in part. They may often be required to do seemingly endless drills without being told why they are important in the whole scheme of things and they lose confidence and develop a learned helplessness. This is especially observed when they have 'in class' support from a teaching assistant (TA) to help them read classwork and write responses.

The systematic, rote, multisensory initial training was in direct contrast to the early years reading and writing teaching ethos and created horror among early years reading specialists who favoured a visual and language based more creative approach. In their system a sight vocabulary was expected to be acquired before phonics work was introduced in the acquisition phase. This was assisted by having a controlled vocabulary in many of the reading schemes.

What was not recognised was that the dyslexics were already three times failures by these normal methods and that the later phonics methods of the 'remedial' teachers were not effective either. The acquisition strategies needed for those who had failed over several years to learn by the usual methods needed to be different from those used in the Reception phase.

When the British Dyslexia Association was established in 1972 one of its goals was to design and seek validation for a course based upon Kathleen Hickey's anglicised version of the G and S programme to teach remedial teachers its principles and practices. In 1975 the Council for National Academic Awards (CNAA) assembled an expert panel of reading teaching college and early years specialists to scrutinise the proposal and they concluded that it could not be validated because its remit was too narrow. The teaching methods needed to be an 'eclectic mix' rather than the pursuit of one method involving such rote training methods.

This eclectic approach was introduced into the BDA curriculum and so the specific training in the G and S methodology was watered down. What it permitted was the introduction of best practice as conceived by the course tutors with the Hickey programme as just one of them. An important opportunity for dyslexics was lost because it did not fit with the current orthodoxy.

It was because of this that Miss Hickey established the Dyslexia Institute at Staines in order to be able to pursue her original programme. She was most concerned that it should remain intact because she had seen it work and knew its results and this is why her executor who had funded the first publication of the programme insisted that the second edition (Augur and Briggs, 1991) should not make any changes to the basic programme despite the new phonological research.

This little piece of history is still being played out today at the expense of dyslexics but it must stop. Learning to read and write in the early years is different to the challenges posed for dyslexics who will fail or have failed to learn by those methods. If they have a dissociation deficit then surely the methods required need to be different. The purpose is to train the areas around the deficit to take over the function, and this takes time and systematic effort. Once the first few initial letters have been learned, however, the remedial teachers report the process speeds up and this is consistent with other brain retraining pursuits.

The nature of these specialist G and S programmes did, however, transfer one feature to the general field and that was the value of an element of multisensory training of phonograms in remedial work. This means that in learning sounds and their symbols pupils must also learn to write the letters linking all three aspects in the 'VAKs' triangle – Visual (grapheme) – Auditory (phoneme) and Kinaesthetic (motoreme) or motor programme in handwriting. What is frequently ignored is the articulatory input.

The importance of articulatory training

On the basis of research (Montgomery, 1981, 1997a), the essential role of articulatory training was established in the Visual-Auditory-Kinaesthetic (VAKs) work. Although the G and S schemes ensure the sounds are articulated correctly dyslexics need more than this. They need articulatory training to reinforce the link between sound and symbol. They need to learn to feel the key articulatory features of a consonant in the mouth. They have to learn that this is the only concrete clue there is when identifying a sound and its symbol. It can give them the clue to spellings because in a syllable one consonant follows another in order or sequence as in C – T for 'cat' and B – D in 'bed' as we speak it. We cannot separate out the spelling of a syllable by ear. This is because syllable sounds are shingled on top of each other and the ear cannot hear them separately (Liberman et al., 1967).

This is why children can correctly clap the syllables in their names and words in general but **cannot clap the phonemes** in a syllable or word correctly unless they can spell it (Montgomery, 1997a). Thus the 'multisensory mouth training' method was incorporated into the Teaching Reading Through Spelling (TRTS) programme (Montgomery, 1984, 1994).

Mouthing their words when spelling was recommended by Monroe (1932) as she observed beginning spellers learning their words. Edith Norrie in 1917 used just such an articulatory method to help her learn to read and incorporated this into her construction of the Letter Case.

Dyslexia and the alphabetic stage

In the 1980s and 1990s it was usual for dyslexics to be identified late in their school careers. Typically when they failed to learn to read in the early years they would be given extra reading and phonics help in the classroom and then when this was unsuccessful they would be withdrawn for one-to-one tuition.

Often it was untrained parent helpers who gave this extra support but over time teachers experienced in remedial work took over from them and many local authorities funded teams of peripatetic remedial teachers and some established Remedial Centres. Referral for this specialist help generally took place after the child had failed in Reception, failed in responding to extra help in the classroom and failed to learn in a school withdrawal setting. They had become three-time failures. By the time they were put on the waiting lists for specialist help they were nine years old and did not receive the necessary help until they were 10 or 11 years old and just about to move to secondary school.

After the 1983 implementation of the Warnock Report (1978) the teachers were renamed 'special needs' teachers and over time their role changed with the pressure for integration and then inclusion. The 'in class' support movement (Fish, 1985) followed and this made withdrawal for tuition outside the classroom less common. The Statementing procedure that was introduced reinforced and formalised the delay in identification.

The Code of Practice (DfEE 2001) and its later revision simply formalised the already present delay in identification of the dyslexic's problems by insisting on staged interventions 'School action' and 'School action plus' prior to Statementing for specialist help. These delays persist even now. The specialist help may also not be so special in that it is more of the same.

Thus in each decade the poor dyslexic has been failed. The needs are not met by the methods and procedures in operation otherwise there would be no need for parents to buy in help, nor for schools to be taken to tribunals for not making adequate provision. It was not surprising that in a survey of remedial provision across the English LEAs, Pumfrey and Reason (1991) found that the remedial provision on offer was not effective.

In a later review of teaching methods for dyslexics and the National Literacy Strategy, Piotrowski and Reason (2000) summarised the predominant features as follows:

The NLS gives:

- a cumulative sequence of phonic targets
- an emphasis on the hierarchical structured study of language
- implicit reference to mastery learning but specified targets

(p. 53)

They identified four elements at Key stage 1 word level work:

- phonological awareness, phonics and spelling
- word recognition, graphic knowledge and spelling knowledge
- vocabulary extension
- handwriting

(p. 53)

There were activity resource sheets promoting onset and rime strategies, single phoneme work and synthetic phonics. Teaching methodology was not detailed.

The important consideration here is that cumulative sequences and hierarchical structures can be based upon very different principles. Hornsby's structure was based upon speech therapy principles and is very different from that of HMLC based upon the dyslexic's learning needs. The NLS claimed to be cumulative, structured and hierarchical but the principles on which it was based were not recorded. What we know in retrospect is that it moved too fast for those with difficulties, especially dyslexics, and too slowly for the most able. The NLS failed to meet the needs of dyslexics.

The research of Piotrowski and Reason moved on to a comparison of different sets of teaching materials for ordinary learners, poor readers and dyslexics. The dyslexia programmes analysed were Alpha to Omega, HMLC and *Teaching Reading and Spelling to Dyslexic Children* (Walton, 1998), which was mainly a phonics programme.

Their analysis graded the schemes from 1 to 3 under the following eight headings: a comprehensive model; progression; speaking and listening; reading and writing; assessing to teach; mastery learning; role of the learner; home and school links.

The analysis did not include any consideration of the effectiveness of the programmes by analysing their outcomes. Anyone can design and develop a dyslexia programme and claim it works for dyslexics because it is structured and cumulative but what we have to do is build the evidence. It exists in the files and records of individual remedial teachers and only accumulates over time. Often a considerable time and researchers may not be prepared to invest in this. It is also the accumulated evidence from single cases.

Piotrowski and Reason concluded:

> In terms of structure and content, the overall framework of the NLS is a positive development that may, in time, prevent and alleviate the difficulties of a dyslexic nature experienced by some learners.

They raised concerns about the pace of learning at the end of Year 1 and the beginning of Year 2 and the need for the NLS evaluations to focus on the 'tail' of underachievement in the UK rather than on those children who have always learnt quite well.

We know now that the NLS was not effective in alleviating dyslexia nor did it address the 'tail' of underachievement. Thus the Rose Review (2006) was set up to diagnose the problems and its main emphasis was on 'phonics first' and 'synthetic phonics'. Yet when we look into Reception and Year 1 classrooms today this is not what we observe. The guidelines become reinterpreted in terms of custom and practice and very little changes. The criticisms have been that teachers did not have a good enough knowledge of either synthetic or analytic phonics.

As already indicated, what is conceived of as 'good' for dyslexics and 'effective' in meeting their needs is not necessarily doing so. Dyslexics still appear in every year and demonstrate that their needs are not being met.

What then are the dyslexic's needs in the alphabetic phase?

The dyslexics identified at the statementing stage show inadequate phonic knowledge, an inability to build words from their phonic knowledge, an inability to develop correct orthography, their reading is poor and halting, their spelling skills are even poorer. A typical profile is that a dyslexic pupil at ten years of age has a reading capacity of a seven or eight year old and the spelling skill of a five or six year old. These features are the reason why the dyslexic is said to be stuck in the alphabetic phase.

Figure 5.2 Danny's writing in Year 6, age 11 in 2001

'My brother is annoying he's silly and dumb and gets on my nerves. Black hair, brown eyes pollrew (??) nose big ears.'

Why does he not have a Statement? If dyslexics also have a handwriting problem, dysgraphia, they will be even more seriously disadvantaged and may fail to learn to read and write at all unless they have very good visual memories.

The results of effective dyslexia programmes

The effective programmes are those that address the dyslexics' needs. They must also give two years progress in each year (see Tables 5.1 and 5.2). Their purpose is to provide a shortened but intensive course over two years in not less than two sessions of 45 to 50 minutes per week. They are programmes that enable pupils to catch up to the level of peers at least at grade level. Their curricula cannot be effectively taught at the same time as a lesson in another subject because of the dissonance and cognitive overload that would create. Therefore in-class support as the only provision does not meet the dyslexics' needs.

Making a few months' progress in a year after no progress is not sufficient to remediate a dyslexic's difficulties. Working with matched pairs was found to give better results than with individuals (Ridehalgh, 1999; Montgomery, 1997a). The reasons for this became apparent when dyslexia teachers on MA SpLD and MA SEN programmes recorded their one-on-one teaching and found they talked far too much and were preventing pupils from engaging in their own inner dialogue, cognitive rehearsal and consolidation. They were also moving the pupil on too quickly to cover more ground rather than moving at the pace of the pupil.

The effective programmes have been termed APSL multisensory programmes. This stands for programmes that are Alphabetic, Phonic,

Table 5.2 The relative effectiveness of APSL and Non APSL programmes

APSL Dyslexia Programmes Progress in 1 Year		NON APSL Programmes in 1 Year		
R. Prog	S. Prog	R. Prog	S. Prog	Researcher
A to O 1.93	1.95	0.53	0.32	Hornsby et al 1990
N=107		N=107 (Teachers' phonic programmes)		
TRTS 2.45	2.01	1.06	0.16	Montgomery 1997a
N=38		N=15 (Eclectic mix by teacher)		
Pairs tuition				
(H & A to O) 1.21	0.96	0.69	0.65	Ridehalgh 1999
N=50		n=50 (SME)		
TRTS 3.31	1.85	2.2	1.14	Webb 2000
N=12		n=12 (SME/TRTS)		
TRTS 4.04	3.00	(no control group)		Gabor, 2007
N=12				
A to O 2.4	2.4	Same group, no progress in previous year		Pawley 2007
N=10				

KEY: R. Prog. – Reading progress; S. Prog. – Spelling progress; TRTS – Teaching Reading Through Spelling; A to O – Alpha to Omega; H – Hickey Multisensory Language Course/ DILP; SME – Spelling Made Easy. (Brand, 1998)

Syllabic and Linguistic – taught in a multisensory way, especially initially. Miss Hickey termed her programme alphabetic-phonic-structural-linguistic.

The characteristics of APSL programmes teach:

- letters in frequency of use order e.g. i, t, p, n, s;
- word building as soon as two letters are learned;
- syllabification and syllable rules and structures;
- cursive writing with loops below the line but not above;
- linguistic rules that aid generalisation; and
- explicitly the morphemic as well as the phonic basis of English.

The above table of results shows that A to O, HMLC, and TRTS were capable of being effective in attaining two years' progress in one year when correctly used.

Ridehalgh (1999) examined the results from teachers who had undertaken dyslexia training courses at Dyslexia Centres around the country. The factors she investigated were length of remediation, frequency of sessions and size of tutorial groups in dyslexic subjects taught by three different schemes – Alpha to

Omega (Hornsby and Shear, 1993), Dyslexia Institute Language Programme (DILP/Hickey, 1995), and Spelling Made Easy (SME, Brand, 1998). She found that when all the factors were held constant the only programme in which the dyslexics gained significantly in skills above their increasing age was Alpha to Omega.

However, in a follow-up she found that the users of the Hickey programme in her sample had found it more convenient to leave out the spelling pack work and the dictations! The data also showed that in paired tuition the dyslexics made greater gains than when working alone with the teacher (see Table 5.2). This is an important consideration in terms of the dyslexics' progress and of economics in schools. All the four tutors in the 1997 TRTS study worked with matched pairs of pupils.

Webb found that she had to cut out the dictations and some of the spelling-pack work because the allocated time for lessons was too short. As can be seen, this has had an effect on the spelling results. She also found that in using SME the pupils were not making progress unless she introduced the multisensory mouth training from TRTS to link the sound and symbol. This accounts for the better SME results than for Ridehalgh's groups.

In Gabor's study at an international school the high progress dyslexics had supportive backgrounds and were encouraged at home to do the homework.

Pawley's study took place with ten pupils placed in a special school for Emotional and Behavioural Difficulties (EBD). In the previous year the group had made no progress with their literacy skills. He found that as their reading and spelling improved the incidence of EBD decreased by 30.7 per cent. Before and after the programme the incidence of behavioural problems were independently recorded on the Conners Teacher Rating Scale for EBD (2007).

Ridehalgh also found that the spelling progress with DILP was 1.06 in the first six months but dropped back thereafter (0.54). This shows the importance of the initial multisensory alphabet and phonics training.

Table 5.3 The impact of pairs versus single tuition and progress in one year

Programme	Reading		Spelling		Totals	
	Single	Pairs	Single	Pairs	R	S
SME	0.71	0.66	0.79	0.5	0.69	0.65
N=50						
DILP	0.69	1.59	0.66	0.96 }		
				DILP/A–O	1.21	0.96
A – O	0.47	1.19	1.19	0.87 }		
N=50						

The use of SME shows pupils regressing in each year in all conditions whereas the use of the Hickey-based DILP programme and A to O show greater progress with pairs tuition (except in spelling for A to O). (Ridehalgh, 1999: 52)

Spelling progress at different years showed:

- A to O was most effective at 7 and 11 years.
- DILP was most effective at 8 years. This was without the use of the spelling packs and dictations.
- SME was of most value at 12 and 13 years.

In a separate project Roycroft (2002) used DILP for four months with ten dyslexics in pairs, twice per week and found that they made 1.4 years progress in reading and 2.5 years progress in spelling. Ten Controls in pairs given standard reading and writing support made 0.2 months progress in reading and 0.1 months progress in spelling in the same four months.

These results suggest that we might use an APSL programme for six months or one semester then stop so that there can be a period of consolidation. One semester or a term and a half should give an uplift of at least one year's progress.

The review should identify whether or not the pupil knows all the names and sounds of the letters and can use them in word building. Handwriting should be joined and legible. If these criteria have been met then the pupil should be introduced to an orthographic phase programme (Chapter 6) in the next term. If some criteria have not been met then the appropriate lessons and methods should be targeted to address these needs before moving on.

Why omit phonological awareness training with dyslexics?

Phonological awareness training consists of encouraging pupils to become aware of the sounds in words, initially in syllables. They are encouraged to say the syllable, often a simple word such as 'sat' and then to separate out the sounds that make it up 's – a – t'. Research has already been cited that showed that splitting syllables in this way 'by ear' is not possible unless we can already spell them. The only feature that is clear is the initial sound with its extra energy. The clues to the separate sounds in the syllable are the articulatory pattern of the consonants and the sequence in the mouth that they follow.

We can in this way detect the 's' and then the 't' or 's-t' and this is why beginning spellers spell in this way. Vowels do not have such a distinct 'feely' pattern. The only other ways that we can split a syllable are by being able to spell it or having it drawn out in speech that tends to distort it.

The Phonological Assessment Battery (PhAB, Frederickson and Frith et al., 1997) is widely used to test phonological skills and takes about 40 minutes to administer individually. There are eight phonological tests and two supplementary tests.

The phonological tests are:

- Alliteration – segment the initial sound, includes digraphs.
- Rhyme – identify same end segments, analogies e.g. c-at, s-at.

- Spoonerisms i) 'cat' with an 'f' gives??
                ii) 'King John' gives 'Jing Kong'
- Non-word reading (phonics needed here).
- Naming speed (pictures).
- Naming speed (digits).
- Fluency (alliteration) generate /k/ words e.g. car, cup, cook.
- Fluency (rhyme) generate '-at' words, e.g. cat, fat, sat .

With the exception of naming speeds, all these tests require secure phonic knowledge. Even naming speed involves verbal processing with which dyslexics are known to have difficulty. More specifically, the other six sub tests can only be undertaken if we have some spelling knowledge, in particular phonics. My argument therefore is why not give them a letter sound test and a graded spelling test and then we would know exactly which sounds they do know. Training could then be more precise using the APSL approach.

Bryant and Bradley (1985) and Bradley (1981) trained their experimental group of pre-readers how phonemes were represented by graphemes using plastic letters to make words (sound–symbol correspondence). After 40 ten-minute sessions over two years the experimental group were four months ahead of the control groups. Another two years later at age eight or nine years they were two years ahead of those controls who had received no training and were three months ahead of the 300 children who had originally performed well on the rhyme test.

Although Bryant and Bradley claimed that the training was 'phonological', it was just another term for teaching a spelling strategy that can be found in dyslexia programmes.

> The particular advantage gained by the children taught to understand the connection between sound categories and orthographic spelling patterns suggests the two together make a formidable contribution to children's early progress is spelling.
>
> (Bradley and Huxford, 1994: 410)

When Simonson (2008) tested the effectiveness of phonological awareness training in her MA SpLD research project she compared the use of HMLC with LTK (Language Tool Kit, Rome and Osman, 1994) she found that the phonological training did improve the phonological skills significantly but did not transfer to the spelling performance on tests and in their free writing. Those trained on HMLC were not so good on the phonological awareness tests but their spelling skills were much improved.

Thus if we get straight on with symbol–sound correspondences and spelling teaching we save time and focus on the very specific needs of the dyslexic.

The characteristics of effective APSL programmes

The structure of an APSL lesson:

1   Alphabet work (see Chapter 7).
2   The reading pack.
3   The spelling pack.
4   Dictations.
5   Games.

Example of the APSL multisensory phonogram training for letter 'd'

After the alphabet work the reading pack work follows. There are 84 cards in the TRTS reading pack and 51 in the spelling pack. The order of introduction of the first 16 letters is i, t, p, n, s, a, d, h, e, c, k, ck, b, t, m, y:

- The teacher begins by presenting the reading pack card 'd'.
- The pupil learns to respond and say /d/.
- They discuss the clueword, e.g. 'dog'.
- The teacher shows the clueword and the pupil responds /d/.
- The teacher shows the name of the letter on the reading pack card and the pupil responds 'dog – D'.
- The teacher says 'd' and asks for the clueword and name of the letter.
- The teacher says 'dog' and asks for the initial letter's sound and name.
- The teacher says 'd' and asks the pupil to repeat the letter and give its name and now also write the letter.
- The teacher scribes the letter 'd' in the air, on a surface, or on the pupil's back. and asks for the clueword, name and sound. The pupil responds.

This process is repeated until the pupil securely responds automatically to all the combinations and the written form has reduced to a normal size.

Work on the spelling pack is as follows:

- The written sound is presented and read by the teacher or the pupil.
- It is repeated by the pupil 'd'.
- The pupil names the letter 'D.'
- The letter is written by the pupil and just beforehand it is named.
- Word building using the letter 'd' and the earlier letters begins, each time the letters are named.

Dictations then games follow this procedure.

Other sounds are added to the letter cards as appropriate, e.g. the 'I' and 'i' card will eventually have '-igh' and 'ie' on it.

It is during this process that pupils must learn to become aware of when their lips are open or closed, where the tongue touches the teeth and whether there is vocalisation or not (feel a vibration in the voice box in the throat).

The vowels are less easily defined and are open-mouthed and this is why they are not always detected by beginning normal writers so they write 'wt' for 'went' and 'str' for 'sister' and so on. Dyslexics also do this once they have begun to acquire phonic knowledge and follow the typical pattern of much younger children's development.

It is not surprising that dyslexia teachers and researchers have found the alphabet training process very repetitive and boring but they are not the concern. It is the dyslexics who need this 'treatment'.

The syllable structure work in the specialist schemes is more than teaching syllables are 'beats in words', that each must have a vowel in English spelling and that the basic structure is consonant-vowel-consonant (CVC). The syllable structures are open or closed and vary when the vowels within them are short or long. They often form what are called 'basewords' to which other syllables are added. These additions are prefixes (pre- fixes) added to the beginning of words, suffixes added at the end of words such as '-ing', plural 's' and 'es', and various forms of final stable syllables such as '-le', and '-ly', and '-tion', '-sion' or '-cian'.

Simple rules govern the use of these syllables and are based in linguistics. Most good spellers appear to learn these implicitly but in a remedial 'catch up' programme they need to be made explicit if correct orthography is to be developed. In classes and individual cases where these rules have been taught they speed up the spelling development of normal readers as well. This is illustrated in the next chapter.

Brain imaging studies

In comparison with controls, brain imaging studies by Blakemore and Frith (2006) found that during reading dyslexic children had reduced activation in the major reading and speech areas. They concluded that if it was true that dyslexics had a serious stumbling block in processing phonemes and relating them to spelling (sound–symbol correspondence) then they could not be expected to learn like normal children.

This does support the ideas set out earlier that a special format or training approach is needed to get over the stumbling block. It was demonstrated with Nicholas in Chapter 1 and reinforced in the chapters on logographic and alphabetic phases.

Although Kappers (1990) was using more limited EEG brain recording techniques he found that when the dyslexia was remediated the activation in the dyslexics' brain areas resembled that of normal subjects, demonstrating that what is observed in many brain activation studies may be the result rather than the cause of dyslexic problems – the long result of time.

Cases showing alphabetic stage scripts

Figure 5.3 displays Martin's script showing he has just cracked the alphabetic code but has a very poor grasp of phonics and some whole word knowledge. He is in Year 4, aged 9, in 2001. He writes:

> *I sloos thz eSohPcols Jaog.* (it is about exercises)

> *1. you have to Jag 2.youlallto sent 3 .haps 3 you have to jumb 10 tImes 4. you have to wnak slnAc up stns 3 tlmes 5 run uP and doun on the spat 6 you have to Jubms Ilrstn (jumbs of strat Jumbs*

He has written 38 'words' in 20 minutes at a speed of 1.9 words per minute. How has he slipped through the system? Even if he has a Statement of Special need (no evidence of this) he has had no specialist provision.

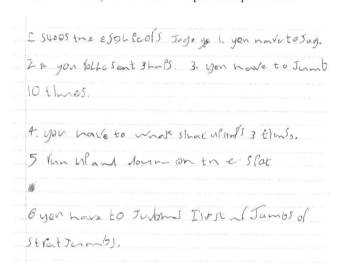

Figure 5.3 Martin's early alphabetic phase script in Year 4 (half original size)

Alphabetic phase programmes for Ordinary learners

Developmental Spelling Programme (Montgomery, 1997b)

This is a handbook of 110 mini lessons written for use by Early Years classroom teachers with ordinary learners. It is based upon the general principles of APSL programmes but without the overtraining necessary for dyslexics. There is no reading or spelling pack but the order of introduction of the letters is in the same use order i, t, p, n, s; letter names are taught, there are dictations, there is multisensory articulatory phonics training and synthetic phonics. It can be used alongside any system or programme of reading teaching.

Table 5.4 SATs improvements in spelling and reading using the *Developmental Spelling Handbook Programme*

	SATs 1997	SATs 1998
Reading	46%	58%
Spelling	16%	44%
Writing	57%	58%
Mathematics	83%	85%

It was written for a particular infant school (Montgomery, 1997b) in which the SATs spelling results were very poor. They were teaching reading by the Look and Say method and spelling and writing by using cursive from the outset in tracing and copy writing. There was no phonics teaching input.

The impact of the Developmental Spelling programme can be seen in Table 5.4. The spelling results have been significantly improved by the programme but so have the reading results. The skills learned in the spelling teaching have been transferred to reading by the learner. However, in the 1997 results the skills learned in reading and handwriting have not transferred to spelling – spelling has not been 'caught' during the reading process. Thus we can see that spelling is enhanced by explicit teaching with normal learners while it is essential for dyslexics.

Example contents list of the 110 lessons in the Developmental Spelling programme

Lessons:

1   Assess marks on paper.
2   Correct pencil grip.
3   Left handers.
4   Fluency in handwriting.
5   Cursive letter 'i' and sound (i).
6   Name I and clueword.
7   Cursive letter 't' and sound (t).
8   Clueword for 't' and name T.
9   Cursive 'p', sound (p), clueword and name of P, word building.
10 Assess writing of 'news'.
11 Syllable beats.
12 Sound 'n', clueword and name of N.
13 sound (s), sibilant sound, clueword and cursive s.
14 Second sound of s (z), capital S and clueword.
15 Word building with i, t, p, n, s.
16 Sound (a) and word 'a'.
17 Rimes –an and –at; analogy strategies. Dictation assessment.

(Handbooks can be obtained at www.ldrp.org.uk)

Five example lessons

After the initial lessons that involve multisensory-articulatory letter training the methods of teaching and learning adopt a problem-solving approach to spelling. The 'engage brain' strategies are designed to help pupils overcome any learned helplessness that has arisen because of the copying methods and rote learning that is so often adopted for spelling. When the programme is used with beginning learners it is designed to prevent learned helplessness arising in the first place. It must include the articulatory training element introduced into the TRTS programme (Montgomery, 1984).

The methods used are also based on the 'engage brain' Spelling Detective Approach that will be expanded upon in the next two chapters.

Lesson 5: Letter i and sound (i)

It is important to teach all the letters in a full flowing ovoid cursive with loops below and not above. Lined paper is also essential. Use a multisensory technique as shown below.

Cursive is essential because handwriting is a motor activity and joining a whole word means that the starting point only has to be found once, not again for every letter or letter part. Cursive enhances fluency and speed and supports spelling. Switching from early print to cursive is problematic for learners, especially those with coordination difficulties, so avoid this.

- Ensure that the classroom assistant has put out lined paper or drawn strong, clear lines with a ruler across the paper with wide spaces between them.

- Show the cursive form of the lower case letter 'i' on the board or whiteboard.
- Explain how it is made by talking them through the letter, e.g. 'Start on the line and flow up then back down and round a little. Now add the dot over the top'. Repeat this several times and ask them to join in the talk through.
- Give them the sound of the letter unless one of the children knows it (i) Talk through the letter once more and get them to do so too and say its sound as well.
- Now demonstrate the formation of the letter in the air with your back to the children. Repeat with the left hand for left-handers.
- Each time the letter is written its sound should be spoken, that is its short sound (i).
- Ask the pupils to imitate the movement in the air all together once or twice and then with hands on the table saying the sound at the same time. Repeat the sequence of 'in air' and 'on table' several times so that every pupil can be observed to check the movement is correct.
- Individuals can be asked to come and show the rest of the class.
- The teacher then writes a large cursive 'i' again on the board and pupils can volunteer to come and see if they can do it too. The model is first covered up and then uncovered to see if the two match well. Small pupil-sized chalk boards can be very useful now for practice especially for those with difficulties. Drawing in the sand tray can also be useful for them.
- When pupils have a feel for the letter they can be encouraged to try to form it on their lined paper, saying the sound as they do so.
- When they have the correct form they can try joined groups of letter 'i's.

Lesson 32: The L-F-S rule

This is a useful rule and simple to learn and apply.

In a closed syllable with a short vowel sound and the characteristic consonant–vowel–consonant (cvc) structure, in the case of l-f and s it is said that they are not strong enough to hold in the vowel on their own and so we must double them, e.g. tell, small, cuff, stuff, puss, less, mass.

There are a few exceptions to this general rule. No other consonants are doubled in this way unless they are a special name such as water butt, bitt to hold up a winch and a putt in golf.

- Present some examples of cases of the rule as follows:
  Set 1: had, mad,, sad, wed, red,, men, ten, pen, win, sin, son, tin, tip, ton. but, wit, ram, bar, tar, saw, raw, stop, step, slip, wax, bed, lip
  Set 2a: call, mall, all wall; tell, fell, well, sell; till will, still, gill, fill: toll, moll, poll, doll; hul, mull, cull full
  Set 2b: off, buff, huff, stuff, muff, ruff, tiff, whiff, toff, buff, skiff, luff
  Set 2c: pass, bass; mess, less: miss, hiss, kiss: toss, boss: puss, cuss

- Find out if the pupils can remember that these words are all examples of single closed syllable words containing the short vowel.
- Tell them to write down the syllable code for each of the four Sets 1, 2a, 2b, and 2c. e.g. 1, cvc, 2a cvcc, 2b cvcc, 2c cvcc. Check they have made the patterns correctly.
- Get them to look at the Sets and the structures and ask how Sets 2a, 2b, 2c are different from Set 1.
- Now ask them to formulate a general rule which would fit all these Set 2 cases or examples. Help them if necessary.

In a closed one-syllabled word we must double the final l, f or s

- Give them a short dictation to help them practice their new knowledge of the new rule:

'*I shall pass you the doll. Take that cuff off. I will fill the well. Do not make a fuss puss*'

Lesson 33: Exceptions to the L-F-S rule

Most rules have a few exceptions. Give pupils all the exceptions if there are only a few as in the l-f-s rule.

- Ask pupils if they can think of any words that do not follow the doubling rule: pal, gal, nil
  of (clue is the pronunciation), if
  yes, bus, gas, us, this, thus, plus
- Ask them to try to make up a sentence that uses all the l-words; then all the f-words and two sentences for the s-words.
- For a homework set the task to find out who can use most or all of the l-f-s exceptions in one sentence.
- Now ask them to hypothesise why we do not double the 's' in the following words:
  has, was, is, as, his
  The reason is of course that 's' is pronounced as (z) and so the rule does not apply. The letter 's' has two sounds (s) and its second sound (z).
- Give them another set of words in which the l-f-s rule does not apply e.g. Curl, girl, furl, hurl, scarf, loaf hoof, heel, peel, peal
- Tell them to note down the consonant and vowel codes for each of the above words, e.g. cvcc, cvcc, cvcc, cvcc, cvcc, cvvc, cvvc, cvvc etc.
- Ask them to try to give an explanation of why we do not double l-f-s in these words, first discussing it with their partner.
- The explanation is that we do not need to double l-f-s after a double vowel or when there is a double consonant already there to hold in the vowel. Doubling is already present in some form.

Lesson 34: The letter 'c' which does not have a sound of its own

If cursive 'c' has already arrived as a letter they needed in the repertoire or was included in a previous lesson then it simply needs to be reinforced as a cursive phonogram.

The main bulk of the session can then be spent upon the two forms of c, (k) and (s), its name and cluewords.

- Teach or reinforce the work already done on cursive c. By this stage they might simply observe it being written on the board, trace it in the air and then put it on the paper, first with the eyes shut and then as patterns with eyes open.
- Explain that the name of the letter is C and that is how its name is written as a large C and no lead in strokes.
- Introduce the first sound of c which is hard – (k) and you can discuss them as 'cat words', cop words and cup words e.g. cat, cap, can, cad, cop, cot, cup, or cut.
- They may well be used to writing the word 'car' by now so they may just need to have the explanation that the 'r' after the vowel slightly lengthens or pulls out the vowel sound – carbon, card, cart, carton.
- You may decide at this point not to introduce the second sound of c in case it confuses and then save it till later. Do not force the pace for the sake of getting through the list.
- The soft or second sound of c (s) is used in other words. Generate a list of words and use it to see if the pupils can work out the rule which governs its use. When do we use the second sound of c? e.g.

  City, cistern, car, circle, card, coat, cot, care, cere, certain, carp cusp, cycle, coffee cyst, cyanide, café, crease, cram, cringe, ceiling, claim, cream, crime, climb
- Pairs should discuss the list and try to work out the rule that governs the use of the second sound. Give them five minutes and then discuss.
- The rule they should evolve is that c is hard before vowels a, o and u and it is soft before e, i and y. Note that y has sneaked in here. It can be both a vowel and a consonant. Discussion of its use can probably be left until later.
- Before consonants l and r, c is hard

Lesson 63: Compound words

Compound words are usually words made up of two full words. Each retains its own spelling. In the German language it is very common to have what are called 'portmanteau' words in which several words are added together to define a new object or situation. In English we usually try to invent a new word and the language is one of the most flexible in this respect. New words are being created all the time.

- Write a set of compound words on the board or give out a worksheet with them at the top for the pupils to inspect e.g.,

  Classroom, timetable, anyone, anything, dustbin, lipstick, alongside, gunshot, waterfall, backdrop, highlight, outdoors, indoors, godfather, grandmother, bandwagon, Bournemouth, Weymouth, seagull, cheekbone, saucepan, upset, backward, uphill, downhill, rearguard, whiteboard etc.

- Ask the pupils to hypothesise what one thing all the words have in common, do not tell them. Let them think, then let them discuss their ideas with their partners before writing down their final answers (Think-Pair-Share).

- Discuss their answers focusing on the fact that all the words are made up of two complete words even when three consonants occur together. Discuss the meaning of selected words.

- They should look up the meaning of the more obscure words in their dictionaries in FOUR moves. See who can be the first to find the answers.

- Return them to a study of particular words and to write them down in two columns.

  Column one: Compound words that have exactly the meaning of their separate parts.
  Column two: Compound words that make a slightly different meaning with either or both of their two parts.

- Give out one page of a daily newspaper to each pair and ask them to skim through it together and list as many compound words as they can find in five (or ten) minutes.

- Collect the new words as a list on the board and ask the pupils to regroup them as far as possible into a new set of categories giving an overall label or classification to them. Do not tell them categories in advance. They might find categories such as: people, sport, events etc.

In a teacher research project O'Brien (2004) compared the spelling progress of matched control and experimental groups of Year 3 pupils with reading and spelling difficulties The 14 controls were taught spelling from the National Literacy Strategy and the 14 in the experimental group were taught from the Developmental Spelling Handbook matching the contents where possible, not the methods. The spelling sessions lasted 30 minutes each week for 9 months.

O'Brien found it impossible to keep pace with the NLS, e.g. teach ee, ea, ai, a-e and ay in one session. She found that the NLS placed emphasis on learning rote letter patterns not cognitive processes. The results were that the experimental group gained five months in spelling skills above the expected nine months and the control group lost a month overall in expected development and made only eight months of the expected nine months progress.

Toolkit for teachers with early or late stage alphabetic phase dyslexics

- Randomise the lower case letters of the alphabet on a card to make a letter sounds test. Make a record sheet to ring omissions and errors.
- Do the same for the capitals for a names test.
- Search out suitable reading and spelling tests in the files and obtain the latest norms, e.g. Schonell, Daniels and Diack, NARA, Vernon.
- Buy tests of IQ that teachers may use such as BPVS and NFER tests.
- Buy a set of the Ravens Progressive Matrices test for the age group (for children who are non-literate or non-English speakers).
- Select an appropriate APSL programme for your dyslexics – HMLC, TRTS, A to O.
- Select or design an appropriate developmental programme for ordinary learners using the model in Chapter 1.
- Practice the specialist programme on individual dyslexics and follow it very precisely for one semester and evaluate.
- Ensure there are pre-test and post-test results for reading, spelling and free writing for the evaluation.
- Keep a record of all outcomes to check effectiveness and to assemble group data.
- When familiar and comfortable with the APSL programme begin matched pairs tuition.
- For class teaching use the *Developmental Spelling Handbook*.
- A dyslexia qualification is a gateway to local authority recognition and employment but a portfolio of effective learning outcomes can be as powerful.
- Keep updated in the theory and research but do not be swayed by the latest fashion. Test it.

Conclusions

In this chapter the key APSL programmes based on the Gillingham and Stillman model were identified. Research on their effectiveness in comparison with other schemes has been presented and evaluated. It has been shown that correctly used the specialist programme can give an uplift of two years in each year and thus it is an effective remedial toolkit in comparison with the other schemes.

It has shown which aspects of the APSL programmes are central to addressing the dyslexics' needs to move them into and beyond the alphabetic phase rather than become stuck in it. The critical elements are the 'cracking of the alphabetic code' and the use of 'phones' in Reception reading and writing and then the use of this knowledge in word-building in synthetic phonics.

The reason for the dyslexic problem is found in a neurological dissociation in an area that would normally allow the sound-symbol and articulatory feel of consonants in particular to be connected. The result is that areas around the dissociation need to be taught to take over what appears normally to be an automatic function. This is why the initial stages of the alphabetic work have to be very slow and very secure with no confusion allowed to set in. A radical rethink of remedial intervention in this respect is therefore needed.

It was suggested that the remedial intervention in the alphabetic phase may in the past have gone on too long because after six months the major effects have been achieved. The pupil then needs a consolidation period to practise the skills that have been learnt, in the wider classroom. At this point the *Developmental Spelling Handbook* approach can be used to support the learning. For some the specialist programme will need to be resumed after the 'rest period', others could profit from moving on to an orthographic phase programme. No pupil should be having remedial tuition for three or four years. It would mean the programme was not effective and must be changed. It is to be hoped that the Alphabetic phase is dealt with by the end of Year 1.

Most dyslexics – except those with the severest difficulties – do eventually begin to learn to read but it is usually some three years late and the spelling remains poor. The spelling problems persist into adulthood and 'phonological' weaknesses and slow processing speeds are still identifiable in adult dyslexics.

If the difficulties could be addressed in the Reception year, as outlined in Chapter 4 and followed up as in this chapter, it may be possible with careful monitoring for the problem to be overcome by the end of the infant stage. Teachers in infant schools should determine to test this through the changes in practice suggested. We could then collect their results through the Learning Difficulties Research Project website at www.ldrp.org.uk and disseminate them.

Dyslexia is widely considered as a 'disorder' but looking at the cases and the progress that can be made, once they do have a grasp of the essentials this may not be true. It appears that their progress follows a normal pattern that resembles the errors and inconsistencies of much younger children in line with their reading and spelling ages. Thus the 'system' does not appear to be disordered, what we observe is the result of a specific delay.

Because of all the different interventions and learning experiences that dyslexics experience, as well as their different levels of motivation, it is not surprising that each presents a unique profile. It is argued by some that this makes dyslexia a many-headed problem, a disorder with sub-groups, or just a problem of poor reading. However, the complexities in the nature of the problems observed it is suggested here is the 'long result of time' caused by the initial delay and then all the attempts over the years to address it that have not been successful.

When remediation has been successful it is still 'a catch up' profile because three years or more of normal literacy experiences have been missed. Eventually reading may be at grade level or better but in many it is slower than it should be and comprehension is more difficult for them especially when new technical vocabulary is introduced. This was noticed in the teacher education programmes when introducing the psychological vocabulary and constructs. Students regularly complained about 'all that jargon' and had problems in spelling it as well as in its comprehension.

Their late dyslexic difficulties were revealed on the Year 4, Learning Difficulties year-long programme when as a result of the studies they reflected upon their own learning histories and came forward to discuss their needs in lunch time 'clinics'. Together we learnt how to deal with them. Similar case histories of dyslexia, dysorthographia and dysgraphia were revealed by mature students on inservice BEd and MA programmes.

The results of the experiments and case work with these 'recovered' dyslexics are discussed in the next chapter and reveal what needs they have in the orthographic phase and how these can be addressed not only with adults but also with pupils in schools even from the earliest ages.

6 Remediating dyslexia in the orthographic phase

Introduction

The residual needs of adult dyslexics were fully realised when marking scripts of undergraduate teacher education students and mature students on continuing professional development programmes. Because the courses were about learning difficulties it seemed incumbent upon the tutor to help them overcome their problems. The students themselves sometimes had only just realised why they had experienced difficulties at school through studying on the programme. Others had histories of dyslexia and too frequently a late diagnosis. Characteristic of the group was that they had all shown great determination and persistence to follow their chosen career and overcome their problems – often with little or no support.

Their spelling correcting strategies were limited to rote learning of the correct versions, visualisation, look-cover-write-check, 'does it look right' and asking a friend to proofread what they had written before they handed any work in. It was in exams that they became most vulnerable to detection for their own proofreading too often missed the errors.

Another major problem identified particularly among the mature students was an inability to present what they knew in a way that would gain them good marks towards their qualification. When this was investigated it was found that they had had no training in study skills and how to structure and write an education essay or essays in general. This was easily dealt with by study skills strategies such as the following and incorporating study skills into the learning programme supported by a study skills book with examples for use in schools (Montgomery, 1993):

- Ringing the key concepts in the question, usually three to five elements – concepts, theories, research, critique, applications.
- Teaching them to write to a structure under the five headings – discuss or explain the concepts in the question, explain at least two theoretical positions, give four pieces of background research, try to criticise them, give practical classroom applications and write a concluding statement.
- They then practised rewriting an essay once and discussed the results.

- They wrote several answer plans on other exam questions and discussed those with the tutor.

The results were that these students who had failed in their previous exams all passed comfortably and were also able to modify the technique and apply it to their other subject areas. It is typical that dyslexics and many others from disadvantaged groups need help with such skills. This is possibly because during their learning history their brain is so engaged with decoding the words and making sense in the process that they miss grasping the overall schema and deep structures that others acquire implicitly. Wider problems with organisational skills can also be a problem associated with dyspraxia. One such student would get lost in Tesco's and have to be rescued by her children.

Gifted underachievers from disadvantaged backgrounds can also miss out on learning such skills. This is because they have such good recall that in the early years they do not have to study texts more assiduously to find the structures and meaning. It is very often only at degree level they begin to fail as memory is not the only requirement for success. There is also too much even for them to remember so that strategic approaches become essential to identify principles and hierarchies of knowledge.

In investigating the students' study skill needs it was realised that a similar set of protocols or procedures was needed to help many of them with their spelling and so a series of investigations began.

The development of the Cognitive Process Strategies for Spelling (CPSS)

Initially a list of strategies was invented that did or might assist in correcting misspellings. These worked out to a maximum of 12, the so-called 'cognitive process' or 'brain engage' strategies that would serve as alternatives to the major rote learning procedures, mnemonics, visualisation and singing and rhyming techniques that were widely used. It was hoped that the 12 strategies would be more effective.

A set of 12 difficult to spell words was selected and were deliberately misspelled to mislead. They were presented visually and were also read to classes of students on ITT and CPD programmes over a five-year period as part of teaching courses about spelling and dyslexia.

The misspelling test:

1 Ass-ee-9
2 Brag-ar-doh-chio
3 Virr-mill-aeon
4 Rare-ee-figh
5 Im-pahst-err
6 Row-cocoa

7 Lick-we-fye
8 Sack-ree-lidge-ious
9 Pav-ill-eon
10 Ack-come-oh-dait
11 Se-pehr-ate
12 Dessy-kate

On each occasion the students were asked to write the words correctly and reflect on their mental processes and explain what strategies they were using. Once again the limited range of most people's strategies was apparent. They syllabified, used phonics and analogies with known words, wrote it then tried to assess if it 'looked right'. Some used meaning and the knowledge of another language. Many suggested how useful mnemonics could be.

However, it was explained that finding a mnemonic (a verse or device for aiding the memory) was often a lengthy process and then only corrected the one misspelling, making it not so useful as they might believe. Strategies were needed that would generalise to a range of words and misspellings. The emphasis needed to be on the strategy not the process of finding it.

The best spellers appeared to have the largest range of strategies. In the developmental period 1,700 subjects had been tested. Over time, several thousand responses have been recorded and no participant ever scored 12. Only a handful of subjects from this large group had scored more than eight correct. Many had scored only one or two points to their great surprise and indignation.

From the outset 12 CPS strategies had been devised and in all the feedback from the subjects no more than these 12 were ever recorded. Each needed an explanation to show how it could be used and then the teachers would have a general toolkit to use to help their pupils and their own spelling development and correct their misspellings.

There was a significant lack of spelling teaching knowledge and research in that period apart from in the traditional phonics teaching programmes and the remedial programmes. The students with the spelling problems came individually for help to the lunchtime clinics and brought a list of their misspellings from a recent essay plus the essay itself so that other errors they might have missed could be found and included. Together we worked on two errors per session. This enabled the 12 CPSS to be tested for their effectiveness in overcoming the students' spelling problems.

Twelve cognitive process strategies for spelling – CPSS

Lower order strategies

• **Articulation** – the misspelled word is clearly and precisely articulated for spelling – citation mode.

- **Over articulation** – the word is enunciated with an emphasis on each of the syllables or unstressed sound, e.g. parli (a) ment, gover (n) ment, w(h)ere.
- **Cue articulation** – the word is pronounced almost incorrectly, e.g. Wed -nes - day, Feb - ru - ary.
- **Syllabification** – the word is broken down into syllables, e.g. misdemeanour – mis / de / mean / our.
- **Phonics** – a comprehensible articulatory skeleton or word scaffold is made to build upon – km, cm then cum, may appear before come.

Higher order strategies

- **Origin** – the root in another language may give clues, e.g. -op / **port** / unity; an opening, a **port** or a haven.
- **Rule** – a few rules can help unravel a range of spelling problems, e.g. the l - f- s rule, these are doubled in one syllabled words after a short vowel sound – ball, puff, dress. The 12 exceptions are made into several sentences e.g. YES, the BUS runs on GAS PAL, IF you pay NIL you get turned off. I before E except after C – receive, perceive.
- **Linguistics** – syllable types open, closed, accented and unaccented need to be taught as well as the four suffixing rules which govern most words, e.g. Add, Double, Drop, Change.
- **Family/base word** – family helps reveal silent letters and correct representation for the 'schwa' unstressed vowel, e.g. Canada, Canadian; bomb, bombing, bombardier, bombardment; sign, signature signal, resign. Basewords can make families of words, e.g. form, reform, forming, deformed, formation.
- **Meaning** – separate is often misspelled as sep / e / rate. The dictionary meaning shows it means to divide or part or even to pare. The pupil then just needs to remember 'cut or part' and 'pare' to separate.
- **Analogy** – comparison of the word or the key part of it with a word the pupil does know how to spell, e.g. 'it is like boot - hoot, root' or 'hazard' is one 'z' like in 'haze' and 'maze'.
- **Funnies** – sometimes it is not possible to find another strategy and so a 'funny' can help out, e.g. 'cess pit' helped me remember how to spell 'necessary'.

The seven-step protocol for using CPSS

Younger pupils and those with poorer spelling will need more of the first five CPS strategies and little or no dictionary work to begin with:

1 The pupil selects **two** misspellings to learn in any one session.
2 The pupil identifies the **area of error**, usually only one letter with help of the teacher or a dictionary.

3   The pupil puts a **ring round** the area of error and notices how much of the rest is correct.
4   The pupil is taught (later selects) a **CPSS to** correct the misspelling, a reserve strategy is also noted where possible.
5   The strategy is **talked over** with the teacher and is used to write the corrected spelling.
6   The spelling is **checked** to see if it is correct – the dictionary can be used again here.
7   If correct the pupil covers up the spelling and writes the word three times from memory in **joined up/full cursive, naming** the letters (Simultaneous Oral Spelling (SOS). It is especially important to use the joined script at least **over the area of error** if full cursive presents a problem.

NB. Mnemonics are no part of CPSS because they do not generalise to new words and are laborious.

Why two strategies are needed to correct a misspelling

Research by Kuczaj (1979) found that the motor programmes for spelling words, particularly their bases and affixes were stored together in the brain. This meant that learning to write syllables and base words as cursive writing units during early learning was an important strategy and could contribute to spelling accuracy. The word meaning in the lexicon (word memory store) has to be consistently associated with its motor memory (motoreme).

The posterior frontal lobe area (usually left hemisphere) organises and initiates the voluntary motor movements involved in forming the individual graphemes and syllables. These are stored in the motor memory and available to be called up during writing. Over time and practice this process becomes automatic so that during essay writing we do not have to think about the details of the spelling.

The problem arises when as young writers or dyslexics we store incorrect spellings. In order to correct them we have to address the error both in the word memory store and in the motor memory store. The CPSS corrects the error in the lexicon and the SOS strategy is needed to correct it in the motor memory. As old memories are not deleted but persist they also will be called up when writing. The CPSS, however, gives the new spelling a higher profile and as the writer writes a sentence and the 'problem' word comes nearer 'warning bells' ring and the writer recalls the strategy, slows down and writes the correct version.

Soon the writer is able to write the correct version without having to pause and recall the strategy. Eventually the correct version arises each time unless under stress when it may pop up again. On these occasions proofreading will clear it out.

An investigation of the types of spelling errors made by undergraduate teacher education students in a three-hour exam was undertaken. All 55 scripts were analysed. There were 165 errors in total and 152 different errors. The estimated number of words was about 3,000 words per script making 165,000 words in total giving an error rate of 0.001 per cent and a modest writing speed of 17 words per minute, taking into account that thinking time was heavily involved.

Table 6.1 The nature and frequency of the undergraduate errors

Error type	Total	Error type	Total
Suffixing	43	Homophones	3
Baseword	36	Long vowel	4
Prefixing	26	Phonetic confusion	3
Roots	19	Short vowel	2
Syllabification	9	Articulation	0
Slip of the pen	7	Noun/verb confusion	0

N=152 errors 55 subjects

The preponderance of errors of the undergraduates fell in the linguistic/morphemic or higher order area rather than the lower order articulation and phonics areas. These higher order errors are not unexpected for an adult group and can be compared with the Year 7 results in Table 6.2 below.

Table 6.2 Spelling error type data analysis in Year 7 cohorts

Error type	% Errors SEN group (N=27) Cohort B	Cohort B (N=160)	Cohort C (N=251)	Cohort C (Error % all words)
SYNTHETIC PHONICS				
Artic/Pronunciation/ Syll	12.4%	11.9%	12.9%	(0.58%)
Phonetic/Phonic	32.8%	28.7%	29.1%	(1.23%)
MORPHEMICS				
Baseword/Origin	28.2%	30.0%	19.6%	(0.82%)
Suffix/Pref/vowel rules	11.8%	18.4%	17.2%	(0.73%)
Homophone	1.4%	3.5%	9.5%	(0.40%)
Grammatical	13.2%	9.7%	11.7%	(0.49%)
Total numbers of errors	773	1953	2651	(4.25%)

Multiple errors of the same words' misspelling by an individual pupil were only counted once.

The main difference between the Year 7s and the undergraduates was that in developmental terms they made slightly more errors of a basic kind such as with articulation and phonics and in their grammatical knowledge. Even pupils classified in school B as having SEN, mostly with specific learning difficulties, showed the *same types of errors as the rest of their cohort*. They also showed a profile of spelling development typical of younger children when compared with results from Year 5 cohorts. In other words their misspellings were not 'bizarre' but merely typical of younger children learning to spell.

Case examples in spelling interventions using CPSS

1. Casework with Kimmi, Year 7 (Ashraf, 2005)

Kimmi is a talented musical performer but has severe difficulties in spelling in English and French. Her spelling in English was referred to as 'dire' and her tutor Myra decided to try the CPSS strategies with her. Kimmi had weaknesses in spelling, grammar and articulation.

Errors from her previous work were collected and given to her in a dictation.

Although she was an enthusiastic pupil, Kimmi began very quietly and nervously with a distinct lack of confidence. The words for spelling were articulated clearly and carefully and put into simple sentences so that the meaning was clear.

There were 17 words in the spelling list and Kimmi found the whole task laborious and there were many hesitations. Some of her words were written with capitals inserted and a heavy pressure was exerted during the writing. Her spellings and misspellings were as follows:

> Freind, danceing, chaze, chazing, Rain, Rainig, aKPlan, cmPLan, cmpLaning, bLush, bLushing, fnchr, capchr, mixchr, paNisment, enJoy, anJoyment.

When Kimmi was asked how she arrived at her spellings she explained that most of the time she was aware that she had misspelt the word and that she found it difficult to keep up with her class teacher during dictation. She confided that she was desperate for help and was positive she could spell well if only her teacher was patient and supportive.

She was assured that she would be helped to learn a few strategies that would improve her spelling and for her teacher to follow with her. They started with helping Kimmi with more precise articulation modelling a few examples and using the words she had misspelled.

She was taught to just draw a ring round the area of error in a word and focus the correction on that because all the rest was correct. They circled the letter 'e' in 'danceing' and then the 'DROP' suffixing rule was explained.

Kimmi was elated that she only had to identify and ring the error and she quickly located the word in the dictionary. After that she circled all the errors and then learnt about syllabification and how easy it was to spell a word when it was broken down into short syllable units. She learnt how important it was for every syllable to have a vowel in it using 'furniture' – her version was 'fnchr' – as an example.

Kimmi then provided examples of multisyllabled words and then tried to spell them using her new strategy, e.g. rhinoceros, hippopotamus, comfort, sister, automatic (her 'otomatic' was close). Myra went on to teach her basewords, prefixes and suffixes as one writing unit to move her from her print writing style. Kimmi was quite willing to learn cursive if it would improve her spelling.

Once she had gained proficiency with single letters she wrote the letters in groups of three in the alphabet sequence. Initially she found this difficult and had to stop to think which letter came next in the sequence. After a week of daily practice she was competent and they continued the spelling practice for a further two weeks. By this time Kimmi was full of confidence and when 13 of the words she had misspelled were dictated she spelled ten of them correctly, misspelling 'rainnig', 'furinture', 'enjoment'.

At the end of a month Kimmi was retested on the original 13 misspelled words again and five new words were added (refreshment, vulture, signature, lecture, development). This time she correctly spelled 16 out of 18 and only added an extra 'n' in one word and vowel 'a' in 'lacture'. Kimmi was delighted with her progress and the class teacher seeing the results tried them out with some other poor spellers. She reported excellent results and declared she would use the strategies in every spelling lesson.

What we can observe in this case is that 'learned helplessness' has been overcome and so much stress and anxiety has been reduced.

2. Casework with Carl aged nine years 11 months (MA SpLD student)

Carl had a spelling age of eight years four months and was diagnosed by an educational psychologist as 'moderately dyslexic'. He was given a 100-word dictation from his Harry Potter reading book. He misspelled 12 words and identified 5 of them:

> monning (morning); itsalf (itself); bewiching (bewitching); foled (followed); turbern (turban).

> and: cristmas, midde, coverd sevulal, foled, punshed, thay

In the period of a fortnight they dealt with his errors, Lesson One follows:

- **Christmas:** Carl missed the 'h' in this word and said he sometimes missed the 'r' as well.

- Cue articulation: 'We pronounced the word 'Christ mas'. We talked about the fact that Christmas is all about Jesus, i.e. Christ. We looked up 'mass' in the dictionary and discovered that it can mean a meal or a body and that at Christmas we have a big meal to celebrate that Jesus came to earth in human body. Carl had never realised the word 'Christ' was in Christmas.
    - 'Funny': As soon as I spelt this word correctly Carl said, 'Oh look my brother's name'. Carl has a brother called 'Chris' whose name he can spell quite happily so it really helped him to remember that the name 'Chris' is in 'Christmas'.
    - SOS: He found it quite hard to make himself use the cursive writing at first but said it got a lot easier as he repeated the word. He also found it easier to remember the spelling if he shut his eyes.
- **Followed:** Carl spelt this as 'foled'.
    - Syllabification: Carl needed help to see how the base word 'follow' can be broken down into syllables, then he spotted the word 'low'.
    - Analogy: He was able to think of a rhyming word for 'foll', i.e. 'doll'. As soon as I mentioned the past tense he remembered he needed a 'ed' ending. (After analogy with doll it might have been useful to introduce the l-f-s rule and/or doubling after the short vowel sound.)
    - At the outset of lesson two he spelt the two words correctly and he and his teacher proceeded with the next two words. After the six sessions he was given the dictation again and Carl correctly spelled all the 12 target words. Initially he resorted to the former spelling of 'covered' and 'punishment' but in both cases he immediately realised his error and self corrected. He was quite hesitant over 'several' but got it correct after some thought. He initially put 'terban' for 'turban' but corrected it immediately. His writing in the post test was more joined.

3. Casework with Maia aged eight years eight months (Morey, 2001)

Maia was diagnosed with specific learning difficulties at seven years one month and was taken into the learning support programme. Two years later her exercise books showed she had received phonological awareness training and some key rules and spelling pattern training. The interventions had been many and varied but no clear-cut structured programme had been provided.

Morey, the Head of Learning Support decided to place her on the APSL, TRTS programme and she began on this in September 1999. Tests showed that at eight years eight months Maia had:

- a reading age of eight years four months;
- a spelling age of seven years five months (15 months below CA);
- her British Picture Vocabulary Test results showed her mental abilities were at the nine years eight months level a year above her CA putting her in the high average range; and

- she had a very good expressive use of language.

She started on TRTS and began with i, t, p, n, s to check and consolidate her initial sounds knowledge. It immediately became clear that she had an articulation awareness problem. When she was introduced to the blends she recognised the letter patterns but was unaware of their articulatory feel.

From September to December 1999 she was given two 35-minute lessons per week in a one-to-one tutorial withdrawn from the class. On each occasion she seemed to do well and then on another she would regress. Her problem seemed to be an inability to see why segmenting a sound was worthwhile for spelling. She would spell 'call' as 'col'. Even when she learned to correct to 'll' she still spelt the word with an 'o' (p. 27).

When her tutor tried to teach her the onset and rime strategy 'c - all' it did not seem to work. Maia did not learn if she was not interested. She seemed to need something more than the structure of the APSL programme and Morey decided to try CPSS with her.

She was given a dictation from Alpha to Omega (Hornsby and Shear, 1993) and a sample of her free writing was collected. It appeared that she used a mixture of phonetics and visual tactics to read and spell. On occasions she would use -ck correctly and then incorrectly as '-c' in the same piece of writing, e.g. 'Nick' and 'Nic' and so Morey began intervention at this point. Maia seemed incapable of self-monitoring and proofreading.

The first two words chosen for correction were 'back' spelt 'bac' and 'they' spelt 'thay' – a common error. The sessions ran as follows:

The importance of proof reading was discussed. Maia could not find all her errors on the dictation and free writing test. It was explained that she should concentrate all her attention on the area of error in a misspelling and put a ring round it. Maia used a coloured marker pen.

- The first strategy used was 'cue articulation'. Maia was to spell the word aloud naming the letters B - A - C - K then say it incorrectly as 'bac-k'with a double /k/. Maia did this then started naming words that rhymed with 'back' and gave them the double /k-k/ treatment. It amused her but she admitted that in English it sounded complete nonsense.
- The second strategy was 'linguistic' and the rule governing '-ck' was explained – in one syllabled words with a short vowel and no other consonant before the last /k/ we use '-ck' for the /k/ sound.

    The story is of, 'kicking /k/ and cushion consonant /c/.

    'Kicking k' is the meanest letter in the alphabet who doesn't like the vowels and eventually turns round and kicks them. The reason is all the vowels have two sounds but 'k' has to share a sound with consonant 'c'. This letter is the cushion that slips between the vowel and the letter 'k'. 'C' becomes breathless by being continually kicked by 'k' and does not say its sound. Hence together '-ck- say one sound.' (Morey, 2001: 28).

Pictures of 'kicking k' and 'cushion c' were used to support Maia. She was asked to identify the initial sound of 'back' then note its short vowel sound and immediately saw her own error and spelled the word 'back' correctly.

She was then taught that when there was an extra consonant or an extra vowel before 'kicking k' they protected the short vowel and the cushion was not needed.

Maia fully understood the process and began to generate her own words to test the rule repeating the various explanations to herself. She remembered she had misspelt 'clock' and saw she had missed out the 'cushion' and said, 'Poor vowel!'. They then used the SOS strategy to reinforce the motor programme and check the spelling.

When she was asked to think of a way of correcting 'thay' she was unable to do so. So together they rehearsed the 'Family' of words – they, them, their etc. Maia called 'they' 'A Yucky word' and the tutor suggested they use this to remind her by calling it 'THE Yucky word'. She had created her own 'Funny' and using SOS was now able to demonstrate she could spell it correctly. Later she reported it had worked in classwork and she remembered the strategy.

Maia then found that the '-ck' rule had failed when she spelled 'speak' as 'speack' in a class spelling test. They revised the rule – 'only after a short vowel sound' and Maia moved on. When she arrived at her next lesson she had found she needed to learn how to spell the /k/ sound at the beginning of words and so they worked on that rule.

Morey, reflecting on the learning experience for both of them, found that immediately the cognitive strategies were introduced there was an overwhelming change in the relationship with Maia in the lead and Morey having to give up her planned programme.

When her progress was checked in July 2000 the results were that while Maia's spelling was still weak CPSS had had a dramatic effect on her reading. Her scores were:

- CA nine years four months.
- RA ten years four months (two years uplift in one year).
- SA eight years four months (11 months uplift in one year).

4. Casework with Jan aged 13 years seven months (MA SpLD student)

Jan is a year 8 pupil (R.A. = 9.1; S.A. = 8.7) and had had small group withdrawal teaching in Junior school for reading and spelling. Now in Secondary school she was in the bottom set for English in a group of 15 with some teaching assistant support. She had a half hour group withdrawal session per week but no special programme was in place.

Jan said she felt stupid, other children laughed at her reading and spelling, often teachers were cross with her for spelling words incorrectly. She really wanted to be a successful reader and speller. Over a period of four weeks in a one-on-one withdrawal session they used CPSS with the following result.

> Jan and I gained a lot from this experience. She said she thought that she'd never learn to spell words that she got wrong and she felt that now at secondary school they had given up on her. She felt by working together that she had used a lot of her own ideas when investigating words and she had enjoyed having the responsibility. She said that when we talked about things together she understood more than if she was just listening........She said she'd always thought she wasn't as clever as other children and had labelled herself as 'thick'.....I had seen a marked improvement in Jan's confidence, enthusiasm and spelling abilities.

6. Casework with Alex aged 13 years (MA SpLD student)

An example of Alex's work before and after five mini sessions of CPSS:

Before
he eat him. now I'm no
exspert but anemals do
behve lick that. and
he did the same to the
others but the had a
difrent larws and the
PLeos cort him eath
is the most stangest plac
J onow Yors fafhly
hoblar

The underlined words were those chosen by Alex to tackle in the sessions.

After
Dear Hoblar
I fanck you for your letter, I've looked up
your animal consirns and animals on earth have a good
reputasn like Robin Hood, the Fox and Bugs Buny. I have
beny watching a lat of films and cartoons and I disagree
with you. For example police dog's save live's and guide
dog's help blind people. I'll meet you at the space cafe on
Wednesday 4th July
See you soon
Blar

This writing was better laid out and more fluent, joined and legible. Obviously more work on spelling is needed but some useful progress has been made.

5. Casework with Natalie aged 15 (Wensley, 2005)

Natalie was a pupil in Year 10 (aged 15). She was somewhat impulsive and had dyslexic type difficulties (spelling age 12.4 years). She had been in the learning support class for three years: 'there are numerous difficulties in school as Natalie does not like to listen to criticism and does not accept help to improve her work.'

Her writing was sometimes difficult to read, especially when writing words she was unsure of. Her written work did not reflect her level of understanding, she wrote the minimum required, did not proofread, made many grammatical errors and was very slow at writing.

In the first CPSS session the teacher and Natalie spoke at length about the strategies and then Natalie was given a dictation. She selected the words 'edge' and 'comfortable' to tackle, put a ring round her area of error, looked them up in the dictionary, and cue articulation was suggested for ED-ge and then a 'funny' which arose when Natalie said she was reminded of a dog called 'Edger/Edgar', then they used the phrase 'edger has the edge'.

Natalie then chose cue articulation for the word com -FORT- able as well as the phrase which amused her 'The fort is comfortable'. She became very keen on using CPSS and over the next few weeks kept asking if she could have her spellings checked and if she could have new ones.

She enjoyed identifying the word, looking it up in the dictionary and thinking of strategies to overcome it. However, what she did not enjoy was the SOS and cursive writing. She was reluctant to use them despite being told why and felt they were too much like other spelling programmes she had been given before but which had failed.

A few days after the first session Natalie came in very excited because she had 'heard alarm bells ringing' when writing the word 'edge' in Food Technology and as a result of 'the bell' she had taken more time over the word and been able to correct her own writing'.

Over the next three weeks they spent ten minutes every learning support lesson reviewing spelling. Only in these sessions could Natalie be persuaded to use SOS. After a few more weeks all the words she had been learning were put into a dictation. Although Natalie complained she had not had time to review them in fact all were spelled correctly except 'thought', which was given as 'though'. She said that now whenever she used the target words the alarm bells would ring although sometimes it took her a while to remember the strategy. For example, she still wanted to spell the word leisure as 'leasure' but now her brain told her not to.

Other important things emerged during the mini lessons and Natalie became willing to share some of the stresses her problems with spelling had caused and opened a floodgate on homonyms that had troubled her for years. She was surprised that no one had thought to teach her the suffixing rules before. As the sessions progressed she gained in confidence and was enjoying studying spelling and getting very obvious benefit which she herself could see and experience.

The dyslexia tutor explained:

> Many of the students I work with have been following dyslexia spelling programmes with private tutors for years with little or no improvement in their ability to spell accurately when under pressure especially in a test or exam. When I first read about CPSS I was a little dubious as it seemed a time consuming way of teaching students correct spelling however I was desperate to find something which would work after years of repeatedly correcting the same errors.
>
> It did not take long for my experimental student to feel confident about what she was doing... it has been an extremely positive experience as it really helped raise her self esteem as well as improving the accuracy of her spelling. I have now introduced the CPSS to all the classes I teach.

An earlier research project by Parrant (1986) had shown effective results in six weeks with classes of 11 year olds. The control class of 23 pupils and the experimental class of 21 pupils, including seven with specific learning difficulties in reading and spelling were given a 100-word dictation pre- and post-intervention. Each week they worked on a set of common errors from the dictation. The control group were taught to use Look-Cover-Write-Check and write the word correctly three times. The experimental group tackled the same errors with CPSS, writing the word correctly three times. Both groups' spelling improved but for the controls there was not a significant gain but the experimental groups' improvement was very significant ($p < 0.01$). Even the group with SpLD improved their spelling significantly ($p < 0.05$). The error rate of the experimental group dropped from 273 to 162.

Parrant also recorded a change to a positive attitude to spelling in the experimental group. They were more interested in spelling and more confident in their writing after the intervention.

Casework by the author, 2014–2016

Casework with John, aged 56

This report is based upon documents submitted by John who referred himself for a secondary opinion diagnosis and help. The documents included a WAIS III IQ test and scores from attainment tests. He was in the process of presenting his doctoral thesis and wished his diagnosis of dyslexia to be taken into account.

Handwriting samples and a list of spelling problems were attached to his documents on request. The general profile that emerged from the test results was:

1   A highly intelligent person with a measured IQ of 132 but which in actual terms is significantly higher, in the region of 142–145. The reason for this difference is that IQ tests are a measure of long-term memory. They assess what an individual has picked up in the environment and acquired in school and committed to memory. Even the immediate memory span tests rely to a significant extent on subskills that are built on learned literacy. The learning disabilities thus depress particular scores on IQ tests in which verbal processing is involved such as Arithmetic, Coding, Information and Digit Span – the ACID profile.
2   A recovering dyslexic in the orthographic stage. As a child he had difficulties in learning to read and write. He now shows all the adult signs of this former difficulty. His high intelligence has enabled him to make much better progress than many other dyslexics. It is indicated in his very good literacy comprehension score and general academic successes. His spelling score is two standard deviations below his IQ.
3   In addition he has a fine motor coordination difficulty that seriously affects his handwriting. It would have made it even harder for him in the early years of school to demonstrate any literacy progress he was making. He would have difficulties making readable marks on paper. It would result in school grades being lower than he should have been awarded.

In personality terms he has shown great determination and persistence with a desire to succeed in what he does that is much to be admired.

It is still perfectly possible to address these spelling problems and gradually remove them.

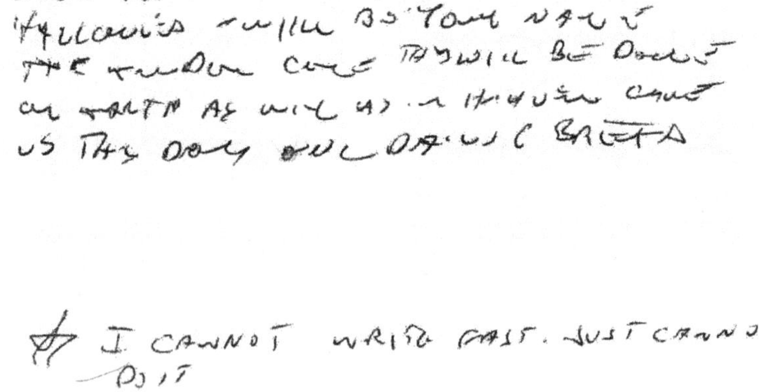

Figure 6.1 An example of John's writing

To resolve the severe handwriting problems that he clearly has had and the dyslexia, he has resorted to writing in capital letters. Many unremediated dyslexic and dysgraphic students have done this. It is of course a problem when any speed is needed in examinations. As he finds word processing a better option he should *never be required* to take any test in which handwriting is required.

His writing difficulties are so severe that when trying to write at speed it was impossible for me to read what he had written except that I also knew the prayer topic. He wrote 32 words (more or less) in one minute which would be a good speed for note taking and exams except that a marker would not be able to decipher most of it.

His other writing in capitals is however very readable and has obviously served him well. It suggests that an early intervention (at five or six years old) using cursive would have worked and supported his spelling better.

His dyslexia requires that he should always be *given extra time* in any examination type task to read and absorb questions and instructions. He may also need some extra time in tutorials to check that he has all the information he needs. Assignments will take him longer to organise and structure and so *extra time* should be negotiated where necessary.

Example spelling problems identified by John

These are all orthographic phase dyslexic-type problems showing John has made a lot of progress over the years. That is, they are advanced orthographic errors and the region of error lies usually with one letter, in one syllable or at a syllable boundary.

John has used as most dyslexics do the basic phonic skeleton drawn from the sounds of the word and then visualisation and rote memory to get to the best fit/correct spelling. This is a good basic strategy that he can now slowly extend if he wishes.

These are the examples of the misspellings given by John that he wanted to correct:

1 typical or typicle?
2 impact or empact?
3 bureau or burreau?
4 recruit or recrute?
5 vendor or vender – both are regarded as correct just use one
6 des or dis at the beginning?
7 proposition – propo-propa-prope-propi?
8 mitigation – miti- mita-mite?
9 first – fist – practise rolling the 'r' to detect it before consonants
10 relevant – rele-reli-rela?
11 decent or desent?
12 deliberately or deliberatly?

The five vowels in English each have two sounds – the short and the long. John needs to check that he can hear and even feel the slight differences in his mouth when he makes them. He then needs to be able to identify them in words. The consonants have much more detectable key features and it is important for him to be able to feel these differences in his mouth as well as hear them.

Addressing the particular problems raised by John

Linguistic rules

There are four suffixing rules ADD, DOUBLE, DROP, CHANGE Double and Drop are the most frequently needed.

Short vowel sounds and the DOUBLING rule:

> Hop, run, sit, tap, pot all contain the short vowel sounds. If we add anything to a single syllabled word after a short vowel we must double the final consonant – hop p ing, hop p ed, runner, running; sitting, tapped, potting, potter, stopping

Long vowel sounds are denoted by silent 'e'. The DROP rule

If we hear the long vowel sound in a single syllabled word it is denoted by a silent 'e' at the end. To add an ending we must drop the final 'e' and just add the ending, e.g.: hope – hop ing; tape – taping; rope – roping; have – having, love – loving, come – coming.

We can also apply the rules to other longer words:

- **bureau – burreau** which has the long vowel sound and which has the short? So which is the correct spelling? 'Bu –reau'. Burreau is pronounced like 'burrow'.

  accommodate, acomodate or accomodate? (Prefix ac –) commo -

Apply the rule – which is the correct spelling?

ADD rule

When adding consonant suffixes to whole or basewords we can just ADD the suffix unless it changes the meaning, e.g. king-ship, man-ly, care-less, wood-s, dry-ness, play-ful, forget-ful

Suffix –ly. This suffix means like (kingly), how (slowly) or when (lately). We simply ADD it after words ending in silent 'e'.

- **deliberate - ly** This word ends in silent 'e' so just ADD the consonant suffix – deliberately.

There are a few (eight) that do not obey this rule, e.g. 'Truly Mr Duly your ninth argument is wholly awful'. Also – judgment and acknowledgment.

More rules – final stable syllables

- **Typical or typicle?**
  a. -le is a final stable syllable for the sound 'L' at the end of words
  It is the most frequent one used at the end of words so when in doubt use -le.
  Use -le after a 'stick' or a 'tail' subtle, puddle rabble, gaggle, trouble, apple, raffle.
  Use -le in three and four syllabled words particle, capable, legible, noticeable, pinnacle.

  b. -el is also a stable final syllable and less frequent for 'L' at the end of words.
  Use -el when there are no 'sticks' or 'tails' before the 'L' sound, e.g. tunnel, funnel, trowel, bowel, towel.
  Use -el to keep 'c' and 'g' soft, e.g. cancel; chancel, angel

  c. -al is also a less frequent final stable syllable for 'L' at the end of words.
  Use -al after whole words, e.g. music -al, tropical, electrical, political, seasonal, sensational, portal
  Use -al after adjectives (describing words before nouns), e.g. local, central, regal, total.
  Use -ical and -al after silent 'e' words, e.g. type – typ -ical but you must DROP the silent 'e' recite – recital.
  A tiny number of words may need a 'funny', e.g. bridal – no dal-liance there!

2. Basewords

Most of the words we use are built on a baseword, e.g. FORM is the baseword for form, formed, reform, deform.

- **proposition.** To correct this spelling we need to use its baseword PROPOSE as the guide to spelling PROP -O-sition.

3. Funnies (or stories) and 'L'

- **principal or principle?** The principal is a person or a PAL. The principle is just a rule.

4. Meanings

- **dis- or des- at the beginning?**
  Dis- is a prefix. Learning the meaning of the prefixes we put in front of words can help. Prefixes such as dis-, re-, pre-, pro-, ab-, anti- etc.

  The prefix 'dis' means 'in two' or 'the opposite of', e.g. agree and disagree; order and disorder; trust and distrust.

  'des' is not a prefix but 'de' is. It means down, from or away and is used on words derived from Latin, e.g. describe de-scribe; de-stroy, de-liberate, de-form, de-struct.

  It helps if when saying these words for spelling that you use 'CITATION MODE' – that is articulating very clearly and precisely for spelling to distinguish, e.g. between dis - turb and de - struct.

5. Articulation – citation mode

- **Im-port or em-port?** These prefixes mean 'in' and 'into' and depending on context are interchangeable with 'in' and 'en', e.g. engage, invade, import, emblazon.

One of the best ways to remember which is correct in context is to ensure that citation articulation mode is used. This means in everyday speech the correct articulation is used, e.g. IM – port; IM-personal; EM – bargo, EM-phasis; IN-trigue, IN-correct; IN-vert; IM-minent, IM-pede, IM-perfect.

Can John hear and feel the articulatory differences between these prefixes? Does his ordinary speech allow him to note the differences?

6. Origins

There are only a few words – like 'relevance' and 'relegation' – that can cause problems. First look up the word in a 'good' dictionary. It will give you five things – spelling, pronunciation, meaning, origin in other languages, related words.

- **Relevant** -RE is the prefix meaning 'again' or 'away'. The word re-levance comes from the Latin 'levans' to raise up or levitate so we must spell it RE-LEvant.

The word 'relegate' comes from the Latin RE-LEGARE, meaning to banish or send away. RE-away and LEGARE to send.

- **Mitigation** miti or mita? Look up the word in the dictionary. It comes from the Latin 'mitis' meaning MILD. I would use the origin and the 'mild' story to remind me how to spell MITIGATION.

7. Phonics

These are the 44 sounds of the English alphabet. Sometimes two letters represent a single sound (e.g. six digraphs ph, th, th voiced, wh, sh, ch and 15 vowel sounds ea, ei ae etc).

There are also some rough generalisations that we learn implicitly during reading and that sometimes need to be taught to dyslexics, e.g.

- **Desent versus decent?** If we hear and feel the soft 's' sound in the middle of a two syllabled word it is usually represented by 'c' (c does not have a sound of its own – it is either 's' or 'k') thus decent, recent (decens and recens are words derived from Latin).

If we hear a 'z' sound in the middle of such a word it is usually represented by 's', e.g. de-serve, re-serve. The clue here is also the base word 'serve'.

If you put 's' between two vowels it usually says 'z': deserve, reserve, rise, use.

8. Cue articulation

- **Recruit or recrute?** There are some words that do not respond to logical analysis. 'Recrute' is an Old French spelling but how it changes is not clear. As there are only a few such words I would use a 'cue articulation' strategy. This means that I would say it as RECRU-IT as I was spelling it and thinking about it. Pursu-it is its friend.

9. Over-articulation

- **First or fist?** To detect the almost silent 'r' in words such as 'first' and 'burst' it helps to practice over articulating them to support spelling. The Scots are very good at this hidden sound and roll the 'rr'.

Thus John's 12 misspellings have revealed a need to extend his strategies for spelling. Nine out of the 12 CPSS have been used to illustrate this. The rest takes us into the realm of useful linguistic rules. There are many rules that govern our spelling system but some have a wider applicability than others. Over time and the case work on error interventions such as with John the most useful have emerged.

Casework with some younger writers using CPSS

1. Louise: six years five months

Transcript:

> 'Once upon \a time in a far away land lived a mer queen and a mer king.
> They had a littel girl called Pearl. Pearl was a beatifel girl but Pearls sister
> was very mean. Pearl did'ent like her xx sister but she dident mind. One
> day Pearl's evil antie made a postion to kill Pearls mum. Years later Pearls
> got rggttose by the minet. Pearls stepmother dide'nt know her mum
> gave Pearl the most preshers shell in the whole world. Pearl had lots of
> frends but her best frend was called Carle'

Louise writes at a speed of 8.3 words per minute, She is right handed and uses
a thumb over grip. This speed is in the average range. She has made eight
different spelling errors apart from one or two squiggles that could not be
read from the copy. There were 12 errors over all. The different errors were:

> dident, littel, beatifel, frends, antie, postion, minet, preshers

This is more than she should be making given her age and high ability
although they might be more typical in an average learner
   To correct these misspellings take just two words at any one time and
choose the most common words first, e.g.:

> **dident** Explain that the base words are 'did not'. In running speech we
> say 'did-nt'. Get her to articulate it as 'did-nt' and explain the comma is
> to show a letter is missing and should be in the place of that letter.
>   **littel** In speech we say 'litl'. Ask Louise to say it correctly for spelling.
> The final 'l' sound in words is represented by the stable final syllable –le.
> It is the most common spelling for the 'l' sound at the end of one-
> syllabled (one beat) words, e.g. litt-le, bubble, trifle, maple, ripple, table.
>   **beatifel** Louise has nearly spelled this difficult word correctly. Get her
> to say it first as she has spelled it e.g. 'beat – i – fell'. The baseword is
> 'beauty' - person full of beauty. The French origin of the word is 'beauté'
> (Think of 'beau', a man attentive to dress such as Beau Geste).
>   Ask her to syllabify and say it correctly as 'beaut-i ful'.
>   **Frends** – this is a common misspelling at this age. To remember the
> silent letter an easy method might be to try a 'funny'. 'I am going to fry
> the ends of my friends' and cue articulate it for spelling as 'fri-ends'.
>   **antie** – if she says this as she has spelled it 'ant – ie' she will hear and
> feel that something is missing. Again the 'u' is needed to draw out that
> sound. 'Auntie needs an uncle to help her out'.

minet – this word is spelled in the same way as something very small but is pronounced differently, e.g. mi-nute – 'A minute is very small, it is minute'.

I would not intervene on the other misspellings at this stage unless they reappear in other pieces of writing. If they do then:

postion – first say the word as she has spelled it: 'post – i – on' or 'pos – shun'.
    If the word is 'poison' it uses the second sound of 's' and that is 'z' as in (poi- zn).

An alternative reading may be that she intended to write 'potion'. In this case she needs to syllabify the word 'po - tion'. This is the open syllable po- with the long vowel sound. The final stable syllable '-tion' is the most common spelling of the (shun) sound at the end of words. Attention, mention, intention, traction, faction, reaction.

preshers – this is something valuable, it has a high price. Use 'price' to remind Louise that the spelling of 'precious' also has the soft second sound of 'c' in it, then syllabify for spelling 'prec - i - ous'.

In the case of a gifted seven year old it can be expected that reading and spelling are at the level of about a nine year old. If such a one produced writing with these misspellings it would raise concerns about the quality of the learning environment and/or potential dyslexic difficulties. If Louise has such difficulties she has done extremely well to make this amount of progress. Her work needs careful monitoring.

2. Alexander: seven years ten months, right handed rigid tripod grip, IQ 137

Information provided by parent:

- Has always avoided activities involving writing. However, always very neat at colouring (he won a prize in Reception for genuinely very neat colouring).
- 'Meltdowns' during Reception and Year 1 when asked just to write just his name on a card at home.
- Episode of significant distress at school during Year 1; told the teacher that he couldn't get what he wanted to write from his head onto the paper.
- Has consistently told us that he doesn't like the feel of the paper; also refuses to write after washing his hands until his hands are completely dry.
- Has refused to use a pencil at home, with preference for a pen.

- Prior to Year 3, used a pen with a rubber on the end so that he could rub out any mistakes. In Year 3, started to use a mechanical pencil that looks like a pen, and then moved onto a 'hexagonal' grip pencil (rather than a rounded grip pencil).
- Repeatedly sharpens pencil, so that it is as sharp as it possibly can be (generally a few times within just a few minutes; pencils don't last long).
- Has always preferred to print letters.
- Has previously refused to write cursive letters: 'Mummy, I don't like the silly squiggles.'
- Teachers' attitude in Years 1 and 2 was that any writing is better than no writing.
- Alexander is in top set for English in Year 3 and is now expected to write cursively (but no help is being given at school).

Other information

- Very early reader (could sign words before saying them).
- 'Streets ahead' according to Reception teacher when first started.
- Verbally articulate.

Transcript:

> Football
> Once apon atime a footballer lived with his wife in a mantion of a bildnd. But one day some antieces went missing! The footballer called the polece. They came in two seconds tlat! Then they called a Decetive. He serced all arond until he called are you sure you bought them!Owe he said I fogot I was gowing to get them for Christmas but I forgot! The end
> Dear mummy I had a relay good time In Denmark. The montains Here are superb! I wish you could be heer. See you In two weeks.
> Love Alexander
> PS I got a nue cat. His name is Mister tar ball. Beli beli

Spelling skill: 16 spelling errors. This is a higher error score than average approaching 15 errors per 100 words. The HMI criterion is that the pupil should make no more that five errors per 100 words by Years 6–7 and younger pupils such as Alexander will make more perhaps up to eight or ten per 100 so a score of 15 is of concern. It will of course be affected by the level of difficulty of the words selected, e.g, antiques, mountains. A list of his misspellings include:

apon, atime, mantion, bildnd, antoeces, polece, tlat, Decetive, serced, arond, Owe, gowing, relay, montains, heer, nue (fogot and forgot)

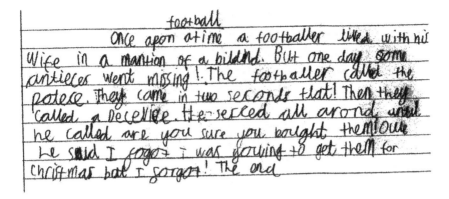

Figure 6.2 Alexander's writing, seven years ten months

Given his high IQ we should expect that he would be writing at a speed of 15 words per minute and spelling correctly all the words he uses in this piece of writing.

The overall impression given the high ability, early verbal ability and early reading competence, plus the overlarge and spiky writing put together with the meltdowns, and some rigidity of responses, the oversensitivity to the feel of paper etc. suggest he might be just on the Asperger dimension.

Premature babies (details in the communications) are more vulnerable to a range of difficulties and the patterns of them are very individual. Given Alexander's undoubted ability he will learn to overcome them.

However, I think the next few years may be critical for him. We want him to settle and enjoy what the current school is offering and also think about getting him ready for the transition to secondary school which may not be easy.

Spelling skills:
The errors show a good vocabulary that because of his reluctance to write has not developed as well as could be expected. Only *two errors* at a time should be addressed and checked to make sure the strategy has been effective.

- The first thing to improve spelling is to ensure that Alexander speaks clearly. He needs to practice **citation** mode for spelling. Listen to his ordinary speech to check he does pronounce words correctly, e.g. 'uh-pon' not 'a-pon'; 'fl-at'.
- He needs to learn to **syllabify** longer words for spelling, e.g. *de - tec - tive*.
- Baseifrds. Many words belong to a FAMILY or have a base word that tells you how to spell them. So it is important for Alexander to discover

the basewords in a paragraph of a story he is reading. He can use a marker to underline or put a ring round the **baseword**. This can begin by word processing his Football story with correct spellings to see if he can find any basewords, especially **Build; search; go; real.**

- There are also **compound words** such as foot ball; Christ's mass; for-got; up-on. Two proper words make up a new one.

As can be seen, beginnings and endings are added to some words to change their meaning. Beginnings are called PREFIXES (a-, ab-, anti-) and add-on endings are called SUFFIXES (-ing; -ed; -er etc.). These that Alexander has used are the most frequent. There are also four main rules that apply to suffixing – ADD, DOUBLE, DROP, CHANGE. These may need to be addressed later if you will collect a list of his common errors.

- To remind him how to spell POLICE I would encourage him to use a 'FUNNY' and MISARTICULATE it as PO - LICE.
- I think the only other error I would address at this point is the diphthong 'OU' in e.g. mountain and around. The sound of 'OU' in words is 'AH-OO'. Check that he can hear it and make the sounds clearly. Can he then reread his piece of text and find the two 'OU' words in it?
- Next get him to try to generate some more 'OU' words and keep a collection of them. How many can he find? E.g. round, found, sound, mound, pound, compound; mount, fount. Can he invent a sentence to include at least four of them to aid memory?

Save the next two misspellings until the need arises:

- There is one other letter combination that makes the AH-OO sound and that is OW but only half the time e.g. COW, CLOWN, TOWN, DROWN, HOW, NOW (how now brown cow)
- In other words OW makes the long vowel 'o' sound, e.g. show, mow, row, throw, tow, grow

The parents were then given details of CPSS, the seven-step protocol and SOS with explanations for why they are needed.

3. Charlotte: eight years five months

Transcript:

> Once upon a time there was a small Karmarlo(?) called Sunny who was quite famos and wanted to discover what humans were 'they are Big for one thing' hissed a snake and very tasty to a dirgo(?). But I'm not a

dirgo' Sunny iameditly replied ' That my friend is erelivent so screw your head back on you wanted to know.

But I dident ask you' he shouted, Well I Can Read Minds!' snake yelled as loud as a rock hiting a planet at high speed eavery thing in the whole world was silent you coud heare a rein drop hit the ground but soon after a stange//

Suggested spelling interventions

1   Ask Charlotte to proofread her piece of work to see if she can identify and correct any of her misspellings. If so she should put a ring round the area of error and concentrate on correcting that segment.

Only tackle two errors in a session and ensure she has learnt them securely before moving on. Tell her she is going to learn to be a 'Spelling detective'.

2   She misspells 'dident' so needs to say the word correctly for spelling in citation mode – 'did not' did-n't.

Some of her errors result from using an advanced vocabulary and she will gradually acquire the correct versions from contact with print. Some need correcting now but go carefully in case she is not yet ready.

The vowels have two different sounds a short sound and a long one in which the vowel 'says its own name' as in A E I O U.

3   **hiting** – Can Charlotte detect the short vowel sounds in one-syllabled words – hit, cap, run, hop as opposed to the long vowel sounds in hite, cape, rune, hope?

HOP and HOPE

If so, the RULE is that after the short vowel sound (in a closed syllable –CVC) when we add -ing then we must DOUBLE the consonant, e.g. hit-t-ing, hop-p-ing, run-n-ing and also hitt-er, hopp-er, runn-er.

The silent 'e' at the end of the word 'hope' is to tell us to make the long sound of 'o'. When we add -ing to this word we must drop the silent 'e' and just ADD -ing, e.g. hop-ing, mak-ing. (These are called suffixing rules and there are four main ones – ADD, DOUBLE, DROP, CHANGE.)

She could try counting how many examples there are of the doubling and drop rules in a page of her reading book to help remember the strategy.

4   **heare** – this is an overgeneralization of the long vowel/silent 'e' rule. When 'two vowels go walking the first one does the talking' (CVVC) and they make the long vowel sound anyway and so we do not need the silent 'e' to tell us this.

5   **eavery** – 'ea' is the long vowel sound (two vowels going walking). Spell 'very' and just add the short vowel 'e' as in 'e-very'

6   **stange** – this may be a slip of the pen or a slight articulation error. Check that she pronounces the three-letter blend 'str-' correctly and can feel the difference in the mouth between 'st-' and 'str-' and also hear it.

7   **famos** – this is a nearly correct spelling. The BASEWORD is **fame**. There are three spellings of the 'us' sound at the end of words – us, -ous and -ious.

   • After nouns we use –us, e.g. crocus, locus, circus, bonus, virus (nouns are the names of things.)
   • -ous is an adjective ending telling us how something is, e.g. famous, nervous, generous, dangerous.

   Keep this one in reserve in case she needs it later:

   • If the word has a 'sh' sound before the 'us' then we use -ious, e.g. vicious, malicious, fictitious, anxious.

8   **coud** – the spelling rationale for this one is lost in the mists of time. A writing strategy is recommended, e.g. 'could' and 'would' and 'should'. (See the writing practice suggested below.)

   The next two are best dealt with by getting them nearer to the correct version than perfect as yet, identify the baseword and articulate it clearly.

9   **erelivent** – start with correct articulation 'relevant' and syllabify i-rele-vant. Later point out the double 'rr' after the short vowel sound.

10   **iameditly** - im - mediate - ly, prefix 'im', we must double 'mm' after the short vowel sound.

4. Felix: 12 years seven months

Transcript:

> Legend has it they road deer carrying all there esentials deep unto the cave of Banishment. What they found was etraordinaryand even they didn't expected it. 10 stationary rock cat statues there eyes made of differant medium tear drop crystals.
>
> A As they enered there crystals glowed brighter and the eyes started to glow. The beast stepped down from their podiums and great them by saying, 'welcome gem masters, to the guild of stone'. After this the largest said
>
> 'I haven't seen young people reach the guild. You are well equiped and you must have been training to beat the creatures that lurck in the depths of the cave. Like you all of us were banesed at 6 six and have our two friends of the other elements. And yet again welcome to the guild.

There are nine different misspellings:

Two are homophones – **'road' and 'there' (x2), esentials; etraordinary; differant; enered; equiped; lurck; banesed**. The HMI criterion is that at this age pupils should make no more than five errors per 100 words. Felix has made 10 in 135 words which is high but not problematic when we examine the types of error.

First ask Felix to proofread his MS and see how many misspellings he can find and correct. List the ones he cannot correct and discuss the correct spelling, some suggestions follow. Do not try to tackle more than two at any session. Check the next day if he can spell the word(s) correctly.

If he cannot go over the explanation again and then ask him to write the word three times in cursive correctly from memory covering the word each time saying the NAMES of the letters.

- **Homophones** are common and are usually picked up in proofreading so Felix needs to reread his MS so that you can check he notices 'road' for 'rode' and 'there' for 'their' and can correct them. If he does not notice them then discuss 'ride' and past tense 'rode' and rodeo for horse riding trials. Point out that the road we drive along has asphalt on it so 'road' must contain the letter 'a' for asphalt. (oa is a vowel digraph and 'when two vowels go walking the first one does the talking – usually.) Here in r-oa-d we hear long vowel 'o' or the 'o saying its own name).

'There' refers to a place as in 'over there'. 'Their' refers to things that belong – their books, their essentials etc. the 'I own' things for them.

- **differant** – use '-ent' when the root word or baseword contains an 'i' or 'e', e.g. different, referent, proficient, recent, obedient, convenient, persistent. Use -ent to keep 'c and 'g' soft, e.g. innocent, intelligent.
- **lurck** – there is no need to use 'c' here. '-ck' is only used at the end of words to preserve the short vowel sound, e.g. back, tick, lock, muck, wreck.

Use '-k' after vowel digraphs, e.g. look, book, teak, leak, peak.

Here -ur and -or (ur) and -er (ur) sounds act like vowel digraphs, e.g. lurk, murk; work, Turk, perk.

Also use '-k' after a consonant, e.g. desk, task, link, tank, milk.

- **equiped** – the base word is equip. To preserve the **short vowel sound** we must follow the DOUBLING RULE for suffixing, e.g. HOP and HOPE.

Hop has the short vowel sound when we add the suffix -ed, -er, -ing we must DOUBLE the final consonant, e.g. hop-p-ed, hop -p -er, hop-p- ing.

If we want to preserve the **long vowel sound** we must DROP the silent 'e' and add the suffix, e.g. hop-ing, hop-ed, hop-er.

Felix's spelling would make us say equipe - d with long vowel 'I'.

The next four words have a characteristic in common:

- **esentials** – the base word is 'essence'.

After the short vowel sound we must use 'ss' to keep the short vowel pattern. Felix may be saying 'E - sential' which is incorrect for spelling.

- **etraordinary** – extra, ex - tra - ordinary
- **enered** enter, en - ter-ed
- **banesed** banish -ed

The main point with this last set of four is to ensure that he is articulating the base words correctly for spelling. He needs to use citation mode for spelling and proofreading as well as clear articulation in running speech and may need some attention to this.

Some final points on the cases

As can be seen, the suggested interventions have as their basis the 12 cognitive process strategies and then the four suffixing rules, the prefixes and suffixes and final stable syllables.

Having devised the CPSS strategies and procedures it was evident that they were just the first step in helping pupils and others correct their misspellings. They were the general strategies that any teacher could learn and use in their subject area as they were moving round the class helping with or correcting work.

The strategies could also be taught as mini lessons in tutor groups when a common misspelling was identified and they could be made part of a subject tutor's introduction of new and difficult or technical vocabulary.

As the numbers of case studies in the research increased it became evident that the linguistic rule category was expanding and required more technical knowledge than most teachers had or wanted. It was essential to try to narrow down these rules to the most essential and most common that would correct the most number of errors.

According to Hanna and Hanna et al. (1966) it is possible to spell 85 per cent of the English language with a knowledge of phonics and some basic rules although spellers complain that it is a very irregular language to learn. These researchers found that it was possible to programme a computer to spell 17,000 basic words with some 300 rules and knowledge of how sounds are transcribed and represented by alphabetic symbols – phonics.

However, they were dealing with rules governing letter order and frequencies often called 'surface rules' rather than with deep structure rules about word and syllable structure, morphemics and linguistics. Henry (1997) in the US suggested that with a knowledge of roots the rules governing only 14 words could teach all the spellings that an elementary school child might be expected to know. Her techniques were based upon different syllable structures but not a problem solving approach and were laborious.

However, these studies led to the idea of finding a set of words in a topic or subject area that would illustrate enough linguistic information to lead to the correct spelling of a large number of words. It was in this manner that **the 15 Spells** were identified.

The '15 Spells' represent 15 words and their structures and rules that when they are understood can lead to the correction of 20,000 or more misspelled words. This is because the English language is much more regular than people think. These interventions are more specialised and based on linguistics and morphemics but some are memorable and children like them. It gives them a feeling of power.

Pupils respond very well to these insights even from an early age and case examples from a range of subjects has been used to illustrate this. These interventions can also be made into mini lessons in class by English teachers and any other teacher who compiles a topic-based list for their subject area. As a school policy underachievement on a wide scale could be lifted by improving spelling and handwriting.

With better handwriting teaching linked to CPSS and the 15 Spells we may be able to reduce barriers to learning and significantly lift achievement.

A school topic-based approach to strategic spelling

In her MA project Schaapkins (2008) decided to test the value of introducing a small version of CPSS in Food Technology with Year 10 pupils. Pupils each year were given lists of technology words to learn but no specific techniques were offered to help them study the words other than to tell them to memorise them.

The spelling list was: design, technology, temperature, coagulation, protein, carbohydrate, analytic, evaluation, hygiene, ingredients, manufacture, recipe, specification, research, vitamin, mineral, polysaccharides, whisk, hazard, nutrition.

There were two mixed ability classes and one served as the control group and the other as the experimental group. The experimental group were given copies of the 12 CPSS list for personal use and each word was syllabified when it was introduced to give them an example to follow. The post-test results showed no significant improvement in spelling accuracy in the controls but significant improvements and a lowering of spelling errors in the experimental group.

'The 15 Spells'

Although many English spellers have learnt to spell accurately without ever having any knowledge of morphemics or linguistic rules, when they are introduced to them it can give them a special interest and pleasure. Spelling teaching instead of being laborious, a 'spelling grind', can be enjoyable and flexible more like a problem-solving piece of detective work.

With this principle in mind it was discovered about 15 words are needed to do this in English. The idea is that every school should develop a policy towards spelling which includes CPSS and every subject area should convert the principles and practices in the 15 Spells to their subject area vocabulary so that all the teachers would be reinforcing the same approaches rather than rely on sightword training alone.

The following is a list of the 15 KEY WORDS built round a trip on a Thames Sailing Barge which pupils from around the country can go on from Essex. They can be changed to fit topics on the Victorians, the Elizabethans and the Second World War in History or topics in Science, PE, Art, geography, and technology or can be devised for year groups and so on.

It incorporates the types of syllable:

- whole words;
- closed syllable CVC, CCVC, CVCC, cut, stop, perk;
- open syllables CV go, to ba-con, o-pen;
- prefixes in-, ad- re-;
- suffixes -ing, -ment, -ship, -ed, -es;
- final stable syllables -tion, -cian, -sion; -le, -ly;
- accented/unaccented syllables – referral, harass.

The list is based on the most frequently occurring errors made in the scripts and the most useful and generalisable rules to correct them. It includes:

- ADD, DOUBLE, DROP, CHANGE the four suffixing rules.
- THE L-F-S RULE.
- LONG and SHORT VOWEL RULES.
- SUFFIXING AND PREFIXING RULES.
- WO- AND WI- RULES.
- DIGRAPHS AND DIPHTHONGS.
- STABLE FINAL SYLLABLES.
- VOWEL R.
- AIR WORDS.

It is not a complete list. There are, for example, other useful hints on accent and stress and foreign words, but the above are more commonly needed. The 'rules' are best learned in context when they are needed. They can be used to 'front-load' the learning of new vocabulary or used to correct misspellings as illustrated in the casework.

The '15 Spells' for the barge trip

1 CUT (cvc) short vowel, closed syllable. DOUBLING rule for adding suffixes - cut-t-ing, putting, running, bedding, hopping, sitting, in polysyllables – rudder, potter, kipper, cutter.

2 HULL (cvcc) short vowel and l-f-s rule. Must double l-f-s after a short vowel in single syllables till, hill, pill; off, boff, sniff; hiss, miss (some exception words – if, gas, bus, yes).

3 ROPE (cvce) After long vowel sound in closed syllable, silent /e/ denotes long vowel sound. DROP silent /e/ when adding suffixes: roping, hoping, riding.

4 SAIL (cvvc) 'When two vowels go walking the first one does the talking, usually' rain, paint, cleats, load, tear. bear Just ADD suffix – raining, painted, cleated, loads.

5 COOK (cvvc) book, look, took, hook, good, double /oo/ short vowel sound, ADD rule, cooking MOON (cvvc) Long vowel sound /oo/ in noon, cool, saloon, zoom, room, tool, ADD rule – zooming.

6 LIST (cvcc) short vowel followed by double consonants simply ADD rule applies – listing, rushed, missed, rusting, posted. Master, lasting, faster, bath – dialect change in south of England from short to longer / ar/ sound.

7 BARGE (vowel r, ge) r changes a in words large, are, art, mart; e softens g -ge

8 WHEEL (wh digraph) teach /wh/ question words as a group. Teach the six consonant digraphs ch, ph, ch, sh, wh and th voiced and unvoiced.

9 LADEN (cvc/ic/id/in) open syllables: These words follow the long vowel rule in open syllables – o pen, ba con, spo ken, la den, to ken. Exceptions are: cabin, robin, rapid, vapid probably pronounced with the long vowels once or the effect of vowel 'i'.

10 WATER (wa /or/ and wo /ir/ rules. W changes the vowel sounds of 'a' and 'o' - war, ward, walk, warm. Work, world, whorl, word, worm, worst.

11 PAY (cvy) CHANGE rule. Change y to i when suffixing. Instead of the regular form payed and sayed we change 'y' to 'I' and add 'd' – paid, said, laid.

12 ROUND (diphthong /ou/ow sound is ah -oo or two sounds) ground, bound, found, sound, hound. rouse, louse; row, cow; oi diphthong in oil, boil, toil. ow is also a digraph low, row, know.

13 SIGN (cv - gn, silent letters) Family words will help with detecting some silent letters – sign, signal; bomb, bombardment. Some letters were once pronounced knife, knight, knave, knitting.

14 STABLE – final stable common syllables e.g. '-le' and '-ly'; '-tion, '-sion' and '-cian', '-us' and '-ous'.

15 PAIR '-air' and '-are' words. Pair, lair, stair and pare, stare, ware.

The Teacher's Orthographic Toolkit

- The Spelling Detective's Dictionary (see Chapter 7).
- The CPSS prompt list (on a green card).
- The 15 Spells on reverse side of the green card for the particular subject.
- A 'good' standard dictionary.
- A list of 10 to 20 subject specific words to practice CPSS.
- A school policy for spelling incorporating references to CPSS and the 15 Spells.
- A list of most frequently occurring vowel sounds, when in doubt choose the most frequent first, e.g.

Long vowel frequencies in rank order (Cowdery et al., 1994)

A a – e, ai, ei, eigh, ea
E ee, ea, ie, c-ei, e – e, eo
I i – e, igh, y – e,
O o – e, oa, ow
U u – e, eu
OO oo, ou, ui

Conclusions

The cognitive process strategies for spelling have been shown to be an effective method for intervening in orthographic phase dyslexic spelling errors. They have worked with undergraduates and now are shown to help dyslexic spellers improve their skills. As the case numbers have increased it was found that at least two years' progress in each year can be achieved with regular mini lessons.

The most important feature is that poor spellers, including dyslexics, can overcome their 'learned helplessness' and actually enjoy problem-solving work on their misspellings.

The strategies can also be imported into ordinary classroom work on spelling development and have also been shown to be beneficial. Capturing further evidence for this now needs a funded research project. The problem has been that once teachers see that CPSS works they just go off and do it incorporating it into their general repertoire because it seems such an obvious way to work. Parrant's research as early as 1988 showed how effective this could be in the general classroom in a junior school for reducing spelling errors.

However, many teachers are anxious about trying to teach spelling because their knowledge of how best to do it is limited and no one has shown them how it might be possible. This is especially important in initial training so that every teacher becomes responsible for spelling development in their subject area as they introduce new vocabulary. Many English teachers will be doing this but they need the support of colleagues and a school policy on spelling and handwriting would help them.

Although schools have been encouraged to record the specialist vocabularies for their subject areas and teach pupils the spellings, the teachers have had limited spelling development knowledge and resort to encouraging rote learning and testing. Thus CPSS and the 15 spells are projects waiting for adoption.

Just as special needs, now termed 'additional needs', is considered to be every teacher's concern so spelling and handwriting needs in the subject areas have to become the remit of every teacher to contribute to their development. This is crucial in the primary or elementary school years to gain the improvements needed and then again in the secondary school to support those with residual difficulties as they acquire new and more technical vocabularies.

7   Teaching dictionary skills and the 'Spelling Detective's Dictionary'

Introduction

Dictionary skills are important and dyslexics in particular need specific help to learn them because they do not just absorb them by being around and using books. We need a secure knowledge of the alphabet in order to use a variety of resources such as dictionaries, indexes, telephone directories, brochures, references and lists of various kinds.

Dyslexics have basic difficulties in learning the names and sounds of the letters of the alphabet although they may be very bright and do not 'crack' this code easily if left to their own devices and by the usual methods of teaching, whether 'Look and Say' or 'Phonics'.

It is most important to buy a 'good' dictionary. This will contain five different types of information on each of its words: spelling, pronunciation, meaning, origin, related words.

Although computers can offer a dictionary and thesaurus, keying in the question does not give all five pieces of information, nor does it give practice in finding the place of the information in a text or list. Very large dictionaries will also contain the history of words and can be used as a classroom resource for the teacher.

In this chapter techniques for supporting alphabet learning are detailed. In earlier chapters (1, 4 and 5), emphasis was given to teaching the letter names as their sounds are being taught. However, the sequence of the alphabet is also useful knowledge and grandparents often enwcourage children to recite it before they go to school. Being able to recite the alphabet does not of course mean that children understand or know how to use it.

Explicit teaching of the sequence of the alphabet during the early years is useful and many teachers group the letters and children sing the alphabet song: 'abcdefg – hijklmn – opqrstu –vw – xyz.'

For dyslexics the problem initially is not one of sequencing but learning the arbitrary sounds and names of the alphabet. Even when they do eventually learn to read and write as most of them do, they then have difficulties with the sequence and need alphabet training, such as that described below which is to be found in all the APSL schemes.

The names of the vowels are particularly useful because the long vowel sound is actually the name of the letter, as in A, E, I, O, U. When we spell a word aloud we need to do it by the names of the letters not their sounds because the sounds will not always make sense, e.g.: s – t – r – e – a – m; s – a – i – d.

Because dyslexics have acquired alphabet knowledge late it will mean their skimming and scanning skills are poor just as their reading is slow and often hesitant. All these skills benefit from direct training and the earlier the skills can be acquired the more fluent they can become.

Left and right confusions

Dyslexics and many other children may confuse left and right, not necessarily because they do not know which is their preferred hand, but because of their labelling or naming difficulties.

One way of helping them with this is to teach them to look at the backs of their two fists, and point the index fingers and thumbs out away from each other as far as possible (right angles). The left hand will make its own capital letter, the capital L shape.

B and D confusions

The lower case letters 'b' and 'd' in the print form look very much like each other and may be reversed in early writing because the eyes may be prone to scanning from right to left, or the child may be mirror writing. Assigning the correct label to two such similar forms can be difficult to do consistently.

One way in which this can be achieved is to use the capital letter forms which are distinct and this is frequently seen in dyslexic scripts. Even when they do know the difference the capitals may have become a motor habit.

During alphabet training and spelling children who have B and D confusion are taught the 'two fists strategy'. Just below the desk line so no one else can see they close their two fists with knuckles together and thumbs raised to 'make a bed'. The left fist shows the 'b' at the head and the right fist makes the 'd', the end of the bed. Eventually a quick left-hand fist will remind them which is which and thus the problem is overcome. This is especially easy where cursive writing with lead-in lines is used as part of the training process.

Alphabet arc

Alphabet training is an essential component of the G and S, Hickey and TRTS specialist programmes. A set of wooden upper case letters/capitals is needed. The pupil is asked to take a pile of the jumbled-up letters and lay them out in alphabetical order in an arc, naming them as s/he does so.

The point at which performance falters is noted and then letter recognition of the letter at which the error occurs is taught by showing, naming and feeling the letter. The pupil is asked to trace it with the forefinger of the dominant hand, and visualise and verbalise what is seen. The letters are put back in the pile and the pupil is asked to lay them out again, naming them to see how far he or she can get this time. Capital letters are used for this because their names are constant.

Use of a 'feelie bag' and alphabet tracking games can be used to promote alphabet knowledge. For example, the pupil draws a line from one alphabet letter to the next in what looks like a random scatter of letters and if they get the sequence correct a dinosaur or rabbit appears. One source of these is *Teaching Reading Through Spelling (TRTS) Book 2* (Cowdery et al., 1994). Felted and sandpaper letters to trace with the forefinger of the writing hand can also be used in the training process.

Dictionary quartiles

Once the alphabet sequence has been mastered then dictionary skills can be taught, e.g.:

- Ask the pupil to open a normal household or school dictionary (Concise Oxford or Chambers) at the approximate mid point by eye ten times in a row and record which letter of the alphabet comes up each time. It will be M. M for Middle.
- Ask the pupil to open it again at the first quarter (quartile) and it will open at E for Eggs.
- Discuss why it could be helpful for finding words beginning with M and E.
- In another session ask the pupil to find the first, middle and third (which will be S for Sausages) quartiles, recording the results each for ten times.
- In subsequent sessions get the pupil to study the letters of the alphabet to be found in each of the quartiles, e.g.:

  1 **A** B C D (APPLES)
  2 **E** F G H I J K L M (EGGS)
  3 **N** O P G R (NUTS)
  4 **S** T U V W X Y Z (SAUSAGES)

Each pupil should invent his or her own mnemonic for A E N S. One pupil in TRTS invented 'African Elephants Need Sun'.

- Ask why the number of letters in each quartile are not equal.
- Put out the first letter of each quartile and ask the pupil to complete each quartile.
- Ask the pupil to find a specific word in the S category but try to do it in only **four moves**.
- Repeat this with the word Dog in the D category.

Make sure this can be done easily before moving on to more difficult locations. Give plenty of practice in this kind of dictionary work but keep the sessions short – about five minutes.

Skimming and scanning skills

Skimming is the ability to run the eyes down a newspaper or page in a book to identify what the text is about or the key points to focus on. It is very difficult for dyslexics initially because of their poor or slow reading and lack of time over the years in experience with text.

They need to be taught that the main points in simpler texts and newspapers are usually to be found in the first and the last sentences or paragraphs.

Titles, headlines and pictures tell what the rest of the story is about and envelopes with several newspaper headlines can encourage pairs work discussions. On other occasions a set of pictures can be set out for pairs to discuss appropriate headlines. The technique is to discuss what the picture is about, write a descriptive sentence about it, then hone this into a headline. It helps if a series of pictures with headlines are discussed to show what sub-editors do. Some pupils will be particularly good at this.

The following extract and exercise was taken from Royce-Adams (1977):

> With a food surplus, the Pueblos were able to turn their attention to other activities besides locating or growing food. In one particular area – pottery making – the Pueblos developed a high degree of artistry. Potters became artists and developed individualised techniques, painting fine-lined geometric designs as well as reproductions or life forms on their vessels. Paints were improved and pottery has been found that contains three or four different colours. (From *Columbus to Aquarius*, Dryden Press 1975).

Identify the main point of this extract and then decide which of the following writing patterns is exemplified in it.

a   illustration – example
b   definition
c   comparison – contrast
d   sequence of events
e   cause and effect
f   description
g   mixture – state which

In pairs, pupils can then discuss how to rewrite the Pueblo passage in each of the different patterns to get the feel of the different options available in writing any passage.

In other sessions they can be given a page of text or a newspaper article and be asked to try to find five facts in one minute.

Scanning is the skill we use when running our eyes down a list or piece of writing to find the one we are looking for. It may be a word in a dictionary or the local plumber in Yellow Pages and a friend in the telephone directory if it is not in the memory of the mobile phone.

In this task we have a word or name in mind and are looking down a list to find it. It is thus important to have good dictionary and spelling skills for this task as well as keeping the focus.

Practice can be given by showing them how to use the forefinger to run down the page or list with the eyes following down to find the key word. Plenty of practice will speed up this skill.

Speed reading

The same technique can be applied to rapidly reading a text in speed reading training. The index finger is drawn down the centre of the page while the eye follows, taking in as much of the text as possible. Over the trials the finger is drawn down faster and faster and surprisingly the sense is not lost in the process.

Speed courses can speed up reading from 400 words per minute to 1,600 words per minute in many cases. A little of this type of training in recovering dyslexics can be helpful because they can become stuck in reading at a particular rate when it may be possible to speed up a little.

Contributions to English spelling

Settlers and successive invaders have left their marks on the English language. After the Iron and Bronze ages the **Celts** were the original inhabitants of the British Isles. They had spread or probably walked across what is now the North Sea from Europe. We call them the Ancient Britons and they spoke Celtic.

The **Romans** invaded in 43 AD from across the Channel and conquered most of the land and eventually settled. They spoke Latin and many Celts, impressed by the Roman way of life, adopted their practices and Latin terms became common alongside the Celtic ones e.g. villa, village, villain, decapitate, expect, just, finish, situate.

In the fifth century the Roman legions were recalled to Rome to defend their homeland from invaders from Eastern Europe. They left behind many Romans who had retired and settled in Britain.

In the seventh century **Anglo Saxons** from northern Europe invaded and settled in the Eastern part of the country with its good farming land. These tribes were mainly Angles, Saxons, Frisians and Jutes from areas now known as Holland and Germany. They brought their own languages, which were mainly Anglian and West Saxon. Anglo-Saxon is what we now call Old English. Essex became the home of the East Saxons, Wessex the West Saxons, Sussex and Middlesex likewise. Some of the words they gave us are shut, fight, strike, new, head.

The **Ancient Britons** were driven to the western parts of Britain and their language survived there as Welsh, Gaelic, Erse (Irish Gaelic) Manx and Cornish.

The **Vikings** coming from what are now Norway and Denmark began systematic invasions from about AD 800 and eventually settled the whole of the eastern part of the country from London to the lowlands of Scotland. Alfred, King of Wessex stopped them from invading the whole country. The language of these invaders was Norse – knife, hut, sofa, stool, and 'by' – the word for a town – Whitby, Ormsby, Grimsby. They also gave us the words – knock, froth, slaughter, ransack and hit.

The **Normans** invaded in 1066. They were 'Northmen' descended from Vikings who had settled in northern France. William of Normandy conquered all of Britain except Scotland and Wales. Norman French was spoken at court and by the aristocracy for the next 300 years – table, chair, palace, duke, estate, mirror, mansion, manor, viscount.

By the thirteenth century there were three languages in use: Latin for the scholars, lawyers, ecclesiastics and philosophers; French for the aristocracy; and English for the rest. English began to be taught in schools from about 1300. In 1362 English became permissible in the law courts and in 1363 Parliament opened up again in English as the French influence declined. Chaucer's *Canterbury Tales* was written in a mixture of English and French around 1373.

In 1477 William Caxton set up the first printing press in Westminster. By this time Northerners, East Anglians, Londoners and West Country people spoke such a mixture of the different languages and dialects emerging from them that they hardly understood each other. Like Chaucer, Caxton selected the language of London and the court as his choice of dialect. 'Modern' English is thought to have originated from about 1500.

The Bible and prayer book were finally printed in this modern English and became distributed widely in Tudor times.

Dr Samuel Johnson published the first dictionary in 1755. It was from this period that 'correct' spelling began to become important. Prior to this, spelling was a matter of individual choice. Clerks wrote and spelled in any way they could that would transmit meaning.

While all this development and change was in progress the language of scholars and the Church was still Latin and Greek. These were originally taught in the emerging school system and without them entrance to universities was prohibited well into the twentieth century.

It is frequently said that English spelling is illogical and confusing but this is not true. It is complex because it is derived from so many roots. Later, as the British Empire extended, new words were acquired from other cultures such as Hindi and Arabic.

English is not to be regarded as a badly organised phonic system that needs simplifying so that it is modelled on phonically regular languages like Italian and Turkish. It is a **morphemic system** based on a phonic structure with several roots. In other words, meaning governs English spelling and has its roots in the rich history of the language. Individual words may be made up from parts in the different languages, e.g.: TELE + VISION (Greek + Latin); BAN – ISH - MENT (OE (ban) + OE (-ish) + Latin --ment).

Other words have been adopted from new European neighbours and old civilisations as and when required. The result is that English is an ever-changing and developing language that has become a world language and the most useful for explaining complex and abstract ideas and phenomena. When we do not have a word for something new we make one up. This is often forbidden by the 'guardians of the language' in other cultures.

New offshoots of the language are also developing. An early one was 'pidgin English' in the Pacific Islands; now we have 'Franglais', 'Spanglish' and 'Pinglish' coming along as well as 'Computerese' and the ever present 'Slang'.

The spelling detective approach

Although some rote learning is necessary, particularly in the early stages of dyslexia, there can be too much of it. Sometimes it is the only strategy that dyslexics know other than visualising. Rote learning is not at all popular with more able and gifted pupils and many dyslexics are in these categories.

Pupils' responses to CPSS in Chapter 6 show their pleasure and relief when they discover they can find a way to spell accurately using a problem-finding and problem-solving approach.

By using a problem-solving approach to detect the structure, origins and meanings of words and a strategic approach to spelling as in CPSS, pupils can learn to enjoy learning to spell and correcting misspellings. It is also creative and relieves them of 'learned helplessness'. It is about 'engage brain' activities.

To distinguish it and encourage them in the problem solving and analysis of their misspellings it was called the 'Spelling Detective Approach'.

However, teachers who were often non-specialists in such studies and had learnt in the Look and Say regime themselves did not always know how to help them. The materials provided by the national guidelines and commercial schemes were heavily based in the rote training ethos with a few rules and structures in support.

Several hundred teachers who had studied on the MA SpLD and MA SEN programmes learned about CPSS and tried it in casework but often found it very difficult to provide the range of strategies that were needed and so the idea of a Misspelling Dictionary developed that would support them. An example of this can be found at the end of this chapter and the full dictionary is at www.routledge.speltec/.

Word structures and spelling

Basewords, roots and affixes have already been referred to. In summary:

- **A baseword** is a word to which affixes are added to change its meaning, e.g. FARM and FORM are basewords for farming and forming.

- **Affixes** are meaningful syllables that can be added to basewords, e.g. prefix re- and suffixes -ing and -ed make FARMING, FORMING, FARMED, FORMED, REFORM, REFORMING.
- **Roots** or **Stems** are not whole words but meaningful units that make words when added to other words or given an affix. FER is a root. With it we can make REFER, PREFER, INFER, REFERENCE, PREFERENCE, INFERENCE, REFEREE.
- **Syllables** are beats in words, e.g. PAN – CAKE has two syllables or two beats. There are six types of syllable:
  - whole words;
  - closed syllables – CVC bed, CVCC best, CCVC spot, CCVCC frost;
  - open syllables – CV to, go, ba-con, o-pen;
  - prefixes;
  - suffixes;
  - final stable syllables – -le, -ly, -ible, -able, -ment, -tion, -al, -el, -sion, -cian, etc.

Prefixes and suffixes have their own meaning and change the meaning of the word they are with which may be a noun or a verb. Added to verbs suffixes are called 'inflectional suffixes' and change the tense, e.g. pass, passing, passed, passes.

It can be very helpful to know the meaning of some of the more common prefixes we use. Suffixes tend to be more obvious. The three main sources of our affixes are Old English, Latin and Greek.

Some prefixes

Old English	Latin	Greek
After-	ambi- before	amphi-
For- away	anti-/ante-/ anci- against,	anti- opposite
Fore- before	opposite	dys- ill, difficult
	dis – in two, negative extra- on	arch- first
	the outside	
Forth-	inter- between	hemi- half
Mid- with	into- into, within	hetero- other
Mis- wrong	multi- many	homo- same
Off- away, from	ne-, non- not	hyper- above
On- on	ob- in front of	hypo - below
Over- above	per- through	meta- among
Sum- half	post – after	mono- single
Thorough-	pre- before	peri- round
Twi- double	re- back, again	poly- many
Under- below	semi- half	pro- before
	sub- under	proto- first
	super-, supra- above	syn- together
		tele- far

Suffixes

Most of the suffixes in common use derive from Old English, e.g.:

- **O.E.**: -craft, -dom, -fast, -hand, -hood, -ing, -ish, -le/-l/-el, -less, -ly, -ness, -ock, -ren, -right, -ship, -scape, -some, -teen, -ty, -ward, -wise, -worth.
- **Latin:** -able/-ible/-uble, -ance/-ence, -escent, -form, -tion/-sion, -ment, -tude, -ism, -ite.
- **Greek:** -isk, -itis, -gen, -et/ -ete, -id.
- **French:** -age, -ure.
- **Spanish:** -dor/dore

Synonyms, antonyms, homonyms and homophones

- Synonyms – different words having the same meaning (Greek – onoma 'name').
- Antonym – words with opposite meanings.
- Homonym – words that sound the same but have different meanings and origins (fair meaning: pale or blonde, just, pleasing looks, bright and clear dry weather, periodic event with stalls and amusements, adjustment of curves in ship-building; (fare meaning: to travel, a fee, food, getting on or succeeding, to happen well or ill, to be in a particular state).
- Homophone – pronounced the same as another word but has a different meaning (to, too, two; bow and bough; fair and fare)

The Spelling Detective's Teacher's Toolkit

- A 'good' dictionary per two pupils.
- A set of wooden capital letters of the alphabet.
- A 'feelie' bag to hold the letters.
- Sets of lower case letter cards for word-building.
- Emery paper cut-out letter cards, lower and upper case.
- A set of local telephone directories.
- A set of age relevant study books for skimming and scanning exercises.
- A collection of newspapers for alphabet exercises.
- 'Surprise' envelopes for pairs containing headlines, no pictures.
- 'Surprise' envelopes for pairs containing news pictures without headlines.
- The Spelling Detective's Dictionary.

The Spelling Detective's Dictionary – some examples

The full version can be downloaded at www.routledge.com/9781138223158 or particular words can be accessed at the same site. Send any good examples of your own (no mnemonics) to www.ldrp.org.uk for inclusion in our dictionary.

Part of the first quartile A to C

a

1   A is the indefinite article and usually has the unstressed short vowel sound (-uh-) as in 'a book', 'a person'.

abroad – (uhbrord)
abrord, abrowd:
1   Syllabify the word for spelling (ab - road) and (a - broad).
2   Teach prefix 'ab' meaning 'from'.
3   Look for the 'road' in 'abroad', 'Get on the road and go abroad'.

absolutely
absouletley, absousletly, absoustly, absulutly, abosultly, aboutaly, aboustly, absolutly, absultly
1   Syllabify and articulate clearly for spelling (ab-so-lute-ly).
2   Identify the basewords 'solve' and 'solution' from the Latin 'absolutus'.
3   Teach prefix 'ab', meaning from.
4   Teach 'so-lute' with long vowel (O) in open syllables: 'so' to' 'no' and 'go'.
5   Teach the long vowel pattern (-VCe), denoted by silent 'e' in (-lute).
6   Simply ADD final stable syllable '-ly'.

actually
actully
1   Identify the base word 'actual'.
2   Overarticulate and syllabify for spelling (act - u - al).
3   Simply ADD final stable syllable -ly after a consonant.

addict
adict
1   Articulate clearly and syllabify for spelling (ad - dict).
2   After a short vowel sound in a two syllabled word there must be two consonants to preserve the short vowel pattern (- VCCV -) and hold the vowel in.
3   Teach the suffix rule DOUBLE 'a - d - dict' to preserve the short vowel pattern, e.g. addict, rabbit, puppet.

adventure
adventurus, eventruse, evetchers
1   Identify the baseword 'venture' with the prefix 'ad-', meaning from.
2   Syllabify for spelling (ad - vent - ure).
3   Note the long vowel sound and pattern (- VCe) denoted by silent 'e' in (- ure).

4   Teach the DROP rule when attaching suffixes to words with silent 'e' endings, e.g. 'ad - vent - ur - ous'.
5   The suffix '-ous' is an adjectival ending, e.g. adventurous, nervous, jealous.
6   The suffix '-us' is a noun ending e.g. circus, virus, bonus and is also an ending for Latin words, e.g. minimus, calculus, Ranunculus, narcissus.

aeroplane, plane, aerobus – but airplane (not airoplane), aircraft, airbus, airport
1   This is a compound word made from 'aero' and 'plane'.
2   'Aero' is a Greek word meaning 'air' – we now use it as a prefix.
3   Other words using the prefix are: aerobatics, aerobics, aeronaut.
4   We can convert the compound word 'aeroplane' to English words 'air' 'plane', e.g. airplane, airbus, airport.

again
agen, agn, agian
1   Articulate clearly and syllabify for spelling (a - gain).
2   Note the long vowel sound and pattern in the second syllable (- VVC).
3   Teach the two vowel rule – 'when two vowels go walking the first one does the talking and usually says its own name', as in (- ai -) again, rain, train, main.
4   (Uh - gen) is what we hear in running speech.
5   'Agian' is a result of 'spelling by eye' and from the over-exercise of Look and Say.

allowed
alowed, aloud, alaud
1   Articulate and syllabify the word for spelling (all - ow).
2   Teach the DOUBLING rule that after a short vowel sound in two syllabled words we need to have two consonants so we double 'l', e.g. 'al - l - ow', swallow, follow, marrow, mellow, tomorrow, yellow.
3   The word comes from the Latin words 'ad - locare' and 'ad laudare'. In English we 'assimilate' ad - low to allow it makes it easier to pronounce
4   'To allow' or permit is the basic verb to which we ADD the past tense ending '-ed', e.g. allow - ed, passed, picked.

always (and already etc.)
alway, allway, allways, allwas, allways, allwaz, allwase,
1   Articulate and syllabify for spelling (all - way -s).
2   Note that it is a compound word made up from 'all' and 'ways'.
3   Teach the 'all, well, full, till rule' that when these words are added to others to make a compound word they must drop one 'l', e.g. all + ways = al - ways, also, alright, already, altogether, almost, welcome, helpful, until.

also

aslo

1   Overemphasis of a Look and Say approach in reading can cause this misspelling.
2   Teach clear articulation and syllabification for spelling (al - so) – the feel of the sequence of the consonants in the mouth gives the concrete clue.
3   Note that it is a compound word made up from 'all' and 'so'.
4   Teach the 'all, well, full, till rule' that when these words are added to others to make a compound word they must drop one 'l', e.g. all + ways = al - ways, also, alright, already, altogether, almost, welcome, helpful, until.

amount

ammount, amout, amant (dialect), amo

1   Articulate clearly and syllabify for spelling 'a - mount'.
2   Teach the 'ou' sound as a diphthong a double vowel sound (ah-oo').
3   The 'ou' diphthong is used in the middle of words and the 'ow' diphthong at the end of words, e.g. a - mount, fount, grout, pout; how, now, brown, cow.
4   Check the articulation of the '-nt' end blend to capture nasal 'n' before 't' – hold nose and try to say some '-nt' words: amount, tent, sent.
5   Very few words beginning with 'am' double the 'm'; they are usually specialist scientific words, e.g. ammonia, ammeter, Ammonite and ammunition.

amusement

amusment

1   Identify the baseword 'muse'; see note 5 above in 'amount'.
2   The long vowel (U) in '- use' is denoted by the silent 'e' pattern (- VCe) as in use, muse, fuse.
3   Teach the ADD suffixing rule – after a vowel just add consonant suffix -ment, amuse -ment, advertisement.

analysis

analiis

1   Articulate clearly and syllabify for spelling: 'an - al - y - sis.
2   It is a Greek word meaning to separate into parts.
3   Misarticulate to -cue for spelling e.g. (ana- ly - sisi).
4   Like lying on a couch for analysis.

angel

agel

1   The misspelling 'agel' indicates difficulties in detecting nasal 'n' before 'g' and 'd' and 't'.
2   Hold nose and try to say words such as 'sing', 'send', 'sent', 'in'.

3   Cue articulate and syllabify for spelling (an - gel).
4   The stable final syllable ending '-el' is used to keep the 'g' and 'c' soft in words, e.g. ang - el, cancel, parcel.

animal
anamal, aminal, animall
1   Syllabify and articulate clearly for spelling (an - i - mal).
2   The doubling rule does not apply at end of multisyllabled words even after the short vowel.
3   The stable final syllable ending '-al' is used for adjectives and nouns, e.g. total, petal, medal, pedal, regal, metal.
4   And when there is a whole word before it, e.g. musical, electrical centrifugal.

annoyed
anoyed, annoying, anoy, anoyying, eynoy
1   Articulate clearly and syllabify for spelling (an - noy).
2   After a short vowel sound we must have two consonants to hold the vowel in so here we must DOUBLE the next consonant a - n - noy, annual, annexe.

another
a nother, anothere, a never, anover
1   Teach this is a compound word made from 'an' and 'other'.
2   'nother' is not an English word.
3   Teach (- th -) sound for dialect (- v -).
4   '-er' is a most commonly used final stable syllable for the unstressed (-ur) sound at the end of words as in other, mother, teacher, learner, baker.
5   '-ere' says (-ear) as in 'here' and has the long vowel sound and pattern (- VCe).

antiques
anteces
1   Cue articulate for spelling, e.g. anti - queues.
2   Use the word family, e.g. anti-quated, anti-quarian, anti-quaries.
3   Emphasise the qu for the /kwa/ sound.
4   Show the French influence on pronunciation as /an-tiques/.

any
eney, eny, anthing, ainything, enything, aney
1   Use cue articulation for spelling and say 'any' as with an Irish dialect.
2   Syllabify for spelling (an - y).
3   The '-y' at the end of words is used for the sound (-ee) as in an-y, mummy, baby, puppy, daddy.
4   'Taxi' is an exception and is an abbreviation of 'taximeter'.

approximately

aproxamatly, approxamatly, approximatle

1   Identify the baseword 'proximate'.
2   Articulate it clearly for spelling (prox - i - mate).
3   The prefix 'ad-' is attached to proximate to make 'adproximate' and by assimilation becomes ap - proximate.
4   We must DOUBLE the consonant after a short vowel sound in a multisyllabled word: a - p - proximate, apple, apply, application.
5   Note the long vowel (A) sound in the final stable syllable, '- ate' denoted by the silent 'e' pattern (- VCe).
6   After silent 'e' endings we can simply ADD consonant suffixes such as '-ly', e.g. approximate - ly, disconsolately, lately, purely, safely.

aquarium

acqweriam

1   Identify the baseword 'aquatic' from the Latin word 'aqua' for water.
2   q is always followed by 'u' in English words – 'qu' as in quake, queue, quick.
3   The sound of 'qu' is (kw) in words – quick, quite, quake.
4   The sound of 'quar' in aquarium is (- kwere -).
5   The final stable syllable is '-ium' a Latin ending for singular items, the Latin plural is aquaria, or we can use the English plural '-s' ending aquariums.

area

earea

1   When vowels are followed by consonant 'r' they change their sounds as in (ar - e - a)
2   The initial syllable also has the long vowel sound because of the following '- e -', e.g. are -a. pare, tare, fare, ware, mare.
3   You might cue or misarticulate it with the long vowel (A) to remind you, as in (A - rea)
4   Or you can link it to another space word, e.g. arena.

argument

arguement

1   Identify baseword 'argue'.
2   Teach suffix rule DROP when words end in silent 'e', e.g. 'argu - ment'.

armour

armer, armor, armur, ama

1   Syllabify for spelling (arm - our).
2   Use meaning to aid spelling, e.g. 'we' protect 'our' 'arms' in armour plated.
3   The US spelling is 'armor' and links with 'armorial' in heraldry.

around

arand, arowd

1   Teach correct articulation in citation mode 'a-round'.
2   Teach diphthong 'ou' sound as 'ah-oo'.
3   Identify the families of words with the 'ah-oo' sound in them, e.g. round, sound, pound, mound, ground, found, bound, bound; out, lout, pout, stout, grout, sprout, trout, bout, rout, doubt.

arrived

arived, arivd

1   Identify the baseword 'arrive'.
2   After the short vowel 'a' we must double the next consonant in two syllabled words to preserve the short vowel pattern (VCCV -).
3   The word derives from the Latin 'ad' meaning to and 'ripa' meaning shore 'adripa', over time is assimilated and 'arriva' arrives
4   When adding past tense endings to verbs ending in silent 'e', we must DROP silent 'e' and attach '-ed', e.g. arriv – ed.

ask, asking

arsk, asing, aks

1   Pronounce the word as with a Northern dialect with short vowel (a) for spelling.
2   Teach end blend '- sk' as a whole joined writing unit in a - sk, task, mask.
3   Simply ADD suffix '-ing' to this blend – asking, masking.

attention

attenshion, atention, attenshun, attentoin

1   Identify the baseword 'attend' and syllabify for spelling (at - tend).
2   Teach DOUBLING rule, that after a short vowel we need two consonants to hold in the vowel so here we must double 'at - t - end'.
3   Teach final stable syllable '-tion' is the most common spelling of the (-shun) sound e.g. distraction, vacation, dictation, insulation, ambition, elation.
4   Note that 'attend - tion' has been assimilated to 'attention', contend to contention.

auntie, aunty

arnty, anty, arntie, anuty

1   This is the one word beginning with 'au' that is not pronounced 'aw' as in Autumn, August, automatic.
2   Use cue articulation for spelling, e.g. 'awn - ty'.
3   Note that the final (ee) sound in English words is represented by final '-y', e.g. aunty, mummy, baby.
4   The diminutive form is to ADD '-ie' to some words, e.g. aunt - ie, nannie.

autumn

atome, autum

1 Syllabify and articulate clearly for spelling (au - tumn).
2 Teach the vowel digraph 'au' is pronounced as (aw - or) in autumn, August, augur, augment.
3 We mainly use 'au' at the beginning of words for (aw) sounds.
4 Check that short vowel (-u-) sound can be identified in the second syllable 'um'.
5 Use family of words to aid correct spelling, e.g. au - tumn, autum - nal (from Latin autumnus).

aviary

avary

1 Articulate clearly and syllabify the word for spelling (a - vi - ar - y).
2 Note the long vowel sound in the first syllable it is called an open syllable as in - a - viary, ba - con, o – pen; there is no consonant to close off the vowel.

baby

babby, babey

1 Identify the base word 'babe'.
2 Note the long vowel sound in the syllable denoted by the silent 'e' pattern (- VCe).
3 Teach the DROP rule for silent 'e' when adding final 'y' to make the (ee) sound – bab - y, mummy, daddy.
4 Note the dialect word 'babby' with the short vowel sound.

back

bake

1 Pronounce 'back' precisely with the short vowel 'a' sound (ba - ck).
2 Pronounce 'bake' with long vowel sound denoted by the silent 'e' pattern (- VCe) to feel and hear the differences between the two words.
3 Some London dialects pronounce the two words similarly.

badges

bages

1 Overarticulate the word for spelling (bad - ges).
2 Link it to other '-dge' words such as bad - gers, hedges, ledges, lodges, bridge.
3 We need to have two consonants after the short vowel sound in the first syllable to preserve the short vowel pattern (- VCCV -); here we use 'd' as in 'bad - ge'.
4 If we were to double consonant 'g' it would not give us the (-dge) sound (bagge).

5   If we pronounce the misspelling it gives us (bages) with the long vowel (A) sound denoted by the silent 'e' pattern (- VCe).

6   When 'e' or 'i' follow 'g' in words they make 'g' say its 'soft sound', e.g. bad - ges, badger, bridging, hedging.

badminton
bamington
1   Articulate clearly and syllabify for spelling (bad - min - ton).

baggy
bagey
1   Teach base word 'bag' with short vowel sound and hard sound of (g).
2   Teach DOUBLING rule when adding final suffix '-y' bag - g - y.
3   We pronounce (bagey) with the long vowel sound and soft 'g' softened by 'e' for comparison.

banished
banesed
1   Articulate clearly, check for correct pronunciation of 'sh' sound.
2   Syllabify, ban - ish - ment, banish-ed.

barbecue
barbque
1   Articulate clearly and syllabify for spelling (bar - be - cue).
2   This spelling is confused with signs indicating Bar - B - Q.

barks
barkes
1   Identify the base word 'bark'.
2   When vowels are followed by consonant 'r' they often change their sounds (-ar) as in bar - k, dark, mark, lark.
3   Add plural 's' as in barks, dogs, cats, pigs, rats and cows.

barnacles
barnickals
1   Over-articulate and syllabify for spelling (barn - a - cl).
2   We use final stable syllable '-cle' in words of three or more syllables – barnacle, chronicle, cubicle.
3   '-cle' is a noun ending – cycle, vehicle, uncle.
4   Endings 'cal' and 'al' are reserved for adjectival endings – musical, electrical, central, local.

base, basically
bace, basicly, basikly, bascilly
1   Identify the base word 'base'.

2 Note the long vowel (A) sound denoted by the silent 'e' pattern (- VCe) in 'base'.
3 The 's' between two vowels usually has the (Z) sound and some people do pronounce the word like this (baze - bazic).
4 Teach that open syllables have the long vowel sound (ba - sic), ba - con, o - pen.
5 We cannot add 'ly' directly to 'basic' but we can add it to 'basical' to get basical - ly, musically, practically, heretically.

basket, basketball
baseballball, bastet
1 Articulate clearly and syllabify the baseword for spelling (bas -ket).
2 A Northern dialect with the short vowel 'a' sound helps the spelling (bas - ket,) and (bask -et).
3 'Basketball' is a compound word made from 'basket' and 'ball'.
4 At the beginnings and in the middles of words we use 'k' before 'e', 'i' and 'y' to make the (- K -) sound, e.g. basket, keeper, baker, king, market, sky.

basking
bascing
1 Teach base word 'bask' as in the sunshine, basking shark and ask.
2 Articulate with short vowel sound as in Northern dialects for spelling (b - ask).
3 Syllabify for spelling (bas - king) or (bask -ing).
4 We use 'k' after a consonant in one syllabled words – bask, task, flask, rusk, bank, desk, milk, pink, folk.
5 To avoid use of 'c' teach 'c' rules, e.g. 'c' has no sound of its own. It has the (s) or soft sound when followed by 'e', 'i' and 'y' – cell, city, cycle, decide.
6 It has the 'k' or hard sound before 'a', 'o' and 'u' or everywhere else – cat, coat, cup, clean, crisp, decay, decoy, decade.

Bassoon
busoon
1 The origin of the word is in 'base' and 'bass'.
2 Syllabify for spelling (bass - oon).

beam
bem
1 Articulate the correct and incorrect spellings clearly (beem) with the long vowel sound and (bem) with the short vowel sound.
2 Ask if the pupil can identify the long then the short vowel 'e' sound.
3 'ee' is the most frequently occurring option for the long vowel sound (E).

4   'ea' is the next most frequent option cue articulate it to remind you (be - am).
5   'ea' is usually found in most words connected with food – meat, feast, tea, bean, cream, yeast.
6   Many words spelled with 'ea' have 'ee' homophones, e.g. meat, meet; bean, been; tea, tee; seam, seem, read, reed; peal, peel.

beaten
betten
1   Articulate the correct and the incorrect spellings clearly with long vowel and then short vowel sounds (beat - en) and (bet - ten).
2   Ask pupil to identify the base word 'beat' with the long vowel pattern (CVVC)
3   Show pupil the homophones 'beet' and 'beat' ask for meanings
4   Suggest memory aids – 'keep all the 'e's in the red beet', 'leave 'ea' in beat, seat and heat.
5   To 'beat' is to batter, and has an 'a' in it. We beat the carpets, we use the hand to beat a ball.

beautiful
butiful, beatifue, beauitfull, beautifull, beatifel
1   Identify the baseword 'beauty'; it comes from the French word 'beauté'.
2   Articulate clearly and syllabify for spelling (beaut - i - ful).
3   Teach the CHANGE suffixing rule – when we add the suffix -ful we must change the 'y' to 'i' in 'beaut - i - ful'.
4   Teach the 'all, well, full, till rule' that when we add these to another word to make a compound word they lose one 'l', e.g. beauty + full = beautiful, awful, helpful, welcome, also, although, until.

because
becuse, beacuse, beacause, becuase, becaurse, becase, bercause, becaus
1   Identify the base word and prefix (be - cause).
2   Use vowel digraph 'au' for (aw / or) sounds at the beginning and in the middle of words – August, autumn, because, clause, pause.
3   We use '-aw' at the end of words law, saw, paw.

bed
be
1   Articulate carefully for spelling, especially the stop consonant 'd' (b - ed).
2   Teach the short vowel sound and closed syllable pattern (CVC).
3   Ask the pupil to feel the articulatory sequence of the word 'bed'. In 'b' the lips start closed and then at 'd' the lips are open, stay open and the tongue strikes the backs of the teeth.

4   Clench both fists with thumbs up straight and put the knuckles together. This will show the places of the ascenders in 'b' and 'd' like in a bed.

been
bean, bin
1   From the verb 'to be', the past participle 'been'.
2   It is often pronounced (bin) in running speech but in spelling retains some of its origins be, been.
3   'Bean' is a vegetable and a noun; many food words use the '- ea -' vowel digraph.

before
befor
1   This is a compound word made from 'be' and 'fore'.
2   The meaning of 'fore' is to be in front of, 'let it come to the fore', forehead, foreland, forebears, forelock.
3   'For' is a preposition meaning 'in place of' because or in respect of 'this was for the bill'.

begged
beged
1   Identify the baseword 'beg' from the verb to beg.
2   Note the short vowel (e) sound and the closed syllable pattern (CVC).
3   Teach the DOUBLING rule that when attaching vowel suffixes '-ed and '-ing' after a short vowel we must have two consonants so here we double the final consonant: beg - g - ed, beg - g - ing, beggar, sagged, tugged, rigged, bugged.

begin
begain, begining, beggining
1   Articulate clearly and syllabify for spelling (be - gin).
2   The past tense is be - gan; note the first syllable is open so (E) has the long sound.
3   Teach the DOUBLING rule that after the short vowel sound in the closed syllable when adding suffixes we must have two consonants so here we double final 'n', e.g. begin - n - ing, running, panning, sunning.

behind
behide
1   Articulate clearly and syllabify for spelling (be - hind).
2   Note any difficulties with end blend '-nd'.
3   Hold nose and try to say behind, kind, hind, rind and (n).
4   The 'n' nasalifies the preceding vowel and is often missed by developing spellers especially in words such as went (wet), bend (bed), behind (behide).

being, be
bieyn, bieying, bieing, bei
1   Identify the baseword 'be' and the verb 'to be'.
2   'be' is an open syllable (CV -) and so the 'e' has the long vowel sound, or it says its own name, as in he, me, to, go, so.
3   Teach the ADD suffixing rule, that after the long vowel sound we simply add the suffix '-ing' – be - ing, see - ing, go - ing.

believe
belive
1   Articulate clearly and syllabify for spelling (be - lieve) and (be - lief).
2   Articulate the correct and the incorrect spellings to point out the differences (be - leev) and (be - live).
3   We put 'i' before 'e' (except after 'c') when the sound is (- ee -), e.g. belief, chief, grief, brief; piece, niece; field, shield, yield.
4   Invent three sentences that incorporate these words to aid memory, e.g 'my belief is that the chief is in grief'.
5   Record other words that have the 'ie' pattern, e.g. wield, priest.

belle
bell
1   The correct and incorrect spellings are homophones so use the meaning to separate them; a bell is an instrument that makes a ringing sound.
2   'bell' follows the 'l - f - s' rule by doubling 'l' to keep in the short vowel sound bell, full, till, mill, sell, well.
3   A 'belle' is a beautiful woman; it comes from French 'She is the belle of the ball'. Remember 'she' and 'belle' must have an 'e' at the end.

best
bes, beast
1   Articulate clearly for spelling (b - est) not (bes).
2   Teach the articulatory feel and sound of the end blend '-st' and as a joined writing unit in best, rest, west.
3   Note the short vowel 'e' sound and the closed syllable pattern (- VCC) in best, lest, west, vest, crest.

biggest, bigger
bigest, biger
1   Identify the baseword 'big'.
2   Teach the DOUBLING rule, that after a short vowel sound in a closed syllable (CVC) we need two consonants before attaching suffixes so we double the final 'g' – big - g - er, big - g - est.

bike, biking

big, bikeing

1 Articulate clearly for spelling especially the end sound (b- ike) with long vowel I.

2 Teach silent 'e' rule and pattern, silent 'e' at the end of a closed syllable makes the vowel say its own name (the long vowel or sustained sound) (b - ike) (- VCe).

3 Find five more words with the same pattern – hike, like, strike, shrike, trike.

4 Teach the DROP rule for adding the vowel suffix '-ing' to words ending in silent 'e', e.g. bike, biking; hike, hiking; like, liking.

birthday

birtday, boithday, berthday, brithday

1 This is a compound word made from 'birth' and 'day'.

2 Articulate clearly to feel the (th) consonant digraph in (bir - th) (b - irth).

3 The word 'berth' means a bed or place usually on a boat so we need to spell our birthdays differently. Try 'the day I was born'.

4 The word 'birth' probably come from the Old Norse 'byrthr' so easily became 'birth' in English.

biscuit

bisquiet, biscet

1 Articulate clearly and syllabify for spelling (bis - cuit) (bis - kit).

2 The word comes from the French 'biscuit'.

3 It originally meant 'twice cooked'; the prefix 'bi-' means two.

4 'c' has no sound of its own to make it say its hard sound (k) we have to add silent 'u' as in 'bis - cu - it'; you can also cue articulate it 'bis - cu - it'.

5 'c' takes the hard sound after 'a', 'o' and 'u'. 'U' is best for the purpose here.

biting

biteing

1 Identify the base word 'bite'.

2 Note the long vowel sound and pattern (- VCe) denoted by the silent 'e' in bite, white, lute, note, mate.

3 Teach the DROP rule when suffixing silent 'e' words; we must drop 'e' before attaching a vowel suffix, e.g. bit - ing, noting, whiting.

bits

bist

1 Identify the baseword 'bit'.

2 Articulate clearly for spelling (b - it) and note the short vowel closed syllable pattern (CVC).

3   Plural ending '-s' can simply be ADDED as in 'bit-s'.
4   Find some other similar CVC words and give their plurals – pots, pans, boys, dogs.

blonde
blond, bond
1   Articulate clearly for spelling (bl - o - nde), check initial blend (bl -) and short vowel (- o -).
2   Say other words beginning with 'bl-', e.g. bleed, block, bling, blunt, black.
3   Say other words with the same end blend sound, e.g. 'end, bend, find, fond, fund.
4   Why does 'blonde' hair have an 'e' when it has no purpose? It comes from the French and is the feminine form, e.g. 'blond' is masculine and 'blonde' is feminine.
5   To remind you it is different say the word with a French accent.

blown
blowen
1   Identify the baseword 'blow'.
2   After the consonant and the long vowel sound (ow) use ADD suffixing rule.
3   Simply add the suffixes, e.g. blow - ing, blow - ed, blow - n, blow - s.

blurred
blured
1   Identify the baseword 'blur' and the closed syllable pattern (CCVC).
2   Teach the DOUBLING rule that after the short vowel sound in a two syllabled word we must have two consonants to keep the short vowel pattern so we double consonant 'r' (- VCCV -) blur - r - ed, blurring; occur, occurring, occurred.

boarded
boaded boarded
1   Identify the baseword 'board' and its meanings such as a 'plank of wood' and to go 'on board' a ship or a boat.
2   Board and boat both have the vowel digraph 'oa' in them, when a vowel is followed by consonant 'r' it changes the usual sound it makes, e.g. 'oar' and 'oa'.
3   Look for the 'oars' on board the boats.
4   Check the articulation captures the final blend '-rd'.
5   Find five more words with the end blend '-rd' – sword, ford, word, bard, nerd.

bodies

bobys, bodys

1 Identify the base word 'body'.
2 Clench the two fists with the thumbs up straight and put the knuckles together to form 'bod' or 'b d' showing where the ascenders should be.
3 Articulate (b - od) feeling the difference in the mouth for 'b' and 'd'.
4 Ask the pupil to describe the feel of these consonants in the mouth, e. g 'b' starts with lips closed.
5 Teach the CHANGE rule for suffixing plurals – after 'y' we must change 'y' to 'i' and add the plural 'es' – bod - i - es, babies, nannies.

Bolognese

bolognase

1 This is an Italian word and keeps the Italian spelling, a sauce made in Bologna.
2 Cue articulate for spelling 'bol - og - nes - e'.
3 Remember it is often nicknamed 'spag bog'.

bomb

bome, bomer

1 Identify the baseword 'bomb'.
2 Remember the silent 'b' by linking it to its family 'bomb', bombardment, bombing, bombers, bombardier.

book

booke

1 Teach the syllable pattern (CV VC) does not need silent 'e' to hold in the vowels.
2 Teach the long and short sounds of (oo), e.g. in a) look, cook, book, soot, foot and b) fool, moon, soon, boon.

Border Collie, border

booda colli, broder

1 Articulate clearly and syllabify for spelling (bor - der coll - ie).
2 A type of dog from the Borders of (England) or margins between countries.
3 Collie – no English words end in (i) we add an 'e' to make Collie, even taxi is a shortened form of taximeter and cauli is short for cauliflower.

bored

board, boreing, bord, board

1 Identify the baseword which is the verb 'to bore' meaning a) tedious or tiresome or b) to drill a hole in something.
2 When any vowel is followed by consonant 'r' it often changes its sound; here it says (-or) as in bore, ore, tore, more, fore.

3   Bored and board are homophones, they have the same sound but different meanings and spellings; remember 'on board boats there will be oars'.

4   Teach the DROP rule for attaching a vowel suffix after a silent 'e' ending, e.g. bor - ing, bor - ed.

5   Keep the 'e' before a consonant suffix bore- dom.

born
borne

1   Born comes from the verb 'to bear' or 'to be born' as babies are.

2   'Borne' is the past tense of the verb 'to bear' and its second meaning 'to carry' – 'the ship was borne away on the tide'.

both
bothe

1   Although (b - o - th) is pronounced with the long vowel sound you will have to learn to say it for spelling with a short vowel sound (both).

2   Link it with Goth, bother, and bothy to remind you.

bought
bough, borght

1   'Ought' in this unusual word says (- ort), it is the past tense of the verb 'to buy'

2   There are four others in this 'family', e.g. ought, brought, thought, fought.

3   Try to make up a sentence that includes all this group, e.g. I thought he ought to.

4   Learn to write the -ought graphemes as a joined writing unit.

bouncy
boncey

1   Identify the baseword 'bounce'.

2   Say it slowly and overarticulate to notice it has the diphthong 'ou' sounding (ahoo) in it.

3   The 'ou' diphthong is used at the beginning and in the middle of words, e.g. out, ounce, bounce, round, ground, found.

4   After silent 'e' at the end of words we must DROP 'e' and simply add final '- y', bounc - y, flouncy; this is because final 'y' already makes the long (E) sound at the end of words, e.g. mummy, daddy, baby, sunny.

bowler
boler, boling

1   Identify the base word 'bowl' as to bowl in cricket.

2   '-ow' is a digraph that makes the long vowel sound of (O), usually at the end of words as in snow, low, blow, follow, tomorrow.

3 Use the word 'bowler' to cue the correct spelling, e.g. (bow - ler).
4 Teach the ADD rule for attaching vowel suffixes after a consonant, bowl - er, bowl - ing, bowl - s.

bracelet
braslet
1 Articulate clearly and syllabify for spelling (brace - let).
2 Look for the (- ace) in 'brace' (br - ace).
3 Note the long vowel sound in the first syllable denoted by the silent 'e' pattern (- VCe).
4 Say the misspelling (bras - let) to show the difference and the value of proofreading.

break
brake
1 'Break' and 'brake' are homophones, words having the same sound but different meanings and different spellings.
2 'Break' generally means to sever or divide; keep the 'e' in sever and in break.
3 Perhaps we once pronounced it (breek) as it comes from Old English 'brecon'.
4 Note other words with the same 'ea' digraph but they follow the 'two vowel rule'.
5 'When two vowels go walking the first one does the talking and usually says its own name', e.g. weak, leak, seat, meat, read, lead.

breakfast
beackdast
1 This is a compound word from the meaning to 'break' your 'fast', e.g. after a night's sleep and a long period without food you have something to eat.
2 After vowel digraphs such as 'ea' always use '- k' alone not '- ck', e.g. leak, cook, freak, meek, seek, book.

bred, breeding
berot, breading
1 The word 'breed' contains the long vowel (ee) sound and pattern (- VVC).
2 'Bred' has the short vowel sound and pattern (- VC).
3 Learn to blend the initial sound 'br -' without the intrusive schwa (uh) sound.
4 'ee' is the most frequently used sound of (E) in words and is therefore first choice; 'ea' is more often found in words related to food as in bread, meat.
5 Teach the different articulatory feel and pattern of final stop consonants 'd' (voiced) and 't' (unvoiced).

bridesmaids
bridesmaides
1   This is a compound word made from 'bride' and 'maid'.
2   'Maid' already has the long vowel pattern (- VVC) as in laid, raid, bead, read, load, road, so we do not need silent 'e' in maides.
3   Maid and maids is the shortened version of maiden and maidens.
4   '- en' is an Old English ending and often makes a plural itself, e.g. brothers, brethren, child, children.

bridge
brigde
1   After a short vowel sound we need to put 'd' before '-ge' in words to hold in the vowel (brid - ge).
2   Overarticulate these words to detect the 'd' in them: badge, cadge, ledge, hedge, wedge, midge, ridge, fridge, dodge, lodger, fudge, judge, nudge.
3   The 'e' makes the 'g' say its soft sound.
4   The misspelling 'brigde' says 'brig - dee'.

brilliant
brilleant, brilliantt
1   Articulate clearly and syllabify for spelling (brill - i - ant).
2   Teach the l - f - s rule, we must double the l - f - and s after a short vowel in a single syllabled word, e.g. brill, tall, fall, mill, all, full.
3   To remember to put 'i' not 'e', think of Lewis Carroll's 'Twas BRILLIG and the slithey toves did gyre and gimbal in the wabe'.
4   '- ant' does not need an extra 't' it already has enough consonants (- VCC) to hold in the vowel, remember the spelling of the insect 'ant'.

bring, bringing
brin, brining
1   Identify the base word 'bring' and articulate clearly for spelling.
2   Teach the end blend (-ng), hold nose and try to say it.
3   Find other single syllabled words ending with '-ng', e.g. sing, long, hang, lung.
4   Teach the ADD rule for attaching vowel suffixes after the short vowel closed syllable pattern (- VCC), e.g. bring - ing, sing - ing, long - ing, hang - ing.

bright
brigt
1   Learn the ending '-ight' (-ite) as a joined writing unit.
2   Learn this friendship group – bright, night, light, fight, might, sight, right, tight.
3   Say 'bright' as it was pronounced in Scots: 'it was a braw bricht moonlicht nicht the nicht'.

Britain
britan
1   Names of countries always take the capital letter to begin their names.
2   Syllabify and overarticulate the name to support the spelling 'Brit - ain'
    Brit – ish.

broccoli
brocoly
1   Broccoli is an Italian word and follows the Italian spelling with double
    'cc' making the sound (- k -).
2   Notice also the 'i' at the end of a word sounding (- ee) is not used in
    English words.

brochure
broshure
1   Brochure is the French word for a pamphlet.
2   In French the (- sh -) sound is represented by (- ch -), e.g. brochure, chef.
3   Cue articulate by saying (bro - chure), e.g. vowels in open syllables have
    the long vowel sound, e.g. bro - chure, o - pen, ba - con.

brother
brouther, broter, brouther, broather
1   Say the word clearly and note that the vowel sound is (uh) or the short
    vowel sound of 'u'.
2   Link it to its relative 'mother'.
3   Syllabify for spelling 'bro - ther'. Note we often use the short form 'bro-'.
4   Note the articulatory feel and pattern of the consonant digraph '- th -'
5   Hold the sound of (- th -) and note the vibration or voicing of this 'hard'
    sound.

brought
broght, brougt
1   The ending '-ought' in this word says (-ort).
2   There are four others in this 'family', e.g. ought, bought, thought,
    fought.
3   Learn them as a group and try to make up a sentence that includes all of
    them, e.g. I thought he ought to ----.
4   Practise writing the '-ought' as a fully joined writing unit.

brown
brow, browen, browne, brow
1   'ow' is one of four diphthongs in English. A diphthong is where two
    vowels blend together; neither vowel keeps its own sound e.g. -ou and -oi.
2   Here 'ow' makes the sound (ah - oo) as in 'how now brown cow'.
3   Check the clear articulation of the end blend (-wn) in brown and frown.

bubbles

bubles

1   Note the short vowel 'u' sound and the short vowel closed syllable pattern (CVC -) in the first syllable 'bub'.

2   Teach the DOUBLING rule that after a short vowel sound in a closed syllable we must double the final consonant before attaching final stable syllable '-le' as in 'bub - b - le' (VC - C - le).

3   Simply add the plural 's' after '-le' in 'bubble - s', nettles, wiggles, settles, muddles.

budgie

buggy

1   Say the full name for spelling (bud - ger - i - gar) and its short form (bud - gie).

2   After the short vowel sound in the first syllable we need to ADD 'd' before 'ge' endings.

3   Overarticulate to feel the '-dge' ending in wedge, hedge, ledge, badge, fudge, budge.

4   The final 'e' in these words is needed to make 'g' use its soft sound.

5   'Buggy' is the name of a small vehicle usually with two wheels and has the hard 'g' sound, fuggy, muggy, doggie. The 'ie' ending is a special diminutive form for little.

built

biult, bilt, buiet

1   In this word 'build' and 'built' the 'u' is silent, and in guilt and guild.

2   Articulate the end blends carefully for spelling (-lt) and (-ld); note the feel on teeth and tongue.

3   Find five more words with these blends – built, spelt, wilt, guild, guilt, gilder.

bullies

bullys

1   In some dialects the word 'bull' is said with a definite short vowel 'u' sound cue. Articulate this to remind you.

2   Teach the CHANGE rule when adding plural suffixes after 'y', e.g. we change 'y' to 'i' and add plural 'es' as in bull - i - es, gullies, fillies, babies.

bureau

burreau

1   Say the correct and incorrect versions – bure-au is the long vowel pattern with silent 'e'. Bureau is a word borrowed directly from the French.

2   Burr-eau is the short vowel pattern spelling in which we double the consonant and is not a correct word. We spell it 'burrow'.

bury, buries, buried

burrie, berdy, burries

1   Identify the base word 'bury' meaning to hide in the ground
2   When a vowel is followed by consonant 'r' it usually changes its sound as here in 'bury' (beri).
3   Teach the CHANGE rule for attaching vowel suffixes and plural '-es'. We must change 'y' to 'i' before adding them, e.g. bur - i - es, bur - i - ed.
4   If we spell it as 'burries' it rhymes with 'hurries'.
5   The double -rr indicates that the preceding vowel is short.

bust

busst

1   Teach the end blend '-st' in bust, last , mast, wrist, fist, whist, most.
2   After the short vowel 'u' two consonants are enough to hold in the vowel (- VCC).

but

bot, bait

1   Teach the short vowel sound of 'u' in the closed syllable pattern (CVC).
2   Find some other words with the same sound, e.g. nut, mud, gut, rut, hut.
3   Even 'put' should be cue articulated with a Northern dialect to belong in this group.

buy

by

1   'To buy' means to purchase for money.
2   Whereas 'by' is a preposition meaning 'near to'.
3   We need a 'u' in 'buy' like purchase to separate it from 'by' the preposition and its homophone meaning.

Postscript: looking to the future

Over four decades a clear picture of dyslexics' needs has emerged from the casework and other research. It suggests that the original problem is a neurological dissociation that prevents sounds being connected with their symbols during the acquisition stage of literacy learning using normal classroom methods. However, there are specific techniques that can overcome the problem and then reading and writing skills appear to develop normally.

The research shows that the dyslexic problem can be identified early in the Reception year in the logographic phase when 'phones' do not appear in free-form writing. It can be overcome by individual and specific multisensory-articulatory phonogram training.

If the dyslexia is not identified until the alphabetic phase as is the current practice the dyslexic is often by then a three-time failure because of all the delays and interventions that have not been effective. At this stage a full remedial intervention programme is needed. The effective programmes give two years' uplift in each year and are completed in two years. These are the Alphabetic-Phonic-Syllabic-Linguistic programmes based on the original Gillingham and Stillman format. The programmes must be followed correctly and give the best results with matched pairs of dyslexics rather than with one-to-one tuition. This is economically advantageous for schools.

As most progress is made on these programmes in the first six months, in many cases they can be discontinued at that point and the pupil transferred to an orthographic phase programme.

The orthographic phase programme detailed is Cognitive Process Strategies for Spelling (CPSS). It widens the range of strategies available and can be used with all poor spellers and as an ordinary classroom technique to develop the spelling of all children. The protocols enable corrected spellings to stay corrected and the techniques can be generalised to correct over 20,000 common misspellings using its 'Detective Approach'.

CPSS can also give two years or more uplift in spelling and has been found to transfer automatically to reading and improve it. When it is made a whole school policy all subject teachers can use CPSS to support the teaching and acquisition of their specialist vocabularies.

Special attention now needs to be given to the teaching of handwriting. It is a skill that has largely been ignored in recent times in English schools. This detailed work should begin in Reception to avoid problem habits developing. For example, Reception children must be given lines to practise their writing on. They must not be allowed to copy and trace letters but to learn to write them free form by tracing in the air and then on paper. Cursive writing form must be taught from the outset and pen and pencil hold and letter formation should be carefully taught and monitored.

As soon as two letters have been learned, joining should be taught, so that word-building skill is developed from the outset and not left to be learned implicitly. At this stage 30 per cent or more children will show some difficulties in coordination. They will need fluency and 'motricity' training to support their writing and a few will need some remedial PE programmes.

About 1 per cent will have such severe difficulties with pencil control that they should be allowed to use their own laptops from the outset. If they are not able to learn rapid word processing skills either then voice recognition systems or a scribe should be acquired to support them. The use of word processors alone in place of writing will slow down literacy acquisition and development as it does not activate the reading areas in the same way as handwriting has been shown to do. It has been found that handwriting also facilitates the generation of more ideas and leads to higher quality composition in the young learner.

Later attention to handwriting should be redirected to improving speed and fluency because they increase legibility rather than pressure for neatness that is common in some classrooms. Automaticity in writing is the essential goal so that ideas generated can be explored fully and answer the tasks set.

Custom and practice in literacy learning and current government guidelines are not serving children well in their literacy learning activities and so they must be changed. Teachers can do this by trying and testing the techniques and examples set out in this book.

References

Aavena S., Snellings P., Tijms J. and van der Molen, M.W. (2013) 'A lab-controlled simulation of a letter-speech sound binding deficit in dyslexia', *Journal of Experimental Child Psychology*, 4: 691–707.

Ainscow, M. and Muncey, J. (1979) *Special Needs Action Programme*, Coventry: Coventry LEA.

Allcock, P. (2001) 'The importance of handwriting skills in Key Stage 3 and GCSE Examinations of more able pupils', *Educating Able Children*, 5(1): 23–5.

Allen, B.V. (1977) *Logical Spelling*, London: Collins.

Alston, J. (1993) *Assessing and Promoting Writing Skills*, Stafford: NASEN.

Ashraf, M. (2005) 'An investigation of the use of CPSS in casework', Module 4, research report. MA SpLD London: Middlesex University.

Augur, J. and Briggs, S. (eds) (1991) *The Hickey Multisensory Language Course (2nd edition)*, London: Whurr/Wiley-Blackwell.

Balcombe, (2004) Handwriting for Windows CD.

Barnett, A., Henderson, S.E., Scheib, B. and Schutz, J. (2008) *DASH – Detailed Assessment of Speed of Handwriting*. Available online: www.pearson-uk.com/dash

Baum, S., Cooper, C. and Neu, T. (2001) 'Dual differentiation: an approach for meeting curriculum needs of gifted students with learning disabilities', *Psychology of the Schools*, 38(5): 477–90.

BDA (1981) Guidelines for dyslexia programmes by the BDA Expert Group. Minutes from the meeting Reading: BDA.

BDA (2000) *Dyslexia Handbook*, Reading: BDA.

BDA (2017) Dyslexia information available online: www.bda-dyslexia.org.uk

Berninger, V.W. (2008) 'Writing problems in developmental dyslexia. Under-recognised and under-treated', *Journal of School Psychology*, 46: 1–21.

Berninger, V.W. and Graham, S. (1998) 'Language by hand: a synthesis of a decade of research on handwriting', *Handwriting Review*, 12: 11–25.

Blakemore, S. and Frith, U. (2006) *The Learning Brain. Lessons for Education*, Oxford: Blackwell.

Boxall, M. (2002) *Nurture Groups in Schools: Principles and Practice*, London: Sage.

Bradley, L. (1981) 'A tactile approach to reading', *British Journal of Special Education*, 8(4): 33–6.

Bradley, L. and Huxford, L. (1994) 'Organising sound and letter patterns for spelling', in C.D.A. Brown and N.C. Ellis, *Handbook of Spelling, Theory, Process and Intervention*, pp. 425–38, Chichester: Wiley.

Brand, V. (1998) *Spelling Made Easy*, Baldock, Herts: Egon.

Bravar, L. (2005) 'Studying handwriting: An Italian experience', Sixth International Conference on Developmental Coordination Difficulties, Trieste, 17–20 May.

British Dyslexia Association (2016) www.bda-dyslexia.org.uk

Brown, G.D.A. and Ellis, N.C. (eds) (1994) *Handbook of Spelling: Theory, Practice and Intervention*, Chichester: Wiley.

Bryant, P. and Bradley, L. (1985) *Children's Reading Difficulties*, Oxford: Blackwell.

Bryant, P. and Chliounaki K. (2007) 'How children learn about morphological spelling rules', *Child Development*, 78(4): 1360–73.

Butt, H. (2003) 'An investigation into CPSS in the development of spelling skills in a group of Year 2 pupils', MA SpLD Dissertation London: Middlesex University.

Campbell, H. (2003) 'The Phonographix methods and ESOL students' 1–18, Leeds: Brudenell Centre Document.

Caunt, J. (2004) 'An investigation into selecting a cursive script for speed and legibility and the setting up of a uniform and coherent policy throughout the Primary section of an International School', MA SpLD Dissertation, London: Middlesex University.

Chall, J. (1967) *Learning to Read: The Great Debate*, New York: McGraw-Hill.

Chall, J. (1985) *Stages in Reading Development*, New York: McGraw-Hill.

Childs, S. (1966) *Child's Spelling Rules*, Cambridge, MA: Educator's Publishing Service.

Chomsky, C. (1971) 'Write first, read later', *Childhood Education*, 47(6): 296–99.

Christensen, C.A. and Jones, D. (2000) 'Handwriting: An underestimated skill in the development of written language', *Handwriting Today*, 2, 56–69.

Clark, M.M. (1970) *Reading Difficulties in Schools*, Harmondsworth: Penguin.

Clay, M.M. (1975) *What Did I Write? The Beginnings of Reading Development*, London: Heinemann.

Connelly, V. and Dockrell, J. and Barnett, A. (2005) 'The slow handwriting of undergraduates constrains the overall performance in exam essays', *Educational Technology*, 25(1): 99–109.

Conners, K.C. (2007) *Teacher's Rating Scale for EBD*, London: Pearson/Psychological Corporation.

Cowdery, L.L. (1987) *The Spelling Notebook*, Wrexham: TRTS Publishing.

Cowdery, L.L., McMahon, J., Montgomery, D., Morse, P. and Prince-Bruce, M. (1983–1987) *Teaching Reading Through Spelling (TRTS) Vols 2A to 2F*, Kingston: Learning Difficulties Research Project.

Cowdery, L.L., Montgomery, D., Morse, P. and Prince-Bruce, M. (1994) *Teaching Reading Through Spelling Series 1-7 Reprint*, Wrexham: TRTS Publishing.

Cox, A.R. and Waites, L. (1972) *Structures and Techniques of Remedial Language Training: Multisensory Teaching for Alphabetic Phonics*, Cambridge, MA: Educators Publishing Service.

Critchley, M. (1971) *Developmental Dyslexia* (2nd edn), London: Heinemann.

Daniels, J.C. and Diack, H. (1979) *The Standard Reading Test*, London: Hart Davis.

DfE (1997) *Excellence for All Children*, London: DfE.

DfE (2014) *National Curriculum, Key Stages 1 and 2. Framework for English and Mathematics*, London: DfE.

DfEE (1998) *The National Literacy Strategy*, London: DfEE.

DfEE (2001) The Code of Practice Revised, London: DfEE.

DfES (2006) *Primary National Strategy: Framework for Literacy and Mathematics*, London: DfES.

DfES (2008) A framework for Understanding Dyslexia. Available online: www.dfes. gov.uk/readwriteplus.understandingdyslexia/

Dias, K. and Juniper, L. (2002) 'Phono-Graphix – who needs additional literacy support? An outline of research in Bristol schools', *Support for Learning*, 17(1): 34–8.

DILP/Hickey (1995) *Dyslexia Institute Language Programme*, Dyslexia Institute.

Downing, J. and Thackray, D. (1970) *Reading Readiness*, London: Unibooks.

Dunn, R. and Dunn, K. (1997) *British Picture Vocabulary Scale 3*, London: G-L Assessment.

Edgington, U. (2017) *Assessing Teaching Through Lesson Observation: The Complexities of Performativity*, Berlin: Springer-Deutsch.

Edwards, J. (1994) *The Scars of Dyslexia*, London: Cassell.

Elliott, J.G. and Grigorenko, E.L. (2014) *The Dyslexia Debate*, New York: Cambridge University Press.

Farnham-Diggory, S. (1978) *Learning Disabilities*, Harmondsworth: Penguin.

Feder, K.P., Majnemer, A. and Bourbonnais (2005) 'Handwriting performance in pre-term children compared with term peers at age 6-7', *Developmental Medicine and Child Neurology*, 47.

Feller, M. (1994) 'Open book testing and education for the future', *Studies in Educational Evaluation*, 20(2): 235–8.

Fernald, G.M. (1943) *Remedial Techniques in Basic School Subjects*, New York: McGraw-Hill.

Ferreiro, E. and Teberosky, A. (1982) *Literacy Before Schooling*, Exeter NH: Heinemann Education.

Fish, J. (1985) *Educational Opportunities for All: The Fish Report*, London: Inner London Education Authority.

Forsyth, D. 1988 'An evaluation of an infant school screening instrument', Unpublished dissertation Kingston upon Thames: Kingston Polytechnic.

Frederickson, N., Frith, U. and Reason, R. (1997) *Phonological Assessment Battery* London: Pearson.

Frith, U. (ed.) (1980) *Cognitive Processes in Spelling*, Chichester: Wiley.

Frith, U. (1985) 'Beneath the surface of developmental dyslexia', in K.E. Patterson, J.C. Marshall and M. Coltheart (eds) *Surface Dyslexia*, London: Routledge and Kegan Paul.

Gabor, G. (2007) 'An evaluation of the process and progress towards setting up a dyslexic programme in an International School', MA SpLD dissertation, London: Middlesex University.

Geddes, W. (ed) (1964) *Chambers 20th Century Dictionary*, Edinburgh: W. & R. Chambers Ltd.

Gelb, I.J. (1963) *A Study of Writing* (2nd edition), London: University of Chicago Press.

Gentry, J.R. (1981) 'Learning to spell developmentally', *The Reading Teacher*, 34(4): 378–81.

Geschwind, N. (1979) 'Specialisations of the human brain', *Scientific American*, 231(3): 156–67.

Gillingham, A.M. and Stillman, B.U. (1956) *Remedial Training for Children with Specific Disability in Reading, Spelling and Penmanship*, Bath: Basic Books.

Gillingham, A.M. and Stillman, B.U. (1997) *The Gillingham Manual: Remedial Training for Students with Specific Disability in Reading, Spelling and Penmanship*, Cambridge MA: Educators Publishing Service Inc.

Gillingham, A.M., Stillman, B.U. and Orton, S.T. (1940) *Remedial Training for Children with Specific Disability in Reading, Spelling and Penmanship*, New York: Sackett and Williams.

Goswami, U. (1994) 'The role of analogies in reading development', *Support for Learning*, 9(1): 22–5.

Goswami, U. and Bryant, P.E. (1990) *Phonological Skills and Learning to Read*, Hove: Lawrence Erlbaum.

Hanna, P.R., Hanna, J.S., Hodges, R.E. and Rodori, E.H. (1966) *Phoneme-Grapheme Correspondence as Cues to Spelling Improvement*, Washington DC: US Office of Education.

Harris, D (ed.) (1963) *The Revised Version of the Goodenough Draw a Person Test*, New York: Grune and Stratton.

Harris, C. (1986) *Fuzzbuzz*, Oxford: Oxford University Press.

Hellige, J.B. and Adamson, M.M. (2007) 'Hemispheric differences in processing handwritten cursive', *Brain and Language*, 102: 215–27.

Henry, M.K. (1997) 'The decoding/spelling curriculum. Integrated decoding and spelling instruction from pre-school to early secondary school', *Dyslexia*, 3: 178–89.

Hepplewhite, D. (2007) Phonics International. Available online: www.syntheticphonics.com

Hickey, K. (1977) *Dyslexia: A Language Training Course for Teachers and Learners*, Staines, Surrey: Dyslexia Institute.

Hickey, K. (1991) *Dyslexia: A Language Training Course for Teachers and Learners (2nd edition)*, J. Augur and S. Briggs (eds), London: Whurr.

HMCI (2001) *The Annual Report of the Chief Inspector for Schools in England*, London: The Stationery Office.

HMI (1991) Letter to the Local Authority copied to the Head of the Kingston Reading Centre.

Hornsby, B. and Farrar, M. (1990) 'Some effects of a dyslexia-centred teaching programme', in P.D. Pumfrey and C.D. Elliott (eds) *Children's Difficulties in Reading, Spelling and Writing*, pp. 173–96, London: Falmer Press.

Hornsby, B. and Shear, F. (1976) *Alpha to Omega: The Teaching of Reading, Writing and Spelling*, Oxford: Heinemann Educational.

Hornsby, B. and Shear, F. (1993) *Alpha to Omega: The Teaching of Reading, Writing and Spelling (4th edition)*, Oxford: Heinemann Educational.

James, K. and Engelhardt, L. (2012) 'The effects of handwriting experience on functional brain development', *Neuroscience and Education*, 1(1): 32–42.

Jeffery, J. (2016) *Teaching Reading Using Games – trugs*. Available online: www.readsuccessfully.com

Jerrim, J. (2013) *The Reading Gap*, The Sutton Trust: Millbank, London.

Johnson, R. and Watson, J. (2005) 'The Effects of Synthetic Phonics teaching on Reading and Spelling development. A 7 year longitudinal study', Edinburgh: Scottish Executive Education Department.

Kappers, E.J. (1990) 'Neurological treatment of dyslexic children', *Euronews Dyslexia*, 3: 9–15.

Kent, C.C. (2014) 'Motricity: Raising confidence in cursive writing', Hastings and St Leonard's Excellence Cluster publication.

Koppitz, E. (1977) *The Visual-Aural Digit Span Test*, New York: Grune and Stratton.

Kuczaj, S.A. (1979) 'Evidence for a language learning strategy in the relative ease of acquisition of prefixes and suffixes', *Child Development*, 50: 1–13.

Lane, C.H. (1990) 'Alleviating children's reading and spelling problems', in P.D. Pumfrey and C.D. Elliott (eds) *Children's Difficulties in Reading, Spelling and Writing*, pp. 237–54, London: Falmer Press.

Liberman, A.M., Shankweiler, D.P., Cooper, F.S. and Studdart-Kennedy, M. (1967) 'Perception of the speech code', *Psychological Review*, 74(6): 431–6.

Liberman, I.Y. (1973) Segmentation of the spoken word and reading acquisition', *Bulletin of the Orton Society*, 23: 365–77.

Lloyd, S. (1993) *The Phonics Handbook*, Chigwell: Jolly Learning.

Low, G. (1990) 'Cursive makes a comeback', *Education*, 6 April 341.

Lyth, A. (2004) 'Handwriting speed: An aid to communication success?' *Handwriting Today*, 3: 30–5.

Marin, M.F., La Voie, N. and Montisinos, L. (2012) 'The effects of manuscript, cursive or manuscript/cursive styles on writing development in Grade 2', *Language and Literacy*, 14: 110–24.

McGuinness, C. and McGuinness, G. (1999) *Reading Reflex – The Foolproof Phono-Graphix Method for Teaching Your Child to Read*, Hemel Hempstead: Simon and Schuster.

Medwell, J. and Wray, D. (2007) 'Handwriting. What do we know and what do we need to know?' *Literacy*, 43(1): 10–15.

Medwell, J., Strand, S. and Wray, D. (2008) 'What should we assess in primary writing?' *Handwriting Today*, 7: 23–28.

Monroe, M. (1932) *Children Who Cannot Read*, Chicago: Chicago University Press.

Montgomery, D. (1977) 'Teaching pre-reading through training in pattern recognition', *The Reading Teacher*, 30(6): 216–25.

Montgomery, D. (1979) *Visual Pattern Recognition Test and Training Materials for Early Reading*, Windsor: NFER.

Montgomery, D. (1981) 'Do dyslexics have difficulty accessing articulatory information?' *Psychological Research*, 43: 235–43.

Montgomery, D. (1984/1994) 'Multisensory mouth training', in L.L. Cowdery, D. Montgomery, P. Morse and M. Prince-Bruce (1994) *Teaching Reading Through Spelling Series 1-7 Reprint*, pp. 237–54, Wrexham: TRTS Publishing.

Montgomery, D. (1989) *Managing Behaviour Problems*, Sevenoaks: Hodder and Stoughton.

Montgomery, D. (1990) *Children with Learning Difficulties*, London: Cassell.

Montgomery, D. (1993) *Study Skills. Teaching and Learning Strategies*, Maldon: Learning Difficulties Research Project.

Montgomery, D. (1997a) *Spelling: Remedial Strategies*, London: Cassell.

Montgomery, D. (1997b) *Developmental Spelling Handbook*, Maldon: Learning Difficulties Research Project. Available online: www.ldrp.org.uk

Montgomery, D. (1998) *Reversing Lower Attainment*, London: David Fulton.

Montgomery, D. (ed.) (2000) *Able Underachievers*, Chichester: Wiley.

Montgomery, D. (2002) *Helping Teachers Improve through Classroom Observation*, London: David Fulton.

Montgomery, D. (ed.) (2003) *Gifted and Talented Children with SEN; Double Exceptionality*, London: NACE/David Fulton.

Montgomery, D. (2007) *Spelling, Handwriting and Dyslexia*, London: Routledge.

Montgomery, D. (2008) 'Cohort analysis of writing in Year 7 after 2, 4, and 7 years of the National Literacy Strategy', *Support for Learning*, 23(1): 3–11.

Montgomery, D. (ed.) (2009) *Able, Gifted and Talented Underachievers*, Chichester: Wiley.

Montgomery, D. (2012) 'The Contribution of Handwriting and Spelling Remediation to Overcoming Dyslexia', in *Dyslexia – A Comprehensive and International Approach* in N. Taeko Wydell and L. Fern-Pollak (eds) InTech Publication. Available online: www.intechpen.com (free access) ISBN 978-953-51-0517-6.

Montgomery, D. (2015) *Teaching Gifted Children with SEN: Supporting Dual and Multiple Exceptionality*, London: Routledge.

Morey, K. (2001) 'Casework with an able dyslexic in Nairobi', *Educating Able Children*, 5(1): 27–30.

Morgan, W.P. (1896) 'A case of congenital word blindness', *British Medical Journal*, 2: 1378.

Mueller, P.A. and Oppenheimer, D.M. (2014) 'The pen is mightier than the keyboard. Advantages of longhand over laptop note-taking', *Psychological Sciences*, 25(6): 1159–68.

Neale, M.D. (1997) *Neale Analysis of Reading Ability* (2nd edition), Windsor: NFER-Nelson.

Norrie, E. (1973) *The Edith Norrie Letter Case*, London: Helen Arkell Centre.

O'Brien, K.M. (2004) 'An investigation of CPSS as a proposed effective intervention to develop or to remediate spelling errors', MA SpLD Dissertation, London: Middlesex University.

OFSTED (1999) *Pupils with Specific Learning Difficulties in Mainstream School. A survey of provision in mainstream primary and secondary schools for pupils with a Statement of SEN relating to specific learning difficulties*, London: OFSTED.

Oliver, T., Alres, R.A. and Castro, S.L. et al. (2009) 'The impact of children's handwriting on text composition', *Handwriting Today*, 8: 14–17.

Ousseren-Voors, R. (1999) 'Write-Dance', *Handwriting Interest Group Newsletter*, 70–87.

Overvelde, A. and Hulstijn, W. (2011) 'Learning new movement patterns: A study on good and poor writers comparing learning conditions emphasising spatial, timing, or abstract characteristics', *Human Movement Science*, 30: 731–44.

Parrant, H. (1986) 'An investigation of remedial approaches to children's spelling difficulties', Unpublished SEN dissertation, Kingston upon Thames: Kingston Polytechnic.

Pawley, J. (2007) 'Dyslexia-the hidden trigger?' MA SpLD dissertation, London: Middlesex University.

Peters, M.L. (1967) *Spelling: Caught or Taught?* London: Routledge and Kegan Paul.

Peters, M.L. (1985) *Spelling: Caught or Taught?* (2nd edition), London: Routledge and Kegan Paul

Piotrowski, J. and Reason, R. (2000) 'The National Literacy Strategy and dyslexia: a comparison of teaching methods and materials', *Support for Learning*, 15(2): 51–7.

Pitman, Sir I. (1961) *The Initial Teaching Alphabet*, London: Pitman Publishing.

Pollack, J. (1981) *Signposts to Spelling* (Repr), London: Heinemann.

Pollack, J. and Waller, L. (2004) *Day-to-Day Dyslexia in the Classroom (3rd edition)*, London: Routledge.

Pumfrey, P.D. and Reason, R. (1991) *Specific Learning Difficulties (Dyslexia.). Challenges and responses and National Survey*, Windsor: NFER-Nelson.

Read, C. (1986) *Children's Creative Spelling*, London: Routledge and Kegan-Paul.

Richardson, M. (1935) *Writing and Writing Patterns*, New education fellowship Conference papers, St Andrews Silver Jubilee Exhibition.

Ridehalgh, N. (1999) 'A comparison of remediation programmes and an analysis of their effectiveness in a sample of pupils diagnosed as dyslexic', MA SpLD dissertation, London: Middlesex University.

Roaf, C. (1998) 'Slow hand. A secondary school survey of handwriting speed and legibility', *Support for Learning*, 13(1): 39–42.

Rome, P. and Osman, J. (1994) *The Language Tool Kit*, Cambridge MA: Educators Publishing Service.

Rose, J. (2006) *Rose Review. Independent Review of the Teaching of Early Reading: Final Report*, London: DfES.

Rosenblaum, S. and Livneh-Zirinsky, M. (2007) 'Handwriting process and product characteristics of children diagnosed with DCD', *Human Movement Science*, 27: 200–14.

Rosencrans, G. (1998) *The Spelling Book. Teaching Children How to Spell*, USA International Reading Association.

Roycroft, S. (2002) 'A study to investigate whether DILP would help Year 3 pupils in mainstream school, showing difficulties with reading and spelling', MA SpLD dissertation, London: Middlesex University.

Royce Adams, W. (1977) *Developing Reading Versatility*, New York: Rinehart and Winstin.

Rutter, M.L., Caspi, A., Fergusson, D., Horwood, L.J., Goodman, R., Maughan, B., Moffit, T.E., Meltzer, H. and Carroll, J. (2004) 'Sex differences in developmental reading disability', *Journal of the American Medical Association*, 291 9 (16): 2007–12.

Rutter, M.L., Tizard, J. and Whitmore, K. (eds) (1970) *Education, Health and Behaviour*, London: Longman.

Ryan, R.M. and Deci, E.I. (2000) 'Self determination theory and the facilitation of intrinsic motivation and social development and well-being', *American Psychologist*, 55: 68–78.

Sassoon, R. (2015) 'Rescuing handwriting from redundancy', *Handwriting Today*. 14 Autumn 27–8.

Schaapkens, T. (2009) 'An investigation into the feasibility of integrating cognitive process strategies into Food Technology lessons for supporting teaching and learning of spelling', MA SpLD dissertation, London: Middlesex University.

Schneck, C.M. and Henderson, A. (1990) 'Discriminant analysis of the developmental progress of grasp position for pencil and crayon control in a longitudinal study', *American Journal of Occupational Therapy*, 44(10): 893–900.

Schonell, F.J. (1979) *Schonell Graded Word Reading Test reprint*, Edinburgh: Oliver and Boyd.

SED (Scottish Education Department) (1978) *The Education of Pupils with Learning Difficulties in Primary and Secondary Schools. A progress Report by HMI*, Edinburgh: HMS.

Seton, E. (2012) 'Handwriting in the 20th Century: Cursive to Manuscript', Maryland US: Loyola University MS.

Silverman, L.K. (1989) 'Invisible gifts, invisible handicaps', *Roeper Review*, 12(1): 37–42.

Silverman, L.K. (2002) *The Upside Down Brilliance: The Visual-Spatial Learner*, Denver: DeLeon Publishing.

Silverman, L.K. (2004) 'Poor handwriting: A major cause of underachievement', Available online: www.visuospatial.org/Publications/ [Accessed April 2007]

Simonson, M. (2008) 'An investigation of two writing approaches in the remediation of spelling difficulties', MA SpLD dissertation, London: Middlesex University.

Singleton, C. (2000) COPS Computerised Cognitive Profiling System.

Smart Kids (UK) Ltd (2014) Letters and Sound Progression Card. Available online: www.smartkids.co.uk

Snow, R. (1973) Theory construction for research on teaching', in R.M.S. Travers (ed.) *Second Handbook of Research on Teaching*, pp. 77–112, Chicago: Rand McNally.

Snowling, M.J. (1991) 'Developmental reading disorders', *Journal of Child Psychology and Psychiatry*, 32(1): 49–77.

Snowling, M.J. (2000) *Dyslexia* (2nd edition), Oxford: Blackwell.

Stainthorp, R. and Rauf, N. (2009) 'An investigation of the influence of the transcription skills of handwriting and spelling on the quality of text writing by girls and boys in key Stage 2', *Handwriting Today*, 8 Autumn: 8–13.

Stone, C., Franks, E. and Nicholson, M. (1993) *Beat Dyslexia*, Cambridge: LDA.

Suggate, S., Pufke, E. and Stoeger. H. (2016a) 'The effect of fine and grapho-motor skill demands on preschoolers' decoding skill', *Journal of Experimental Child Psychology*, 141: 34–48.

Suggate, S., Pufke, E. and Stoeger. H. (2016b) 'Do fine motor skills contribute to early reading development?' *Journal of Research in Reading*, 1–19. DOI: 10.1111/1467-9817.12081

Thomas, F. (1998) 'Une question de writing. A comparative study', *Support for Learning*, 13: 43–5.

Thomas, T., Singleton, C. and Horne, J. (2006) *LASS Junior*, Beverley: Lucid Research Ltd.

Tucha, L., Tucha, O., Wailtzar, S. et al (2007) 'Movement execution during neat handwriting', *Handwriting Today*, 6 Autumn: 44–8.

Tymms, P. (2004) 'Are standards rising in English primary school?' *British Educational Research Journal*, 30(4): 477–94.

Upton, J., Duckett, J. and Boardman, M. (2008) 'A Motorway to ABC', *Special*, Nov. 17–19.

Vallence, C. (2006) Case study Module work for MA SpLD, Middlesex University, London.

Vallence, C. (2008) 'An investigation into the design of a multisensory reading, spelling and handwriting curriculum in a small independent primary school', MA SpLD thesis, London: Middlesex University.

Van de Craen, P. (2016) 'Fostering Talent through Multilingual Education', EU Conference on the Development of Giftedness and Talent, Bratislava, Slovakia September.

Vellutino, F.R. (1979) *Dyslexia: Theory and Research*, London: MIT Press.

Vellutino, F.R. (1987) 'Dyslexia', *Scientific American*, 256(3): 20–7.

Vellutino, F.R. and Scanlon, S.M. (1998) 'Research in the study of reading disability. What have we learned in the past 4 decades?' Paper presented at the annual conference of the American Educational Research Association, April, San Diego, CA.

Vellutino, F.R., Fletcher, J. Snowling, M. and Scanlon, D. (2004) 'Specific reading disability (dyslexia) what have we learned in the past four decades?' *Journal of Child Psychology and Psychiatry*, 45(1): 2–40.

Waldie, K.E., Haigh, C.E., Badzakova-Trajkov, G. and Kirk, B.J. (2013) Reading the wrong way with the right hemisphere, *Brain Sci.* 3: 1060–1075.

Wallen, M., Bonney, M.A. and Lennox, L. (1996) *The Handwriting Speed Test*, Adelaide: Helios.

Walton, M. (1998) *Teaching Reading and Spelling to Dyslexic Children*, London: Routledge.

Warnock, M. (1978) *Children with Special Educational Needs: The Warnock Report*, London: HMSO.

Webb, A. (2015) 'Current issues: a compilation', *Handwriting Today*, 14 Autumn: 27–37.

Webb, M. (2000) 'An evaluation of the SEN provision to improve literacy skills of Year 9 students at Nfields', Unpublished MA dissertation, London: Middlesex University.

Wedell, K. (1973) *Learning and Perceptuomotor Difficulties in Children*, New York: Wiley.

Wendon, L. (2003) *ABC Letterland*, London: Letterland International.

Wensley, S. (2005) 'An investigation of the use of CPSS', MA SpLD Programme Module Project, London: Middlesex University.

Whitehead, M.R. (2004) *Language and Literacy in the Early Years* (3rd edition), London: Sage.

Whitmore, J.R. (1982) *Giftedness, Conflict and Underachievement*, Boston: Allyn and Bacon.

Wilson, J. (1994) 'Phonological awareness training. A new approach to phonics', *PATOSS Bulletin*, November 5–8.

Yule, W. and Rutter, M.L. (1985) 'Reading and other learning difficulties', in M.L. Rutter and L. Hersov (eds) *Child and Adolescent Psychiatry: Modern Approaches*, Oxford: Blackwell.

Some example resource sources

Abc Joined Up – an iPad application for KS1 children: www.abcjoinedup.com

Bic Kids – Handwriting tools: www.bickids.co.uk

Callirobics – graphical patterns traced when listening to music: www.specialdirect.com

Crossbow Education – www.crossboweducation.com

Edding – Education Writing Range: www.edding.com

Lucid Exact – a computerised resource to meet the examination access requirements: www.lucid-research.com

National Handwriting Association – Newsletter and Journal *Handwriting Today*

Nexus – pegboards and rollerball etc.: www.nexus-euro.com

Occupational Therapy: www.otforkids.co.uk

Special Direct – support for handwriting skills: www.specialdirect.com

Stabilo pens – www.stabilo.co.uk

Index